More Precious Than Gold

Written and Compiled by,
Edwin & Jody Mitchell

All Scripture quotations are from the King James Holy Bible.

A Tribute to the Faithful...

We acknowledge with deepest respect and appreciation the brothers and sisters in Christ whose teachings, exhortations, admonitions, reproofs, warnings and testimonies are assembled in these pages. These beloved saints have been used of God in their generations to bring to light the wondrous Way of the Cross that leads to Eternal Life with the Father and the Son. Some in their number *"loved not their lives unto the death"* and now await us under the altar *(Rev. 12:11)*. Their writings carry eternal weight, having proceeded from the inmost heart as a last will and testament, free from worldly considerations and confirmed by a holy life and innocent death. May we (one and all) be gathered with them when Jesus appears in the clouds.

CONTENTS

That the trial of your faith, being much more precious than of gold that perisheth, though it be tried with fire, might be found unto praise and honour and glory at the appearing of Jesus Christ.   1 Peter 1:7

CHAPTER ONE

A Dream Come True

In the summer of 2017, the Lord sent a prophet into our lives who had a dream about us, and along with it, a prophetic Word. From that day forward we have *"kept"* the things spoken *"and pondered them"* in our hearts *(Lk. 2:19; Dan. 7:28).*

"And it shall come to pass in the last days, saith God, I will pour out of my Spirit upon all flesh: and your sons and your daughters shall prophesy, and your young men shall see visions, and your old men shall dream dreams: and on my servants and on my handmaidens I will pour out in those days of my Spirit; and they shall prophesy."   Acts 2:17-18

...Don't remember every detail. Two things, however, remain embedded in our recollections: One, he saw a chain around my neck with a gold key dangling from it for use in setting even the most grievously vexed captives free. This has been a long standing desire of mine. ...No secret to anyone that knows me. Whether the cause be spiritual darkness and Gospel-hardness; or, utter helplessness under the crushing weight of seemingly insurmountable odds, this key would turn the lock. Secondly, he saw my wife Jody *"pregnant"* — not with a child per se — but *"with a book."* Those words, in particular, cut to the heart. Sarah laughed when she was told she would conceive *(Gen. 18:12).* Jody blushed. But, being olive-skinned like so many of her Jewish kinsmen, her surprise at being found out did not show "on her sleeve." *"How did he know?"* That's just the point: he didn't.

" . . . When the word of the prophet shall come to pass, then shall the prophet be known, that the LORD hath truly sent him."   Jeremiah 28:9b

Now, roughly four years later, the appointed *"time of life"* has arrived *(Gen. 18:10 14)*. The Word we received is coming to pass two-fold. After much travail we are giving birth—not to one book—but two! The first out of the womb is *More Precious Than Gold*; and the second, *We Meet at the Cross* (God willing), is soon to follow. Once we hit 400 pages we realized we were carrying twins. Oh what a God of bounty and blessing we serve! He does *"exceeding abundantly above all that we ask or think"* *(Eph. 3:20)*. Just ask David:

"He [the king] asked life of thee, and thou gavest it him, even length of days for ever and ever. . . . Thou hast given him his heart's desire, and hast not withholden the request of his lips. Selah."   Psalms 21:4, 2

For years my wife has been telling me of her great yearning for us to put together a book on how to lay hold of the healing power of Christ. On one occasion, when her faith appeared to be at its lowest ebb amidst a health crisis, she cried out to God begging His forgiveness for the sin of unbelief and asking Him to give her *"the faith of Jesus"* so that she could not only emphatically trust the Lord in her own hour of need; but also, continue walking side-by-side with me in ever increasing faith, preaching the Gospel and ministering deliverance and healing to others *(Rev. 14:12)*. Here's the passage that dropped into her heart as she prayed:

"And as ye go, preach, saying, The kingdom of heaven is at hand. Heal the sick, cleanse the lepers, raise the dead, cast out devils: freely ye have received, freely give."   Matthew 10:7-8

In other words:

"The husbandman that laboureth must be first partaker of the fruits."   2 Timothy 2:6

Freely receiving through one faith-building experience after another would be (for her) the necessary precursor for freely giving to others.

"Blessed be God, even the Father of our Lord Jesus Christ, the Father of mercies, and the God of all comfort; Who comforteth us in all our tribulation, that we may be able to comfort them which are in any trouble, by the comfort wherewith we ourselves are comforted of God."   2 Corinthians 1:3-4

That precept, if reduced to a single word, spells out like this: "T R I A L S."

"I counsel thee to buy of me gold tried in the fire . . ."
Revelation 3:18a

Yet, the mere thought of undergoing an acceleration of circumstances related to health that would bring us once again to the end of ourselves and put us in the position to cast ourselves wholly upon God for remedy still unsettled her.

"But we had the sentence of death in ourselves, that we should not trust in ourselves, but in God which raiseth the dead."
2 Corinthians 1:9

Andrew Murray, a Scottish minister to South Africa that was divinely healed after his own soul crisis in the late 1800's,[1] put it like this: Those who desire to give themselves to the fullness of the Great Commission must wholly abandon themselves to the challenges that precede it...

. . . So that their faith acquires sufficient vitality and strength to enable them to wrestle courageously with all the doubts and difficulties . . . [of others].[2]

". . . *Doubts and difficulties of others*"??? ...Jody had enough trouble wrestling what remained of her own. As needy as she still felt herself to be in this area of her life, however, so great was her desire to reach out. God's love conquers all! Jesus Christ, the "*author and finisher of our faith*," is more than able to give us the courage and fortitude to go with it *(Heb. 12:2; Job 23:6)*.
Alluding to the birthing of a book, she would plead:

...From cover to cover we could wallpaper its pages with testimony back-to-back with Scripture attesting to the authenticity of every modern day miracle we document.

Amidst some of our most heated trials in years gone by we actually did *"wallpaper"* — not a book — but the inside of our camper with picture plaques overlaid with Scripture. ...So many, that a person would be hard pressed to find a single bald spot big enough to add another. We surrounded ourselves with the Word of God. Even the mirror in our restroom was covered except for a tiny outside border. On it was a choice nugget of counsel imparted by a martyr to his wife in his uttermost extremity. We hung it up at a time Jody was wrestling with trusting the Lord for the healing of an unsightly and painful growth that popped up on her eye. Every time she looked in the mirror her heart melted. Sure enough, as soon as the plaque went up the tables turned. Every time she read the words her faith soared until at last her long awaited healing by the stripes of Jesus came. ...Can't help but sing His praise! ...Never did remove the plaque. It was far more glorious to look on than our own fading reflections.

... It is a little matter to be patient, so long as it goes well with a man — that cannot be called patience; but to be patient when it goes ill with one, and then to be able to preserve moderation, this is certainly a great power of faith. Hence, . . . I pray you . . . that you would be patient, and thank God with resignation of heart, saying: "Lord, thy will be done;" . . . O Lord, strengthen my faith and confidence, that I may never become fainthearted, disconsolate, despairing or doubtful concerning Thy promises, but may trust God, for His promises shall never fail; He is much too faithful that has promised it, and there will never be any failure on His part . . .
Raphel van den Velde, A.D. 1576
Slain by fire for his unwavering faith in Jesus Christ[3]

Love... she would say: *We could use my life as a former cripple in regards to faith and good health to show how even the weakest among us (no matter how severe and seemingly hopeless the illness ...the oppression ...or the addiction) can reach up to the heavens with the two hands of repentance and faith and lay hold on the blessing Jesus purchased at Calvary for every one of the lost sheep He brings into His Fold. Then we could send it out far and wide as a door of hope that God could use to open up His tender mercies in the lives of others. We could pick out an assortment of wonders that we have personally experienced. ...Share about our manifold breakings at the altar of repentance in desperate pursuit of our Master's touch ...our lonely nights and bitter tears ...our wrestlings with the devil ...our battles to conquer unbelief and fear. We could tell of the remarkable healings we've witnessed with our own eyes – things which we have seen and heard and handled of the "Word of life" (1 Jn 1:1). ...We could tell about how Jesus heals from the inside, out. ...That His first priority – as the "repairer of the breach" between man and his Maker – is always the healing of our relationship with the Father and the nurturing of an indomitable faith in His loving care, come what may (Isa. 58:12). Plus, we could add accounts of the "valiants of faith" that have gone before us on the road to recovery, beginning with those listed in Scripture and traveling forward from there.*

I've been all for it. Our Beloved Jesus has shown Himself to be *"the LORD that healeth thee"* so often and so preciously (yea, so intimately!) through one severe trial of faith after another that we both want to tell the world *(Exo. 15:26b).*

"For we cannot but speak the things which we have seen and heard." Acts 4:20

We're like the leper of Mark Chapter One (and many others) that simply could not hold their peace after receiving the touch of Jesus and believing the Word that proceeded from His blessed mouth.

"And there came a leper to him, beseeching him, and kneeling down to him, and saying unto him, If thou wilt, thou canst make me clean. And Jesus, moved with compassion, put forth his hand, and touched him, and saith unto him, I will; be thou clean. And as soon as he had spoken, immediately the leprosy departed from him, and he was cleansed. And he straitly charged him, and forthwith sent him away; and saith unto him, See thou say nothing to any man: but go thy way, shew thyself to the priest, and offer for thy cleansing those things which Moses commanded, for a testimony unto them. But he went out, and began to publish it much, and to blaze abroad the matter, insomuch that Jesus could no more openly enter into the city, but was without in desert places: and they came to him from every quarter."   Mark 1:40-45

Yet, we've been hard pressed with ministry, both domestically and internationally. So much so, that we didn't "think" we had the time to embark on the project. A book on healing would of necessity have to be a book centered in the restoration of the Cross to its vital place of emphasis in the life of the Church. Tackling that subject would be a monumental task.

If we were going to burrow in and give ourselves to another book, I'd say, our first priority needs to be a treatise revealing the glory of the original Gospel of Christ in its native colors (no dumbing down, no cow-towing to the religious establishment), against the contrasting backdrop of the candied "gospels" leavened with heresy ...gutted of the Cross ...and tailored to the appetites of the flesh. I loathe them, one and all (Rev. 2:15)!

Nothing more grossly mitigates against the free flow of the Holy Ghost and the healing virtue of Christ than *"doctrines of devils"* and unscriptural traditions introduced under the Christian label by unregenerated men *(Mk. 7:13; 1 Tim. 4:1).*

"But there were false prophets also among the people, even as there shall be false teachers among you, who privily shall bring in damnable heresies, even denying the Lord that bought them, and bring upon themselves swift destruction. And many shall follow their pernicious ways; by reason of whom the way of truth shall be evil spoken of."   2 Peter 2:1-2

The Apostle Peter's Warning

If you're galloping through this introductory chapter right now so as to plunge directly into the heart of the book, we urge you to pull back on the reigns, slow down and let the preceding passage impact you, beginning with the words:

"Denying the Lord that bought them!?!??!"

Whoa! How is it possible to be sitting under teachers preaching in the Name of Jesus Christ, who are at the same time "*denying*" Him? Questions immediately arise. What "*christ*," then, is being preached? Could it be another "*christ?*" ...Perhaps one amongst numerous "*false christs*" of whom Jesus and His apostles cautioned us to be wary?

"For there shall arise false christs, and false prophets, and shall shew great signs and wonders; insomuch that, if it were possible, they shall deceive the very elect. Behold, I have told you before." Matthew 24:24-25

"But I fear, lest by any means, as the serpent beguiled Eve through his subtilty, so your minds should be corrupted from the simplicity that is in Christ. For if he that cometh preacheth another Jesus, whom we have not preached, or if ye receive another spirit, which ye have not received, or another gospel, which ye have not accepted . . ." 2 Corinthians 11:3-4a

Think of what Paul is saying here. In the last days preachers will appear who seem to be men of honesty and righteousness — but who are actually ministers under the influence of Satan himself. They will be of another spirit entirely, introducing another christ, another spirit, another gospel.[4]

One thing is sure: Something is wrong. For we have in our day a very sick Church. ...One whose "gospel tonic" does not seem to be working as it should.

When sitting in meetings, I have often been astonished when the appeals for healing come, and almost everyone comes out of his seat. I have never seen such a sick Church everywhere, and I think that we will continue to be sick, both physically and spiritually, so long as we live essentially egocentric lives.[5]

Rather than the Church leading the world to the altar as its first recourse for remedy and witnessing the signs and wonders that followed the early Christians, the Church is travelling along with the world on the well worn road to doctors, hospitals and pharmacies.

". . . Is not the LORD in Zion? is not her king in her? . . . Is there no balm in Gilead; is there no physician there? why then is not the health of the daughter of my people recovered?"

Jeremiah 8:19, 22

Certainly health care has its proper function in any civil society. But shouldn't we, if we truly possess *"the faith of Jesus Christ" (Gal. 2:16)*, be flocking to Him first—yea, tearing the roofs from our homes (so to speak), if need be, in order to make direct contact with our Healer?

"And they come unto him, bringing one sick of the palsy, which was borne of four. And when they could not come nigh unto him for the press, they uncovered the roof where he was: and when they had broken it up, they let down the bed wherein the sick of the palsy lay. When Jesus saw their faith, he said unto the sick of the palsy, Son, thy sins be forgiven thee. . . . And immediately he arose, took up the bed, and went forth before them all; insomuch that they were all amazed, and glorified God, saying, We never saw it on this fashion."   Mark 2:3-5, 12

Our condition (as a people) is not much different from that of the Jews and their leaders when Israel's Messiah walked the earth. So far had they veered from the true Spirit of the Mosaic Law, that they no longer bore the distinction of its blessing. On the streets ...in the Holy City ...and right there inside their synagogues, God's chosen people were ailing and clamoring for deliverance and cure *(Lk. 4:33-36; Jn. 5:1-17; etc., etc., etc.).*

"And when they were come out of the ship, straightway they knew him, and ran through that whole region round about, and began to carry about in beds those that were sick, where they heard he was. And whithersoever he entered, into villages, or cities, or country, they laid the sick in the streets, and besought him that they might touch if it were but the border of his garment: and as many as touched him were made whole."

Mark 6:54-56

Moving onward in Peter's warning, we read:

"And many shall follow their pernicious ways; by reason of whom the way of truth shall be evil spoken of."

Again, ponder the gravity of what's being said. Peter is telling us that these false shepherds are going to be used of the devil to alienate a great number of professing Christians from the very faith they believe themselves to have embraced; and in so doing, deny them access to the one and only true Jesus of Nazareth that shed His blood for our sins and opened the door for reconciliation with the Father and the recovery of our blessings *(1 Cor. 8:5-7a)*. In other words, rather than pointing the way into the Throne of Grace, they are going to be turning unwitting souls away from it.

"Woe unto you, lawyers! for ye have taken away the key of knowledge: ye entered not in yourselves, and them that were entering in ye hindered."   Luke 11:52

Peter's warning does not stop there. He then goes on to say that Satan is going to use those that are taken in by these errant *"gospels"* to blaspheme the true Gospel *(Gal. 1:6-9)*, an action which most often culminates in the marginalization, intimidation and persecution of the precious *"few"* that cleave to (and preach!) the narrow way to life.

"Enter ye in at the strait gate: for wide is the gate, and broad is the way, that leadeth to destruction, and many there be which go in thereat: because strait is the gate, and narrow is the way, which leadeth unto life, and few there be that find it."

Matthew 7:13-14

We're witnessing this "big time" in our day. Satan's primary means for accomplishing this end has been the introduction of heretical doctrines that separate God's promises from their conditions, thus robbing the Church of an effectual faith rightly placed in the blood of Jesus and administered to us based upon our willingness to conform our lives to the Gospel Covenant and to repent and amend our ways when we fall short. This is the *"Way of Truth"* that Peter alluded to in his warning.

> . . . What a good ointment and blessed doctrine this is which Peter has here taught us by the Holy Ghost. O yes, what a precious medicine this is which the Lord has left us by His apostles, by which the soul can be purified and [both soul and body] healed. . . . Hence . . . let us hear this truth, and obey it; for He proceeded from the Father, yea, came from and was sent by Him, a teacher from heaven, to teach us the way of truth, and the life, which He was Himself; and all that He has heard and seen from His Father, He has taught us, in order to purify our souls, [heal our bodies] and save [us] for ever . . .
>
> Hansken van den Wege, Bold in the faith, A.D. 1570
> Strangled & Slain by fire under Roman Catholic decree[6]

It's also the *"way of holiness"* that Isaiah relayed in his prophecy *(Isa. 35:8)*; and the *"Way of the Cross"* walked faithfully by the penitent, God-fearing, truth-loving martyrs that laid down their lives in defense of its veracity.

> … Adhere all the days of your life to that which you voluntarily so willingly accepted, since it is the true ground, foundation, and way to eternal life. Oh, there shall never be found another, than this way of the cross… A.D. 1564
> Jelis Matthijss, Slain for His Steadfast Stance in Christ[7]

Links on a Chain

Simply put, the *"Way of Truth"* is comprised of a series of links on a chain. The first link connects faith to repentance.

". . . Repent ye, and believe the Gospel." Mark 1:15b

...The second connects repentance to forgiveness:

"If we confess our sins, he is faithful and just to forgive us our sins, and to cleanse us from all unrighteousness."   1 John 1:9

...And the third connects forgiveness to healing, as well as God's other manifold blessings *(Ps. 103:2-3)*; including salvation itself.

"And the inhabitant shall not say, I am sick: the people that dwell therein shall be forgiven their iniquity."   Isaiah 33:24

Knowing this, Satan (thief that he is!) does everything within his power to keep us from discovering (and recovering!!!) these links. He's got most of the "church" locked into the material world, indifferent to the reality that we are three part beings (spirit, soul and body) and that God heals (and deals!) with us as such *(1 Th. 5:23)*.

"And Jesus knowing their thoughts said, Wherefore think ye evil in your hearts? For whether is easier, to say, Thy sins be forgiven thee; or to say, Arise, and walk? But that ye may know that the Son of man hath power on earth to forgive sins, (then saith he to the sick of the palsy,) Arise, take up thy bed, and go unto thine house. And he arose, and departed to his house. But when the multitudes saw it, they marvelled, and glorified God, which had given such power unto men."   Matthew 9:4-8

The Golden Key

Nailing down this *"foundation of repentance from dead works, and faith toward God"* that Paul described as bedrock elements of victory in the life and salvation of a believer *(Heb. 6:1)*, the

Apostle John likewise emphasized soul prosperity as the key on the chain that unlocks the door to good health.

"Beloved, I wish above all things that thou mayest prosper and be in health, even as thy soul prospereth."   3 John 1:2

Without turning that "key" (the "golden key" that the prophet who visited us saw in his vision) by the prescribed biblical means (repentance and faith), there is no sure promise of bodily health *(Jam. 5:13-16).*

"Confess your faults one to another, and pray one for another, that ye may be healed. The effectual fervent prayer of a righteous man availeth much."   James 5:16

Conversely, with the turning of that key comes forgiveness under the atoning blood of Jesus where complete restoration on every level is to be found. Hallelujah! Washed in His blood and forgiven of all of our iniquities, the *"Valley of Achor"* (i.e. "trouble") where our sin is exposed and judged is then turned into a *"Door of Hope,"* just as it was for the Israelites after their defeat and subsequent victory at the Battle of Ai *(Jos. 7)*; and as it will be again for the Jewish people when Christ returns to earth to establish His Millennial Reign *(Hos. 2:15).*

> For us all, dear friends, it is true. In all our difficulties, [diseases] and sorrows, be they great or small; in our business perplexities; in the losses that rob our homes of their light; in the petty annoyances [and relationship conflicts] that diffuse their irritation through so much of our days; it is within our power to turn them all into occasions for a firmer grasp of God, and so to make them openings by which a happier hope may flow into our souls. But the promise, like all God's promises, has its well-defined conditions. Achan has to be killed [meaning sin has to be acknowledged] and put safe out of the way first, or no shining Hope . . . The tastes which knit us to the perishable world [as they did Achan], the yearnings for Babylonish garments and wedges of gold [things like

possessions, pleasure and prestige], must be . . . subdued [and surrendered to Christ at His Cross]. Swift, sharp, unrelenting justice must be done on the lust of the flesh, and the lust of the eye, and the pride of life, if our trials are ever to become *doors of hope*. . . . All depends on how we use the trial, or as I say-first stone Achan, and then hope![8]

Stretch Forth Thy Withered Hand

God sends so many to us that are wounded without and within and we so much desire to see every one — without exception — restored to health; spirit, soul and body. Surely, that is God's intent for us all. But without the full force of the Gospel (nothing added and nothing taken away) and the realignment of our lives to "that Gospel," or what Jesus called: *"this Gospel of the Kingdom" (Mt. 24:14)*, we are not going to see the *"greater works"* He foretold before His departure *(Jn. 14:12)*.

If the Church were to see anew springing up within her, men and women who live the life of faith and of the Holy Spirit, entirely consecrated to their God [and wholly grounded in the unadulterated doctrines of Christ and His apostles], we would see again the manifestation of the same gifts [including healing] as in former times.[9]

We can't be intimidated by anyone — no matter how well accepted their doctrines, denominations or traditions may be. Like the deformed man in the synagogue on the Sabbath Day, we've got to *"rise up"* at Christ's command, *"stretch forth"* our *"withered hand"* (even if amidst a potential sea of reproach and opposition) and allow our Healer to restore it *"whole"* as the other *(Mk. 3:1-6; Lk. 6:6-11)*.

That amounts to "pulling out all the stops" and making a 100% U-Turn back to the original Gospel; not only in relationship to its transformational doctrine on the Cross, but every other teaching as well. That includes the unabashed welcome of the Baptism of the Holy Ghost with all of the wonderful supernatural God-given manifestations and gifts that go with it. It also includes the opening up of our hearts to all five of the leadership offices Jesus gave to His Church; apostles, prophets, evangelists, pastors and teachers *(Eph. 4:11)*. Granted: All of these things (as well as the Bible itself!) have suffered shameful exploitation and distortion. But let not that be an occasion for the devil to trick us to dismiss them, and in the process miss our blessing.

I can just see Jody's face right now pondering the difficulty of conveying all this to readers in a way they can wrap their arms around it and apply it in their own lives. There I am looking across the table and seeing her forehead scrunched up and that look of both zeal and reticence in her eyes. On one side she's super excited and already at the other end of the field looking over her shoulder waiting to catch a pass. On the other, she's apprehensive, see-sawing back and forth with question marks, wondering what the venture will require, and reaching for acceptance:

> *But, Love... So MUCH rubbish (Neh. 4:2).*
> *Where do we begin?!"*

Well, no need to try to figure all this out. ...Couldn't anyway, hard as we might try. Christ Jesus is the initiator of new life and He had a plan—something we could never "in a million years" have come up with on our own.

Meet the Brethren

It all started with a letter we received from our brothers and sisters in Zimbabwe—a *"faithful"* church leader by the name of Raymore *(Col. 4:7; 1 Cor. 4:2)*, his God-fearing wife Linah and their three Holy Spirit filled daughters. ...A true family *"in the Lord" (Rom. 16:11)*. You'll see their names laced through these pages from time to time. With Bishop Raymore taking the lead, they are presently overseeing eight mushrooming home fellowships in the desperately oppressed land of their nativity; a country known at a peak of its prosperity (before its implosion and current collapse), as *"the Jewel of Africa."* The most exciting part of all this is that they are doing it in harmony with the New Testament pattern, completely outside of the institutional frame.

"And they, continuing daily with one accord in the temple, and breaking bread from house to house, did eat their meat with gladness and singleness of heart, praising God, and having favour with all the people. And the Lord added to the church daily such as should be saved."   Acts 2: 46-47

Both Raymore and Linah were born into the Anglican church, but were led out due to the doctrinal error and hypocrisy they discovered. Raymore received the Lord at a tent meeting and the two of them met at a Full-Gospel Church, which, to their great grief, became corrupted by the false material prosperity message, as well as other heretical influences of our day, prompting them both to come out and be washed of those influences, too.

Our lives intersected back in the nineties at a time when mosques were springing up in their country and Christians were becoming increasingly alarmed. Somehow they got a hold of our book, *The Two Headed Dragon of Africa*,[10] containing a copy of a secret OIC[a] document revealing an Islamic conspiracy to turn the entire continent of Africa (as another step towards world domination) into an Islamic Sultanate. It really struck a chord with this couple, being that the pages were lined with testimonies of fellow believers (primarily, but not exclusively, Nigerian church leaders) telling of the frightful escalation of merciless persecutions. Pastors and their congregations were being rounded up and locked inside their churches. Then the structures were doused with fuel and set on fire. The horror of it all struck very close to home.

As time went on, this zealous brother, already involved in ministry, became a true son in the Lord, one that I very soon began to disciple, one-on-one, much like the Apostle Paul did Timothy and Titus when they were ushered into the fullness of

[a] Organization of Islamic Conference, now called the Organization of Islamic Cooperation.

their God-given callings. ...Except, in our case, due to the distance between us, our interaction has been solely via the postal system, emails and our distribution of Bibles and hard-hitting Gospel materials. ...Not your typical Sunday School type stuff; but rather, anointed books and recorded messages from centuries past all the way up to this present time. Now, over two decades later, though we've never been together face-to-face, we are still "*stand[ing] fast in one Spirit, with one mind striving together for the faith of the gospel*" *(Phil. 1:27).*

"For I have no man likeminded, who will naturally care for your state. For all seek their own, not the things which are Jesus Christ's. But ye know the proof of him, that, as a son with the father, he hath served with me in the gospel."

Philippians 2:20-22

Here's a clip from an email that came in from the family amidst the writing of this book. It'll give you a "pulse" on the spirit of humility and devotion that characterizes their lives and propels them in ministry. They speak English, as well as Shona, their native tongue.

Going through [the manuscript you emailed] took some time [due to perpetual power shortages]. Today we completed reading it, slowly, but surely. The reason is we got something [from it that] we either further discussed or prayed about after going over each paragraph. Thank you for showing us the order that is expected of servants of God beginning in the home; from there to church; and then into the community that we serve. It helped us to do real examination of our lives before we try to offer others help. Teachers of the Word are to be judged with a more severe judgment [Jam. 3:1; Mt. 23:14], as according to what Scripture says. The relationship between husband and wife has to be sound, having the Lordship of Christ in full operation. Children ought to portray to the outside world that they have been well cultured [in the "nurture and admonition of the Lord" — Eph. 6:4]. They are like a mirror showing the world how a home where God is at the centre should look. You revealed to us how well those who are taking a lead in the house of God should do so first in their own homes. We really appreciate all this and are praising God that we have done our best to bring up our daughters in the Lord. God helped us and you as well made vast input in the way our children are demonstrating the life of Jesus day after day in their own lives. Their mother, Linah, has been, and is still, an example before them by the way she fits into our marriage relationship and by the way she offers support from so close of a position — not exercising authority over her husband or any other men in church. Because of this her sweet spirit is also evident in our daughters and in the ladies that are in our fellowship. This we are going to teach in the churches.   8 September 2019

...Oh hallelujah!

"[We] have no greater joy than to hear that [our] children walk in truth."   3 John 1:4

Plundered!

Back in early September of 2018 Bishop Raymore's three decade old car (which we now affectionately call *"The Gospel Chariot"*) was plundered while parked outside the home of some fellow believers where the family had gone for their usual mid-week Bible Study. Shaken by their deep sense of vulnerability, they reached out relaying the episode and seeking counsel ...understanding ...and guidance.

Why? Why? Why?

...Robbed while being in the center of what they believed to be God's perfect will??? What was the Lord speaking into their lives through this perplexing providence? ...The "iron was hot." Their ears were tuned. Their eyes were on Jesus. The Lord had their full attention. Together as a family they were in a posture of brokenness, ready to listen (and even repent and amend, if need be) with renewed entreatability to His answer.

The amazing thing about all this is that the Lord graciously turned what Satan meant for evil into good by leading Bishop Raymore and two others to the doorstep of the young marauders, opening the opportunity for them to introduce the Gospel (*Gen. 50:20*). The Holy Spirit moved wondrously on that day, prompting the return of the stolen goods from the willing hands of these aimless youth and making it possible for Bishop Raymore and the family to "*recover all,*" as did David when his camp at Ziglag was invaded by the Amalekites *(1 Sam. 30:1-20)*. No small miracle on both accounts!

> . . . We visited the boys' home and met the mother, only to discover that the boys are still of school going age, ages ranging from 15, 9 and 6 years old. The love of God moved us . . . . We started to prayerfully interrogate the boys whilst the mother was persuading her boys to open up and they each started to disappear and later appear with the items they had stolen. Within no time we had everything back. It was a miracle! We preached the love of God to them. It was all tears on their faces. Then we prayed with them as they received the Lord and [committed] that they will never do it again. We hope to see them in Church on Sunday. We are reminded of the Apostle Paul and the Jailer, how the whole family was saved.   6 Sept. 2018

The Time of the End

In spite of the glorious outcome, Bishop Raymore knew that a full understanding of God's multiple purposes behind the circumstance was a chief part of the prize.

"Wisdom is the principal thing; therefore get wisdom: and with all thy getting get understanding."   Proverbs 4:7

Exactly how are we—as believers—to prepare by faith for the escalating ravages of crime, civilian strife, natural disasters, plagues, pandemics, political corruption and persecution leading to the appearance of our Lord? The tendency for all of us when the seemingly far off warnings in Bible prophecy suddenly arrive on our doorstep, as they have in the recent pandemics of disease and violence, is to begin to seek out (and rely upon) various types of worldly "*battlements*" to create a refuge (if at all possible) from the storms. ...Things like elaborate alarm systems, expensive health care plans, diverse insurance policies, firearms, stockpiles of food, etc. This adamic penchant towards "self"-preservation by natural means was one of the primary reasons for Bishop Raymore's deprecations in the aftermath of his trial.

> This dawned on me that there was a time . . . a man who fixes car locks and repairs car cables encouraged me to have an alarm put on the car. . . . I never thought much about it, but I am feeling I sinned, for I did not share it with anyone.   6 September 2018

Offensive measures can be appropriate, if the Lord (for His appointed purposes) inspires and mandates them *(Gen. 41)*.

"By faith Noah, being warned of God of things not seen as yet, moved with fear, prepared an ark to the saving of his house; by the which he condemned the world, and became heir of the righteousness which is by faith."   Hebrews 11:7

But if prompted by worldly ingenuity, impulse, or panic they can also be a breach of faith and trust in our Father's promise to cover and protect His own. (See Psalms 121 and 91 to name just two.)

"The horse is prepared against the day of battle: but safety is of the LORD."   Proverbs 21:31

In such a case, the added cushioning of our lives will contribute to (rather than alleviate) our vulnerability.

"Go ye up upon her walls, and destroy; but make not a full end: take away her battlements; for they are not the Lord's."

Jeremiah 5:10

"Woe to the rebellious children, saith the Lord, that take counsel, but not of me; and that cover with a covering, but not of my Spirit, that they may add sin to sin: that walk to go down into Egypt, and have not asked at my mouth; to strengthen themselves in the strength of Pharaoh, and to trust in the shadow of Egypt! Therefore shall the strength of Pharaoh be your shame, and the trust in the shadow of Egypt your confusion."   Isaiah 30:1-3

> Those that cannot find in their hearts to trust God forfeit His protection and thrust themselves out of it.[11]

Faith has many faces. That's why we've got to be so diligent about maintaining right standing with the Lord and becoming more and more deeply acquainted with His Word, His Will and His ways. Only then can we hear rightly from the Holy Spirit and not mistake His voice on account of fleshly impulses, fear, or worldly ways of doing things. Sometimes adding a natural buffer might be the proper course of action. At others, however, it may be something that the Lord distains. The bottom-line is faith: meaning, doing everything *"as to the Lord"* *(Eph. 6:7)*, trusting that it meets with His approval *(Rom. 14:23)*.

The danger of reliance on natural buffers is that they can weaken faith, our most *"precious"* commodity, rather than restore it (as God intends) to the strength possessed by the great patriarchs that went before us *(1 Pe. 1:7)*.

...Men like Moses, who led the Israelite Exodus, relying wholly on the Lord's guidance and the blood of the Lamb for provision and protection.

"Through faith he kept the passover, and the sprinkling of blood, lest he that destroyed the firstborn should touch them. By faith they passed through the Red sea as by dry land: which the Egyptians assaying to do were drowned." Hebrews 11:28-29

...Zealots like Ezra and the entourage of Levites and priests that accompanied him on the dangerous journey from Babylon to Jerusalem in the aftermath of the seventy year captivity. Rather than petitioning a pagan monarch for protection against potential plunder, they put everything at risk, trusting solely in the Lord to cover them. ...And He did. ...Marvelously!

"Then I proclaimed a fast there, at the river of Ahava, that we might afflict ourselves before our God, to seek of him a right way for us, and for our little ones, and for all our substance. For I was ashamed to require of the king a band of soldiers and horsemen to help us against the enemy in the way: because we had spoken unto the king, saying, The hand of our God is upon all them for good that seek him; but his power and his wrath is against all them that forsake him. So we fasted and besought our God for this: and he was intreated of us."   Ezra 8:21-23

Not only was the priesthood kept in safeguard in that memorable incident; but also, as a result of the faith they issued, they left behind a powerful witness of our Father's divine protection over the lives of the faithful, in contrast to the judgments sure to befall those that forsake Him. What a glorious Lord we serve! ...He is the very same Lord revealed in the fiery furnace to Nebuchadnezzar and the Babylonians when Shadrach, Meshach and Abednego similarly trusted in God, putting life and limb at risk, rather than bowing down to any saviour but their own *(Dan. 3:1-30)*.

"Then Nebuchadnezzar the king was astonied, and rose up in haste, and spake, and said unto his counsellors, Did not we cast three men bound into the midst of the fire? They answered and said unto the king, True, O king. He answered and said, Lo, I see four men loose, walking in the midst of the fire, and they have no hurt; and the form of the fourth is like the Son of God."
Daniel 3:24-25

The list goes on...

"And what shall I more say? For the time would fail me to tell of Gedeon, and of Barak, and of Samson, and of Jephthae; of David also, and Samuel, and of the prophets: Who through faith subdued kingdoms, wrought righteousness, obtained promises, stopped the mouths of lions."   Hebrews 11:32-33

Faith Our Alarm System

Immediately after receiving Bishop Raymore's letter, we went into prayer. The result was a ten page letter titled "Faith our Alarm System. It covered all kinds of basics on our common need for steadfast faith in God and discernment on how to rightly interpret and respond to the Lord's providential hand in the manifold circumstances surrounding our lives.

As we labored, "out of the blue," Jody was smitten with a distressing infirmity that unnerved her and put her in the challenging position of living out every stroke of the message on faith that we brought forth from behind the keyboard of our computer. This was our hour of visitation, too. Different scenario, but the same Faithful God calling us all to the Cross.

"Beloved, think it not strange concerning the fiery trial which is to try you, as though some strange thing happened unto you."
1 Peter 4:12

Once we came out on the other side of both the letter and our own particular trial, Jody was "chomping at the bit" to get out a follow-up letter testifying to the battle that ensued; the divine healing that followed; and the victory won in multiple areas of our lives. That letter then grew into what has now become two new books — the fulfillment of the prophet's dream and our secret desire, as well.

CHAPTER TWO

And Then the World Changed

The irony of all this is that the books were held up in the birth canal for a protracted length of time. This was cause for continual concern until the COVID-19 pandemic broke ...anarchy was ignited in our streets ...medical fascism was set in motion and a whole new array of antichrist decrees were introduced.

"And he [the Antichrist] shall speak great words against the most High, and shall wear out the saints of the most High, and think to change times and laws: and they shall be given into his hand until a time and times and the dividing of time [three and a half years.]"   Daniel 7:25

It was then that the timing for the release of the books came into view and along with it a panorama of End-time events. There they were in plain sight though shrouded beneath an overlay of media propaganda. ...Biological warfare; i.e. plagues and pestilence. ...Masks, "social distancing," lockdowns. The manipulation of the public via pseudo-science (1 Tim. 6:20). The divide of the world between the "vaccinated" and the "unvaccinated." The prohibition of religious assembly. The throttling of the world economy. Supply chain interruptions resulting in the creation of food and fuel shortages. The detonation of an international Kristallnacht in the aftermath of the heinous (and unjustified) murder of George Floyd; the rise of Antifa; the riots; the opening of our borders; the assault on law and order; the attacks on churches and synagogues; the transformation of the media into a Ministry of Propaganda for Globalism; the widespread demonization of Christians; big tech censorship and the de-platforming of conservatives; the redefinition of prejudice to mean anyone that does not concede to the demands of the LGBTQ community and organizations like Black Lives Matter whose stated ideologies are both Marxist and antisemitic;[1] military decisions favoring Communist China, Russia and Iran; and finally, (though the list goes on) the fraudulent election of a United States president whose party is in the process of rewriting history, removing our nation from its Judeo-Christian foundation, dismantling our constitutional frame, and if left unchecked, handing our national sovereignty over to the Global "Community."

We (as a generation of people) have spiritually passed through what they call in aeronautics the "Kaman line." ...Except in this case, instead of passing through the magnetic field dividing earth from outer space, we have passed from normality into the surreal. The cumulative weight of unrequited sin has thrust the nations of the world over a "tipping point," ushering us into a kind of peril uniquely characteristic of "*the time of the end*" *(Dan. 12:4, 9).*

"The earth shall reel to and fro like a drunkard, and shall be removed like a cottage; and the transgression thereof shall be heavy upon it; and it shall fall, and not rise again."   Isaiah 24:20

Whatever vestiges that still remain of the world as we once knew it are rapidly being eclipsed by the momentum of a seemingly unstoppable acceleration of uncanny events. No doubt about it: The "Cultural Revolution" of the coming Antichrist has made a landmark surge forward. ...Can't help but reflect on the image of a poster hoisted above the crowds in the days of the Communist takeover of China when Mao tried to "purge" the land of the "old" elements of society so as to set up his imagined Utopia. Featured on the poster is the outline of an angry man, sledge hammer overhead, cross under heel, and a caption reading: "*Break the old world. Establish a new world.*"[2]

The Mark of the Beast

The video of a minister on YouTube thundering a "wake-up" call to his "sleepy listeners" back in early 2020 comes to mind. It was forwarded to us by a Nigerian church leader on the heels of explosive news documenting globalist plans to use the pandemic to introduce the proposition of mandatory vaccinations (some of which have been proven to altar human DNA). Along with their administration would come the application of a technologically discernible Quantum tattoo or the insertion of a tiny microchip capable of storing all of the recipient's personal information,[3] financial records, vaccine verification and "*contact tracing*" history.[a]

> The Covid vaccines are intended to work in tandem with the digital ID technology being sponsored by some of the same sources that are funding the vaccines. The globalists involved in "solving" the Covid crisis are putting in place a one-world cashless commerce system that will include a "device-free" digital identification mark/ number for every human being.[4]

Alarm bells immediately started going off throughout the Christian community--especially after further documentation surfaced revealing the possibility that the substance from which the mRNA "vaccines" are made could prove to be the "*platform*" for the Biblically prophesied Mark of the Beast.[5]

"And he causeth all, both small and great, rich and poor, free and bond, to receive a mark in their right hand, or in their foreheads: and that no man might buy or sell, save he that had the mark, or the name of the beast, or the number of his name."
Revelation 13:16-17

Suddenly End-Time Reality was upon us. Clearly, the manipulation of the pandemic by an elite body of globalists could be nothing other than the outworking of the devil's plan in the last hours of his power to create a one world Beast

---

[a] "In public health, contact tracing is the process of identifying persons who may have come into contact with an infected person and subsequent collection of further information about these contacts." Wikipedia

System of government complete with a cashless currency and international ID database designed to mark, monitor and bring into subservience every kindred, nation and people to the rule of his coming Antichrist; or else, if captured, face annihilation.

"And he [the False Prophet] had power to give life unto the image of the beast [the Antichrist], that the image of the beast should both speak, and cause that as many as would not worship the image of the beast should be killed."

Revelation 13:15

The United Nations (including the WHO), the World Economic Forum, the Vatican and other key players have an agenda that involves the creation of a global system of government and the introduction of a worldwide cashless economy utilizing digital currency (an electronic monetary unit) for all personal and corporate transactions. The ultimate aim: Full control over every move of every individual on the planet via a health-imposed economic dictatorship. This agenda is moving forward in the name of democracy but is actually being driven by Marxists dedicated to the cause of world government and in some cases to Lucifer (Satan) himself. We are witnessing the fruits of raw evil playing out in real time. These sinister forces are using the engineered Covid crisis and push for a mandatory vaccine as a means to their ends, implementing their agenda under the guise of "taking necessary health measures" to save humankind. Those of us refusing to take the vaccine— thereby directly interfering with their agenda—will be targeted and blamed for the continued spread of Covid variants. This is not about science, it is about forcing the people of the world into a diabolical snare that, as we will see, has eternal ramifications.[6]

Even now as a prelude to this eventuality, cash is being removed from commerce.[7] For those of us that know our Bibles, questions immediately arise:

How long do we have before our choice not to submit to vaccination will result in ...the denial of travel? ...education ...employment ...commerce ...health care ...etc.?

Many nations are already requiring vaccination documentation via scannable ankle bracelets, "vaccine passports" and/or phone apps designed for verification as a condition for travel, employment, education, entrance into gyms, restaurants, theaters, etc. Next on the agenda is grocery stores. Also, many medical insurance companies are increasing premiums on the unvaccinated. These alarming developments sweeping the globe appear to be amongst the devil's final steps of coercion just prior to the implementation of the Mark itself.

Looking into the future many years ago, one pastor wrote:

. . . Satan certainly will use this system to deny medical care to all who refuse to accept the mark of the beast. . . . The ability to control who receives health care will be another weapon . . . used to force people into the new economic order. If someone refuses to yield to the edicts of those who control the cashless/RFID system,[b] they will be denied treatment for their medical condition.[8]

Still more serious of a consideration is this:

What will be the fate of those that DO concede to vaccination (and ongoing "boosters") once these procedures are married into Mark of the Beast technology; and not only health care, but access to all public facilities, services, provisions and amenities are contingent upon their receipt?

"And the third angel followed them, saying with a loud voice, If any man worship the beast and his image, and receive his mark in his forehead, or in his hand, the same shall drink of the

---

[b] RFID: "Radio Frequency Identification" is circuitry (with an antenna) added to microchips that makes possible the communication of financial accounts and other data necessary for conducting commerce via a low power radio signal.

wine of the wrath of God, which is poured out without mixture into the cup of his indignation; and he shall be tormented with fire and brimstone in the presence of the holy angels, and in the presence of the Lamb. And the smoke of their torment ascendeth up for ever and ever: and they have no rest day nor night, who worship the beast and his image, and whosoever receiveth the mark of his name."   Revelation 14:9-11

Surely, our faith (or lack thereof) in the healing and protecting power of Christ's atoning blood are going to be (if they aren't already) one of the most telling issues of our time. *"Skin for skin,"* reviled the devil in his efforts to condemn Job in the eyes of his Maker...

". . . Yea, all that a man hath will he give for his life. But put forth thine hand now, and touch his bone and his flesh, and he will curse thee to thy face."   Job 2:4-5

It is comparatively easy to forsake husband, wife, children, father, mother, sisters, brothers, houses, or fields, for the name of Christ; but when it comes to a man's own person, and his life is concerned, then it is that he is truly tried and refined, for a man will give skin for skin, yea, all that he has, for his life, as it is written in Job. But Christ says that one must hate and forsake all this, and his own life also, and take up the cross, and follow Him. And whosoever does not do this, cannot, He says, be His disciple. Lk. 14:26, 27.   Matthias Servaes, Tortured & Slain by Sword by Catholic Decree, A.D. 1565[9]

No wonder the visionary in the video was so passionate in his appeal for sobriety. Paraphrased, he cried: *"Get your heads out of the sand. 'Normal' is a thing of the past."*

Absolutely! Persecution of untold proportions lieth at the Door.

Not a single true minister of the Gospel will be immune.[10]

"Yea, and all that will live godly in Christ Jesus shall suffer
persecution."   2 Timothy 3:12

"And ye shall be hated of all men for my name's sake: but he
that shall endure unto the end, the same shall be saved."
                                                        Mark 13:13

A Living Faith

I am reminded of a prophecy that I received nearly six
decades ago at the outset of my Christian walk. As the word
went forth, impression after impression in harmony with
Matthew 24, Mark 13, Luke 21 and the books of Daniel and
Revelation swept over my entire being. *"Perilous times"* of great
stress and trouble, exceeding anything else known to man loom
on the horizon and our Heavenly Father wants His people
spiritually armed and prepared to faithfully endure through
them without denying Christ *(2 Tim. 3:1)*. Through the fires of
adversity, it is His determinate purpose to prepare a Bride
without *"spot, or wrinkle, or any such thing,"* ready to be received
by His Son at His appearing *(Eph. 5:27)*. These twin books (if
God so choose to anoint them with His power) are part of that
preparation *(Eph. 1:3-12)*.

David Wilkerson likewise saw the formation and
beautification of this *"underground"* Church amidst trying
times, as well as the tidal wave of persecution from which it
would emerge, but in much more vivid detail. In his 1973
Vision he described the ferocity of the latter as *"a supernatural
demonstration of demonic powers."*[11]

I see an hour of persecution coming such as mankind has
never before witnessed. This will be a persecution of true
Jesus believers that will soon arise like a many-headed
monster out of the sea. It will begin slowly and subtly,
coming at a time when religious freedom appears to be at
a peak. It will spread throughout the United States,
Canada, and the entire world and will finally become a
kind of madness.[12]

Way back then he warned of *"legions of lying spirits"* being *"turned loose upon the world with the single purpose of accusing Christians through gossip and slander."*[13] It is *"the turning of things upside down"* foretold by the prophet Isaiah *(Isa. 29:16).*

> I know of nothing that so securely and firmly holds men in the sleep of sin till the Lord comes as a thief in the night, as to call good evil (Isa. 5 :20), the Gospel a sect (of which all manner of evil and falsehoods are spoken), and to change the truth into lies. The Christians are called heretics and deceivers; every good work, virtue and righteousness is so misnamed, perverted, painted in such abominable colors, and the worst construction put upon them, so that men are afraid of them . . . . The devil, on the other hand does not appear half so ugly . . . but disguised by a beautiful semblance of love, and changed and transformed into an angel of light, as though he were sent of God, and were himself God. II Thess. 2:4. Then are his lies called nothing less than Gospel and truth; [and] Babylon is called the church of God . . .
>
> Valerius Schoolmaster, A.D. 1568
> Wrote 2 books in prison before slain by Catholic Decree[14]

Even now, through the exploitation of the pandemic and countless other "crises" (some spontaneous and others manufactured), we are witnessing the underlying working of these demonic forces. Masterminds of propaganda and their minions in government, Hollywood, technology, journalism, sports, academia, and religion are indoctrinating the world with the wild notion that Christians are the cause, and that the remedy is the creation of an International Utopian Society that has no place for the God of Abraham, Isaac and Jacob; nor His Son, Jesus Christ; nor His faithful followers and Conservative Jews in it. This is where alien ideologies like Marxism, Critical Race Theory, Climate Change and Gender Equality now creeping into "mainstream" America are aimed at leading us: directly into the arms of the prophesied Antichrist who is to rule the world from the Temple Mount in Jerusalem till his ultimate overthrow *(Isa. 14:13-14; Dan. 11:45)*.

"And there was given unto him [the Antichrist] a mouth speaking great things and blasphemies; and power was given unto him to continue forty and two months [three and a half years]. And he opened his mouth in blasphemy against God, to blaspheme his name, and his tabernacle, and them that dwell in heaven. And it was given unto him to make war with the saints, and to overcome them: and power was given him over all kindreds, and tongues, and nations. And all that dwell upon the earth shall worship him, whose names are not written in the book of life of the Lamb slain from the foundation of the world."   Revelation 13:5-8

Beloved readers: If there were ever a time in the history of the Church that we, as the Body of Christ, needed a *"living faith"* ...absolute soundness in doctrine and life ...and an unfettered love for Jesus, that time is NOW!

"For then shall be great tribulation, such as was not since the beginning of the world to this time, no, nor ever shall be."
                                        Matthew 24:21; See also Daniel 12:1

O my brethren, knowledge or talk is of no account here, but a living faith which is adorned with the power of love, patience, hope, and with obedience. . . . Give diligence to walk with a pure conscience in the truth before God, that in the melting furnace (if you should get into it yet) you will have no regrets to cause you to prove dross or to look back. For . . . in this trial a dead faith is of no account, however glorious the same may seem in the eyes of men, and with however many Scriptures it may be clearly demonstrated, and professed with the mouth; much less will it avail before a strict God and His righteous judgment; for whatever is to stand here and there must be genuine; yea, it must be done through a living faith which works by love.
                                        Matthias Servaes, A.D. 1565[15]

The Melting Furnace

To one degree or another we are all being vetted in a particular "furnace" of our Father's own engineering. Like a master chemist *"who subjects an imperfectly known substance"* to a variety of conditions in order to ascertain its *"nature and affinities,"* even so the *"Searcher of hearts"* is similarly subjecting us to a diverse combination of circumstances so as to *"make manifest the latent possibilities of . . . [our] character,"*[16] to see whether or not we will remain true to Him and *"keep His commandments"* to the End *(Mt. 10:22; 24:13).*

"And thou shalt remember all the way which the LORD thy God led thee these forty years in the wilderness, to humble thee, and to prove thee, to know what was in thine heart, whether thou wouldest keep His commandments, or no."
                                                                Deuteronomy 8:2

Herewith the Lord proves me, even as He proved His dearest chosen ones, as to whether I fear Him, sincerely, trust Him in the greatest distress, and love Him from the heart.   Jan Wouterss Kuyck, Brave & bold till the end, Tortured & Burned Alive by Catholic decree, A.D. 1572[17]

Though the heat for many of us may not yet be up sevenfold, as it was with Shadrach, Meshach and Abednego *(Dan. 3:19);* or even as it is with our brethren presently suffering horrific persecutions in other lands; the refining fire still burns.

We are now under the test; the almighty God grant us His grace, that we may not be found to be hay, straw and stubble, but gold, silver and precious stones. 1 Cor. 3:12.
            Joost Verkindert, Slain by Catholic decree, A.D. 1570[18]

Hour by hour we are each being made subject to divine appraisal and Holy Ghost evaluation; and shall continue to be sifted, along with the Church and the rest of the world all the way up to the Last Day *(Lk. 21:31-32; Rev. 3:10).*

"But who may abide the day of his coming? and who shall stand when he appeareth? for he is like a refiner's fire, and like fullers' soap: and he shall sit as a refiner and purifier of silver: and he shall purify the sons of Levi, and purge them as gold and silver, that they may offer unto the LORD an offering in righteousness." Malachi 3:2-3

Such was the case with Hezekiah; one of the most notable kings to reign in Judah; a man proved to be true in one trial after another, *until* snared in his latter years by an element of pride that surfaced in his dealings with the princes of Babylon. Thank God that we, like this patriarch, likewise have the opportunity to confront our adamic propensities and repent.

"In those days Hezekiah was sick to the death, and prayed unto the LORD: and he spake unto him, and he gave him a sign. But Hezekiah rendered not again according to the benefit done unto him; for his heart was lifted up: therefore there was wrath upon him, and upon Judah and Jerusalem. Notwithstanding Hezekiah humbled himself for the pride of his heart, both he and the inhabitants of Jerusalem, so that the wrath of the LORD came not upon them in the days of Hezekiah. . . . And Hezekiah prospered in all his works. Howbeit in the business of the ambassadors of the princes of Babylon, who sent unto him to enquire of the wonder that was done in the land, God left him, to try him, that he might know all that was in his heart." 2 Chronicles 32:24-26, 30b-31

Time of Grace

If we will not trust the Lord in the little things, how shall we trust Him with the large *(Lk. 16:10)*?

"If thou hast run with the footmen, and they have wearied thee, then how canst thou contend with horses? And if in the land of peace, wherein thou trustedst, they wearied thee, then how wilt thou do in the swelling of Jordan?" Jeremiah 12:5

If we insist on getting our own way now (playing both sides to the middle between God and mammon), how shall we let the Spirit rule over our flesh when confronted with accelerated reproach and persecution *(Mk. 14:38)*? Slothful Christians in such a state will be *"like a city that is broken down, and without walls" (Pro. 25:28)*. Unable to put the brakes on their sins, they will be in great danger of falling away at their latter end.

"Having eyes full of adultery, and that cannot cease from sin; beguiling unstable souls: an heart they have exercised with covetous practices; cursed children: which have forsaken the right way, and are gone astray, following the way of Balaam the son of Bosor, who loved the wages of unrighteousness."

2 Peter 2:14-15

At whose feet shall we ultimately bow when pushed to our uttermost extremity? Shall we turn with unwavering faith to the Lord Jesus Christ and God the Father for our protection and provision, come what may?

"All this is come upon us; yet have we not forgotten thee, neither have we dealt falsely in thy covenant. Our heart is not turned back, neither have our steps declined from thy way; though thou hast sore broken us in the place of dragons, and covered us with the shadow of death. If we have forgotten the name of our God, or stretched out our hands to a strange god; shall not God search this out? for He knoweth the secrets of the heart."

Psalm 44:17-21

Or, will we weaken in resolve as the price climbs, and at an appointed juncture of suffering or self-denial that God already knows, deny Christ and turn to the world, our former *"gods,"* and the Antichrist system for sustenance and survival *(Jon. 1:5; Jn. 6:66-67)*? Will we continue to take the Gospel to the lost though all the world forbid us and *"bonds and imprisonment"* await us *(Heb. 11:36)*? Big questions. The way we choose to live today may very well affect our ability to stand sure-footed in the Lord tomorrow; not only for our own soul safety; but also, as examples of faith and courage for our brethren.

"And the Lord said, Simon, Simon, behold, Satan hath desired to have you, that he may sift you as wheat: But I have prayed for thee, that thy faith fail not: and when thou art converted, strengthen thy brethren. And he said unto him, Lord, I am ready to go with thee, both into prison, and to death. And he said, I tell thee, Peter, the cock shall not crow this day, before that thou shalt thrice deny that thou knowest me."

Luke 22:31-34

Who among us will be able to stand in the power of his testimony when the *"hour of temptation . . . [is] come upon all the world,"* showing in very deed, even at death's door if need be, that we *"can do all things through Christ which strengtheneth"* us *(Rev. 3:10; Phil. 4:13)?*

"And they overcame him [Satan] by the blood of the Lamb, and by the word of their testimony; and they loved not their lives unto the death."   Revelation 12:11

The Great Shepherd of the sheep, in His great love, is bringing us all to the Touchstone now just as He did Peter in days gone by so that when the storms come and the floods rage, we will be *"stedfast, unmoveable, always abounding in the work of the Lord"* (1 Cor. 15:58). Yea, our *"mountain"* will *"stand strong"* (Ps. 30:7).

It is nothing but sheer mercy; a gift from our loving Heavenly Father (who understands the weakness of our frame, as well as the craftiness of the enemy, and above all else, the redemption available through the blood of His Son); to use what the martyrs called this *"time of grace"*[19] to unearth whatever is buried in our hearts that could trip us up.

". . . Cast ye up, cast ye up, prepare the way, take up the stumblingblock out of the way of my people."   Isaiah 57:14

He is gracious and *"longsuffering to us-ward, not willing that any should perish, but that all should come to repentance"* (2 Pe. 3:9b). Many interpret that verse as targeting unbelievers. But careful study reveals it to be an exhortation directed first to *"us-ward,"* meaning to born again Christians, like you and like me.

"For the time is come that judgment must begin at the house of God: and if it first begin at us, what shall the end be of them that obey not the Gospel of God? And if the righteous scarcely be saved, where shall the ungodly and the sinner appear?"

1 Peter 4:17-18

We pray that the Holy Spirit will take the testimony of Scripture revealed in these pages through the prism of our lives and use it to speak into the life of every reader so that together we may be healed of our infirmities and equipped to stand *"stedfast with God"* from this present Hour all the way up to the First Resurrection; in Jesus' name, amen *(Ps. 78:8).*

"A good man sheweth favour, and lendeth: he will guide his affairs with discretion. Surely he shall not be moved for ever.... He shall not be afraid of evil tidings: his heart is fixed, trusting in the Lord."

Psalm 112:5-6a, 7

CHAPTER THREE

O Magnify the Lord with Me

Beloved Brothers and Sisters in Jesus... This is Sister Jody now sharing ...and with such gratitude and joy! ...At about two am one morning in September of 2018 after the completion of the ten page epistle, "Faith our Alarm System," to our Zimbabwean brethren, I was awakened together with Apostle Edwin with a verse ringing in my spirit. I couldn't wait to get up and search it out in the Bible. But first, as is our usual manner when we rise up early in the predawn hours to seek *"hard"* after our Lord *(Ps. 63:8)*, I wanted to warm up a hot cup of tea to get us going. *"Quiet Time"* with Jesus is the foundation of our days.[1] We wouldn't trade it for anything this world has to offer! We're like Zaccheus in a tree *(Lk. 19:1-4)*. We want to see Jesus. We want to hear from our Lord. Here's the verse:

"Come and hear, all ye that fear God, and I will declare what he hath done for my soul."   Psalms 66:16

> *Yes ...yes! I so MUCH want to share, oh my Lord, what YOU have done for my soul.*

"And Mary said, My soul doth magnify the Lord, and my spirit hath rejoiced in God my Saviour. For he hath regarded the low estate of his handmaiden . . . . For he that is mighty hath done to me great things; and holy is his name."   Luke 1:46-48a, 49

"O magnify the LORD with me, and let us exalt His name together. I sought the Lord, and he heard me, and delivered me from all my fears. They looked unto him, and were lightened: and their faces were not ashamed. This poor man cried, and the Lord heard him, and saved him out of all his troubles."

Psalm 34:3-6

Divine Providence

Little did we know at this pivotal time how profoundly the hand of God was in the mix, both here and overseas. Multiple purposes were in play. Not only had He miraculously turned the plunder of Bishop Raymore's car into an occasion for preaching the Gospel and an opportunity for us to put together an End-Time teaching on the finer points of faith-building; but He was also answering my prayers by honing in on my great need for "ever increasing faith" in regards to healing. Praise God! As one brother used to say: "*God is quite the Economist.*" He never wastes an opportunity to "put His finger" on the unique needs of us all.

"Then Jesus beholding him loved him, and said unto him, One thing thou lackest . . ."   Mark 10:21a

"I know thy works, and charity, and service, and faith, and thy patience, and thy works; and the last to be more than the first. Notwithstanding I have a few things against thee . . ."
                                              Revelation 2:19-20a

Plus, the trial of our faith throughout the formation of the letter and in the aftermath marked the conception of the book you now hold in your hands. ...The very book the prophet saw in his dream over a year earlier. ...A book we initially foresaw as a book on healing, but was later transformed into a tool for the preparation of the saints for the First Resurrection and the perils and persecutions that are to precede it.

A chapter called "Made Perfect in Weakness" from Andrew Murray's biography comes to mind. Much like us, this fellow laborer had difficulty finding enough time for writing, too, until the Lord intervened.

"Stop preaching at once!" Such an order from Andrew's doctor must have come as a great shock and test to the untiring, fiery minister. . . . Because he did not immediately heed the warning, from 1879 he lost his voice for nearly two years. . . . But the sovereign God had been working a perfect plan which did not allow for unexpected detours. While unable to speak, Andrew naturally turned to more intensive writing, for which he might not have found much time if he had continued in his ever-accelerating preaching schedule. . . . "Strange that I marked out the plan for a certain book some ten or twelve years ago, and now it is all at once flowing from my pen so easily."[2]

Strange Outbreak

Writing "Faith our Alarm System" was more like an experience than the setting forth of words. It seemed as though all hell was moved against us with every stroke on the keyboard. I did the typing and Edwin did the directing and covering. It took roughly four days.

Shortly after we started a small bump surfaced on my neck about an inch back from my chin. It itched tremendously. Being that we were set up in our RV[a] in a wilderness setting, I thought that I had gotten bit by some kind of an insect. Perhaps a mosquito? But the next day I noticed about three little bumps at that same spot, sort of linked together, and each one had a tiny head on top that felt like fire if touched or scratched.

My immediate response was conviction. Perhaps this was my Heavenly Father's chastening rod? Admittedly, however, my reaction was lacking in a corresponding spirit of worship and thanksgiving. Had I been as seasoned as Job, then faith in the Sovereign Hand and goodness of our Great God, "through thick and through thin," would have prompted that reaction.

"Then Job arose, and rent his mantle, and shaved his head, and fell down upon the ground, and worshipped, and said, Naked came I out of my mother's womb, and naked shall I return thither: the LORD gave, and the LORD hath taken away; blessed be the name of the Lord."   Job 1:20-21

---

[a] RV (Recreational Vehicle) — A self-contained mobile camper-like vehicle common to Americans with multiple uses. Ours serves as a home, writing studio and office.

Acceptance and praise *should* have been (but were not) my reflex responses.

"In every thing give thanks: for this is the will of God in Christ Jesus concerning you."   1 Thessalonians 5:18

IN TIME OF TROUBLE SAY: First . . . It is by [God's allowance] that I am in this place. In that I will rest. Next--He will keep me in His love and give me grace in this trial to behave as His child. Then--He will make the trial a blessing, teaching me the lessons He intends me to learn, and working in me the grace He means to bestow. Last--In good time He can bring me out again--how much and when He knows.[3]

"What could this be" I wondered. *"The Lord must be dealing with me."*

"When thou with rebukes dost correct man for iniquity, thou makest his beauty to consume away like a moth: surely every man is vanity. Selah."   Psalms 39:11

Then, came fear. ...Actually, a mix of fears. My initial fear was the fear of God—a blessing indeed! That kind of fear, if reacted to in faith, leads to one place: the altar of repentance and renewed worship. It leads to amendment of life and steadfast adherence to the Lord and His Word. ...And, at its end, is both healing and eternal life.

"Be not wise in thine own eyes: fear the LORD, and depart from evil. It shall be health to thy navel, and marrow to thy bones."
          Proverbs 3:7-8

"And I will make an everlasting covenant with them, that I will not turn away from them, to do them good; but I will put my fear in their hearts, that they shall not depart from me."
          Jeremiah 32:40

It's actually one of many manifestations of the seven-fold Spirit of God.

"And the spirit of the LORD shall rest upon him, the spirit of wisdom and understanding, the spirit of counsel and might, the spirit of knowledge and of the fear of the LORD; and shall make him of quick understanding in the fear of the LORD . . ."

Isaiah 11:2-3a

The other fears sprang out of unbelief and self-preservation.

How far is this going to go?

I told Edwin about it the next day and asked for his prayers—which (of course!) he was *more* than happy to render. And not just once! Every time I reached for him he was there to undergird me with prayer and words of encouragement. He was juggling several other responsibilities pertaining to the Kingdom at the time, on top of the writing. It brought a degree of peace to me, knowing that my husband was at my side and if he discerned a breach opening me up that I had not detected myself (meaning an inroad caused by sin), he would surely make it known. Notwithstanding, it was necessary for me to discipline my mind (with the help of the Holy Spirit) so as not to drift into questionings. ...Not to scratch haphazardly due to an element of anxiety that I sensed working in my heart. ...And most importantly, not to get distracted from piecing together the letter. It takes so much exertion and focus to plainly set forth the Truth and a break in concentration makes the challenge all the more difficult.

"No big deal," I commiserated myself. "*Must have been some kind of a spider or what's called a no-see-um.*" That's a tiny little bug whose bite can leave behind a venomous swelling, depending on how a person's body reacts.

The next thing I knew, a string of similar bumps popped up on the back of my neck in my hairline. Concerns about my standing with the Lord pressed in mightily upon me. Then an added string of bumps surfaced on the back of my right ear. Plus, the ones near my chin opened up like wounds and burned like fire, so much so, that it became increasingly difficult to remain zeroed in on the letter.

"I am afflicted and ready to die from my youth up: while I suffer thy terrors I am distracted."   Psalms 88:15

Oh Lord, I prayed, *reveal my heart and grant me the grace to recognize and own up to Your reproof, in Jesus' name, amen.*

"I will say unto God, Do not condemn me; shew me wherefore thou contendest with me."   Job 10:2

Taking Hold on the Horns of the Altar

My concern heightened and again I went to Edwin, asking him to pray with me. Four decades walking together through one faith venture after another and there I was getting shaky over a proportionally small issue! It's so important to face our weaknesses and open up. We're all prone to overestimation and self-deception; that deplorable tendency in the adamic nature that prompts us to favor, justify and defend our own cause (even recast ourselves as something we're not); rather than look honestly into the Word when the searchlight of the Holy Ghost is on so as to determine whether or not our lives measure up.

"All the ways of a man are clean in his own eyes; but the LORD weigheth the spirits."   Proverbs 16:2

"For I say, through the grace given unto me, to every man that is among you, not to think of himself more highly than he ought to think; but to think soberly, according as God hath dealt to every man the measure of faith."   Romans 12:3

An outside view from a God-fearing saint who truly loves us with the love of the Lord, yet whose perspectives are not affected by emotional biases, selfish interests or errant beliefs, is an indispensible help *(Eph. 4:15).*

"Open rebuke is better than secret love. Faithful are the wounds of a friend; but the kisses of an enemy are deceitful."
                    Proverbs 27:5-6

Man's love is a love that makes excuses. God's love is a love that redeems.[4]

Thank God for such a gift. It is the Body of Christ!

"But exhort one another daily, while it is called To day; lest any of you be hardened through the deceitfulness of sin."
Hebrews 3:13

Then, humbling myself *with my husband* in prayer, I asked the Lord to forgive me (as I am often compelled to do) for all the lingering sins in my life that I in any wise let slide; even the *"little foxes"* like picking at tidbits of food while cleaning up the dishes when nobody is looking *(Son. 2:15)*. I asked my Lord Jesus and my husband to forgive me for every trace of the spirit of the Queen of Heaven that shows its face from time to time *(Jer. 44:17)*; every proud look, every ounce of disrespect, complaining and contention.

...I asked for forgiveness for the sinful disposition of my old nature that can often be hidden behind a form of outward submission. God *"desirest truth in the inward parts "* *(Ps. 51:6)*. *"Of great price"* in His sight is a truly constant and affectionate spirit of loving support and surrender in the lives of Christian wives *(1 Pe. 3:1-6)*. Like the Word says: It's one thing to give and quite another to be a *"cheerful giver"* *(2 Cor. 9:7)*. The distinction is heart attitude, not the mere act *(Acts 8:21)*.

"Let all your things be done *with charity*." 1 Corinthians 16:14

It's all about what David Wilkerson described in *The Cross and the Switchblade*: *"change."*[5] It's about *"New Beginnings."*[6] About being *"renewed in the spirit"* of our minds *(Eph. 4:23)*; about having a *"right spirit"* *(Ps. 51:10)*, come "rain or shine," about everything we say and do. ...And think, too *(Acts 8:22)*!!

A false heart . . . [is] willing to have his sin . . . [forgiven], but the sincere [soul] desires [that] his nature may be cured and cleansed [as well].[7]

"Create in me a clean heart, O God; and renew a right spirit within me."   Psalms 51:10

"Who can understand his errors? Cleanse thou me from secret faults. Keep back thy servant also from presumptuous sins; let them not have dominion over me: then shall I be upright, and I shall be innocent from the great transgression. Let the words of my mouth, and the meditation of my heart, be acceptable in thy sight, O Lord, my strength, and my redeemer."   Psalm 19:12-14

"And whatsoever ye do in word or deed, do all in the name of the Lord Jesus, giving thanks to God the Father by him."
                                        Colossians 3:17

Gratitude ...Respect ...And Devotion

Don't let the detail in Colossians 3:17 just quoted pass you by. Thanksgiving is one of the key manifestations of a *"right spirit."* It is our open acknowledgment of God's supremacy and creative power; of His righteousness and goodness; of His prerogative to do as He pleases. We owe Him everything, whereas He owes us nothing. Yet, *"of His own will begat He us"* *(Jam. 1:18)*, giving us every good thing He has to offer in the Person of His Son *(Col. 2:10)*. What a merciful Father we serve!

"Let us come before his presence with thanksgiving, and make a joyful noise unto him with psalms. For the LORD is a great God, and a great King above all gods. In his hand are the deep places of the earth: the strength of the hills is his also. The sea is his, and he made it: and his hands formed the dry land. O come, let us worship and bow down: let us kneel before the LORD our maker. For he is our God; and we are the people of his pasture, and the sheep of his hand . . ."   Psalm 95:2-7a

Wherever thanksgiving and deference of this kind are lacking, you will most often find unbelief, discontent and complaining against both God and man. These are manifestations of unacceptance and rebellion that spring from deep roots in the adamic nature of pride and self-will.

". . . They believed not his word: but murmured in their tents, and hearkened not unto the voice of the LORD."

Psalm 106:24b-25

If left unchecked, that kind of disposition lends itself to self-pity and presumptuous sin. Next follows darkness (self-deception), degeneracy, apostasy and ultimately, wrath. To get a full view of the declension read Romans Chapter One.

> Losing a reverential, worshipful spirit is the first step down into the spiral of degradation. . . . Romans 1:21 describes a person who has begun to turn away from the Lord in his heart. He may still continue to go through the outward motions of a believer, but something within him is drying up. He is losing his sense of adoration for the God who has saved him.[8]

"For the invisible things of him from the creation of the world are clearly seen, being understood by the things that are made, even his eternal power and Godhead; so that they are without excuse: because that, when they knew God, they glorified him not as God, *neither were thankful*; but became vain in their imaginations, and their foolish heart was darkened. Professing themselves to be wise, they became fools, and changed the glory of the uncorruptible God into an image made like to corruptible man, and to birds, and fourfooted beasts, and creeping things. Wherefore God also gave them up . . ."

Romans 1:20-24a

Knowing this, I also asked for forgiveness for the ways I take our bountiful blessings lightly. I'm not talking about material things, though we are grateful that our needs, even in lean times, have always been met without fail. Rather, I'm referring to the "best of blessings." ...Things like Jesus as our Lord; an apprehension of (and belief in) the real nectar of the Organic Gospel; our wonderful marriage and the Great Commission which has been at the heart of our union since "day one" *(Phil. 1:5)*; healing as a way of life!; our bond with committed Christians *(1 Th. 1:2)*; the spirit of repentance that

God has granted to us in His great magnanimity *(2 Tim. 2:25)*; our zeal for the Cross and its glorious work of transformation; my discipling under the tutelage of a God-fearing and faithful 21st century apostle *(Eph. 5:25-26)*... I could go on ...and on! I am a truly BLESSED saint and I need to be thanking my worthy Lord more often (yea, continually!) for the price He paid for our redemption; rather than bewailing (in times of anguish and distress) the opposition and challenge that go along with apostolic ministry in a Gospel-hardened land.

"At midnight I will rise to give thanks unto thee . . ." Ps. 119:62a

What a PRIVILEGE it is to serve!! And oh what a wretch I've been! ...So sing we ALL in harmony with John Newton in his famous hymn *"Amazing Grace."* Truly, we meet at the Cross. It's a day by day transformation of character and nature until at last we reflect in every way the beauty of the Lord Himself.

"But we all, with open face beholding as in a glass the glory of the Lord, are changed into the same image from glory to glory, even as by the Spirit of the Lord."					2 Corinthians 3:18

Layer by layer every trace of the rebellion and self-will that spoiled the disposition of so many of my Jewish ancestors (not all by any means!) is being washed away in the blood of Jesus *(Deu. 9:7;1 Pe. 1:18)*. If I continue to walk this narrow Way of the Cross (the way of repentance and faith); then, following in the footsteps of the Apostle Paul after his conversion, I'll be able to more and more effectually support my husband in extending a compassionate (but firm) hand to others from all walks of life in our common struggle to "surrender all" to the Lord, even when they put up a fight *(2 Tim. 2:24-26; Eze. 2:7)*.

"This is a faithful saying, and worthy of all acceptation, that Christ Jesus came into the world to save sinners; of whom I am chief. Howbeit for this cause I obtained mercy, that in me first Jesus Christ might shew forth all longsuffering, for a pattern to them which should hereafter believe on him to life everlasting."
1 Timothy 1:15-16

Not that I can "light a candle" to Paul, but rather that I can identify with his rescue and recovery from the curse of ignorance and unbelief and the misdirected zeal it begets.

"Who was before a blasphemer, and a persecutor, and injurious: but I obtained mercy, because I did it ignorantly in unbelief." 1 Timothy 1:13

Together at the Cross

Edwin took my hands as I opened my soul to the Lord. As usual, he then went on to help me to examine the larger issues which most often take the preeminence in his soul searching. ...Things like accountability regarding the integrity of the Gospel we preach and the spirit in which we approach others.

Have we come up short, O Lord, in anything with anyone? And conversely, *Have we stepped into terrain we don't belong? Have we missed a step of obedience ...neglected to make a call ...presumed upon Your grace ...squandered a moment of Your time ...overlooked a divine appointment? Have we been lagging in fervency ...slack in the investment of our "talent" (Mt. 25:14)? ...negligent in prayer? Forgive us for our moments of distraction when we get off guard and our thoughts run amuck. Are we unwilling to bow to your will on any matter? Have we been intimidated by the "face of man" (Deu. 1:17)? Have we shrunk back from preaching Your Cross (Acts 20:20-27)? Are there any traces of unforgiveness blinding our eyes ...silencing our prayers ...or inhibiting us from reaching out to new people brought into our lives?*

...Much to consider. Once our burdens were cast upon the Lord, we arose from prayer. I sensed a subtle wellspring of hope and directed it toward walking more diligently than ever in *"newness of life" (Rom. 6:4)*. My steps, however, were yet a bit timid and my eyes often filled with tears.

"Surely it is meet to be said unto God, I have borne chastisement, I will not offend any more: that which I see not teach thou me: if I have done iniquity, I will do no more."
Job 34:31-32

CHAPTER FOUR

The Old Time Gospel

Onward we pressed with the ten page epistle to our Zimbabwean brethren. Here's a tiny clip to show you the glorious truths that the Holy Spirit was bringing to the fore at the same time that the devil was probing for weakness in my life. His strategy was to undermine, distract and unnerve me with self-absorption and fear.

> The Apostle Peter taught us that "the trial of [our] faith" is "much more precious than of gold." He also taught that this "precious" virtue was going to be "tried with fire" for the ultimate purpose of purification that it might be "found unto praise and honour and glory at the appearing of Jesus Christ" (1 Pe. 1:7). Being that faith is an indispensible lifeline necessary for carrying us safely under the blood of Jesus to the First Resurrection, we need to guard it with the utmost care and exercise it to the FULL at every given opportunity in order to strengthen it and keep it lively. Never lose sight of your accountability to God. We as Christians, and leaders in particular, are duty bound to maintain a disciplined walk of faith on all fronts [Heb. 13:7]; not only for our own spiritual welfare; but also, as an example and inspiration to others. Like Linah reminds us: "Our lives must teach."[1]

The Gospel of the Cross

While I typed I was reminded of a meeting I attended where Apostle Edwin was preaching on the stripes of Jesus and the promise of healing that goes together with repentance. It's hard to explain, but it was as though I personally (as well as others) were hearing (I mean *really* hearing) the Good News of the

Gospel for the first time. The power and anointing that carried Edwin's message was utterly divine—completely outside of a great deal of what has come to be accepted as the conventional religious norm.

"And they were astonished at his doctrine: for he taught them as one that had authority, and not as the scribes."   Mark 1:22

Yet, it was nothing new. Just the opposite! It was the "old time" Gospel of the Cross centered in the transformation of our lives from the old creatures we once were into new creatures in Christ, from the first day of conversion till the end of our lives. Apart from that daily change, everything else in our Christian lives (no matter how religious or seemingly noble) is vain.

"But God forbid that I should glory, save in the cross of our Lord Jesus Christ, by whom the world is crucified unto me, and I unto the world. For in Christ Jesus neither circumcision availeth any thing, nor uncircumcision, but a new creature."
Galatians 6:14-15

Hard as he could, Edwin was preaching the link that Jesus established between *"repentance and remission of sins,"* and the healing that follows. ...A divine connection imparted by the Lord to His apostles and from them passed down to faithful saints of subsequent generations, many of whom defended it with their lives. Still further, he was preaching the baptism of the Holy Ghost as the God-given power to walk in the rigors of the Gospel and take it to the ends of the earth.

Jesus said: ". . . Thus it is written, and thus it behoved Christ to suffer, and to rise from the dead the third day: and that repentance and remission of sins should be preached in his name among all nations, beginning at Jerusalem. And ye are witnesses of these things. And, behold, I send the promise of my Father upon you: but tarry ye in the city of Jerusalem, until ye be endued with power from on high."   Luke 24:46-49

You could hear a pin drop as the Truth marched on. The reason for Edwin's thunder was the fear of God. He knew beyond the shadow of a doubt that the unadulterated Gospel was sure; and that anyone who dared to tamper with its integrity by slackening its conditions, altering its structure, or rupturing the connection it makes between ongoing repentance and remission (even if he be the Apostle Paul) was in danger of losing his part in the Kingdom of God.

"But though we, or an angel from heaven, preach any other gospel unto you than that which we have preached unto you, let him be accursed. As we said before, so say I now again, if any man preach any other gospel unto you than that ye have received, let him be accursed."   Galatians 1:8-9

Edwin's Foundation

Clearly, Edwin was "at home" in the message. The Holy Spirit had implanted it in his heart as far back as 1964, fifteen years before I ever came along. It took root along with a solid foundation of faith after three landmark experiences in the aftermath of the death of his wife.

The first was the supernatural healing of their cherished six month old son from asthma in answer to the fiery prayers of an elderly Pentecostal housekeeper he had hired to help take care of the baby while he worked extra hours to cover the medical bills incurred by his wife's illness. Edwin returned home from work one day to find that all the baby's medications were gone, but to his utter amazement, gone were the wheezing and hacking, too. *"Who is this Jesus"* he wondered, *that I have only known as a historical figure my whole life long?"*

The second was the "Damascus experience" he touched on in Chapter Two *(Acts 9:3)*, when he was struck down by the Holy Ghost, enveloped by the Shekhinah glory of the Lord, and given an End-Time prophecy that uprooted him from his Methodist upbringing and changed his life forever.

And the third was actually a series of adventures that took place when the Lord teamed him up with a completely unconventional itinerant evangelist that was fanatical about spontaneously obeying the unction of the Holy Spirit. From the sounds of it, the brother wasn't intimidated about being a "fool for Christ." He had been set free from homosexuality and miraculously healed from cancer and he wanted to let all the world know about it, using the Word as his platform. He'd actually toss a great big Bible onto the floor at meetings; place both feet squarely on top of it; and say *"I'm standing on the Word of God"* before he launched into prayer. The gifts of the Spirit freely operated through his life in like manner as was witnessed in the Book of Acts. On two occasions Edwin heard him speaking in other tongues in languages that were unfamiliar to the brother himself, but native to a cross-section of people who rallied around his preaching. That kind of "living faith" soon captured Edwin, too, and was reinforced in a really big way when a couple stood up in a meeting to testify of the clean bill of health that their cancer ridden son received shortly after being placed in Edwin's lap for prayer. Praise the Name of Jesus! There is nothing *"too hard"* for Him *(Jer. 32:17)*.

The Stripes of Jesus

With all that behind him, Edwin stood before us preaching the wonderworking power of the Cross. Sin and disobedience, he taught, not only separate us from God *(Isa. 59:2)*, but are often tied to sickness, and the way to break the chain is repentance; turning from the pursuit of our own way to the discovery of God's Will.

"But he was wounded for our transgressions, he was bruised for our iniquities: the chastisement of our peace was upon him; and with his stripes we are healed. All we like sheep have gone astray; we have turned every one to his own way; and the Lord hath laid on him the iniquity of us all."   Isaiah 53:5-6

There is a close relationship between sin and sickness. How many know that their sickness . . . [may be] a direct result of sin? I hope that no one will ask to be prayed for who is living in sin. But if you will obey God and repent of your sin and quit it, God will meet you, and neither your sickness nor your sin will remain. "The prayer of faith shall save the sick, and the Lord shall raise him up; and if he have committed sins, they shall be forgiven him" (James 5:15).[2]

That golden nugget of Promise was novel. It was powerful!!! ...So powerful that over four decades later I *still* remember the scenario in which it was delivered. ...So potent that once it was published in our first paperback with all the supporting Scriptures and carried unbeknownst to us into Nigeria by a man who we later found out was a visiting Ogboni chief, set off what our African brethren call a *"harmattan bushfire."* The next thing we knew letters started filling our mail box from what eventually mushroomed into 41 African countries — beginning with our first response from a Ghanaian young man converted and miraculously healed by the power of Christ as he received the engrafted Word printed on those pages. Hungry souls wrote beseeching us for books, cassette messages and Bibles. *"Why had this old time Gospel in its full salt and purity been hidden for so long?"* Can't tell you how many times that question was put to us. The testimonies were spectacular! ...People trekked long distances by foot and even by canoe just to lay hold on the Gospel of the Cross. It was Acts Chapter 29; a windfall exodus from the shackles of Catholicism; healing and deliverance included; Muslims risking their lives to embrace Christianity; Baptists touched by fire and filled with the Holy Ghost; prison cells and thatched huts turned into sanctuaries; a bar turned into a church; all kinds of people "set ablaze" for Jesus.

A similar awakening took place in the life of Frank Buchman at the turn of the 20th Century when he heard a devout sister in what one author described as *"simple, artless words"* tell the same story of *"Christ crucified"* *(1 Cor. 1:23)*. Not coincidentally, that revolutionary hearing came at a time when Buchman was mourning his *"failure and futility [in] life and ministry"* on account of the *"lack of the power of God"* in both.[3]

There in the little Cumberland chapel Frank Buchman had a sight of the Cross. Truly, a man may look at a thing nine hundred and ninety-nine times and not see it once,

and then look for the thousandth time and see it for the first time. . . . As she spoke the pilgrim saw the Cross as he had never seen it before and through the Cross he saw himself. That is what the Cross does for us. It throws the searching light of God into the dark places of our hearts and lays bare the things we try to hide even from ourselves. It strips us of the silken robes of self-excusing and tears off the masks wherewith we disguise our condition. This is the light that hurts and heals.[4]

I was fairly new in the Lord then. We were not married at the time. Even though many of those present had professed Christ for years, most of us had never laid hold of the efficacy in Christ's blood as God would have us to understand it.

"For thou bringest certain strange things to our ears: we would know therefore what these things mean."   Acts 17:20

Our understanding of what famed British reformer John Wesley called "*Heart Religion*" was very shallow. Sadly, there are multitudes of professing Christians that have all the advantages; yet, as he so bluntly put it, know "*as much of heart religion, of scriptural Christianity,*" and its connection to health, "*as a child three years old of Algebra.*"[5]

Oh, that we could learn to believe in the promises of God! God has not gone back from His promises; Jesus is still He who heals both soul and body; salvation offers us even now healing and holiness, and the Holy Spirit is always ready to give us some manifestations of His power. Even when we ask why this power is not more often seen, He answers us: "Because of your unbelief." The more we give ourselves to experience personally sanctification by faith, the more we shall also experience healing by faith. These two doctrines walk abreast.[6]

Jesus gave His life, so that everyone of us, without exception, could be saved from our destructions (our sins); and as a result, be made "*every whit whole*" (*Jn. 7:23*).

He is always the same Saviour, both of the soul, and of the body, equally ready to grant pardon and healing.[7]

"Bless the LORD, O my soul, and forget not all his benefits: Who forgiveth all thine iniquities; who healeth all thy diseases; who redeemeth thy life from destruction; who crowneth thee with lovingkindness and tender mercies."   Psalm 103:2-4

The [connection between heart washing and healing]. . . is clearly important, for to treat [natural] symptoms and ignore their [spiritual] cause is to invite the recurrence or continuation of the disease. To attain the fullness of Christian health for ourselves or for others, it is necessary to recognise symptoms and discern the sins which cause them, that so we may suffer the sins to be forgiven and [our whole beings] cured.[8]

Over and over again the same theme is woven into the tapestry of Scripture. Psalm 107 in its entirety is a prime example. Chastisements of whatever form they take, whether as sickness or some other manifestation of adversity that disquiets our souls, are all for the purpose of getting our attention; building our faith; bringing us to our knees in repentance; and turning our eyes away from the world and our flesh to God. In a nutshell, they're about restoring our lives in totality to the Lord *(3 Jn. 1:2)*.

"For He commandeth, and raiseth the stormy wind, which lifteth up the waves thereof. They mount up to the heaven, they go down again to the depths: their soul is melted because of trouble. They reel to and fro, and stagger like a drunken man, and are at their wit's end. Then they cry unto the Lord in their trouble, and he bringeth them out of their distresses. He maketh the storm a calm, so that the waves thereof are still. Then are they glad because they be quiet; so he bringeth them unto their desired haven. Oh that men would praise the Lord for his goodness, and for his wonderful works to the children of men! . . . Whoso is wise, and will observe these things, even they shall understand the lovingkindness of the Lord."

Psalms 107:25-31, 43

Art Katz sums it up like this:

> More often than not, there is a conjunction between sin and ill health, and God does not necessarily want it magically relieved. More importantly, He reserves the prerogative to want to deal with the root cause of the "dis-ease" . . .[9]

Yet, for the most part, that's not what's being taught from today's pulpits. It's not a very popular message because those that are walking in the flesh (no matter how great their need) prefer to have their ears scratched *(2 Tim. 4:2-4)*, rather than hear the necessary reproof that can set us free.

"Thy prophets have seen vain and foolish things for thee: and they have not discovered thine iniquity, to turn away thy captivity; but have seen for thee false burdens and causes of banishment." Lamentations 2:14

> Very few of God's people want to face the issues of truth in an intensive way. That is why we have fellowships that prefer to turn up the amplifiers, establish and promote worship leaders, and employ music to bring the sense of spiritual euphoria and the impression of an alive church, but without the foundational and unmistakable reality of true fellowship. A good definition of much of present Christendom is that it wants the sense of the power and gifts of God, but without the Cross of God. Truth is powerful; it makes a requirement; it is challenging and it brings conviction. Truth calls us to the cross.[10]

Compromise on this issue is one of the main reasons why many of God's children are wandering around bleeding.

". . . Woe be to the shepherds of Israel that do feed themselves!
should not the shepherds feed the flocks? . . . The diseased have
ye not strengthened, neither have ye healed that which was
sick, neither have ye bound up that which was broken, neither
have ye brought again that which was driven away, neither
have ye sought that which was lost . . ."   Ezekiel 34:2b, 4a

Their shepherds are so busy taking care of themselves and
trying to keep everybody happy that they've lost sight of their
accountability as stewards of the Gospel to preach a complete
message that addresses our common need for healing from the
inside, out. We need to be taught the Way of the Cross.

Ministry to the Whole Man

Yes, Jesus is our Healer, but His interest in our well being
extends much further than the healing of our bodies. He's after
the redemption of the whole man: spirit, soul and body; and
often times in that order.

"And the very God of peace sanctify you wholly; and I pray
God your whole spirit and soul and body be preserved
blameless unto the coming of our Lord Jesus Christ."
                                         1 Thessalonians 5:23

That's what Christ's crucifixion and resurrection were all
about: our 100% restoration to God; our sanctification; and our
steadfast stance in Christ from now till the First Resurrection.

What is the enduring benefit of merely receiving
alleviation from the symptoms that were the
consequences of serious defects of character [that could
profoundly affect our salvation and ultimately send us to
the Lake of Fire]? Surely those same character defects
remain with us until [we address them at the Cross of
Jesus in repentance and] the process of sanctification has
done its work.[11]

Christ's unspeakable sacrifice is all about our complete deliverance from the arrogant, unyielding, independent, self-absorbed nature we inherited from Adam — a miracle equally as wondrous (if not more so) than the mending of our bodies.

> . . . It . . . [can be] a long painfully slow job, having the roots of selfishness and bad temper and irritability and laziness, and all the other sins and defects so natural to human nature, put to death. A much more difficult job than being delivered from infirmities and handicaps. But His . . . patient love never . . . [fails]. How skillful He is.[12]

It's about the recovery of a union lost between man and his Maker when Adam and Eve made the fateful choice to eat the forbidden fruit and depart from the commandment of God.

> . . . All this was done [in the divine Plan of the Father and the Son] with the one purpose of bringing us fallen men with our sinful, proud, unbroken natures back to that relationship with God of submissiveness and God-centeredness that was lost in the Fall — that position where once more He can delight in us and we in Him.[13]

"Now the God of peace, that brought again from the dead our Lord Jesus, that great shepherd of the sheep, through the blood of the everlasting covenant, make you perfect in every good work to do his will, working in you that which is wellpleasing in his sight, through Jesus Christ; to whom be glory for ever and ever. Amen."   Hebrews 13:20-21

Errant Beliefs

Many are under the false impression that the working of this perfection is all wrapped up in an *"initial repentance"* and subsequent *"conversion,"* not realizing that the born again experience, when the Spirit of Christ first makes His entrance into our hearts (if He really has), is *"merely the gateway onto the road back to fellowship with God"* (*Gal. 4:6; Jn. 3:3, 7; 1 Pe. 1:23*).[14]

[Yet] . . . it is only when we get on the road that God can start dealing with our self-centered wills . . . [15]

From that turning point onward, the healing, development and maintenance of our relationship with God is hinged upon our willingness to take up Christ's Cross; leaving the world behind and making the Father and the Son the primary object of our attention and affections *(Col. 3:1-2)*.

"And he said to them all, If any man will come after me, let him deny himself, and take up his cross daily, and follow me. For whosoever will save his life shall lose it: but whosoever will lose his life for my sake, the same shall save it."   Luke 9:23-24

What is the first question you raise when you leave the building Sunday morning? Is it, "What did you think of the speaker? Did you like him? Did you like the worship? Did you like the sermon?" Is what you like still the center of your essential will and being? We are still the center, and it is no wonder that we are sick; no wonder we need continually to be healed. Until we make God, His glory, His honor, His name and His eternal purposes the center, we will continue to be sick until our false center is displaced.[16]

Pointing us in that direction is the primary purpose of all of the circumstances brought to bear in the lives of God's children *(Amos 4:6-12)*.

If to bring us back into this relationship with God is the whole purpose of His creation and then His redemption of us, we can be quite sure that this will be the one great object of all His present dealings with us. If an airplane designer designs a plane to fly at a certain altitude and finds that it will not leave the ground, he will bend every effort to make that plane do that for which he designed it. So does God bend every effort to bring us back to Himself.[17]

"He causeth it to come, whether for correction, or for his land,
or for mercy." Job 37:13

Yet, so many in the church today, not knowing how to
recognize and rightly respond in faith and repentance to the
Designer's working, especially chastisement, fail to profit
thereby *(Heb. 12:5-13)*.

"Yea, the stork in the heaven knoweth her appointed times; and
the turtle and the crane and the swallow observe the time of
their coming; but my people know not the judgment of the
LORD." Jeremiah 8:7

> That is a hard word for the many thousands who have
> made a "decision for Christ," or walked down the aisle of
> a church to "invite Jesus into their heart," in their minds
> settling in with confidence that they are now "saved" and
> looking to see what benefits they will now receive.[18]

From their point of view, it's the Lord's obligation to remove
His children from suffering, not to use it, as the Word teaches,
as an instrumentality of sanctification for our ultimate good.

"For which cause we faint not; but though our outward man
perish, yet the inward man is renewed day by day. For our
light affliction, which is but for a moment, worketh for us a far
more exceeding and eternal weight of glory; while we look not
at the things which are seen, but at the things which are not
seen: for the things which are seen are temporal; but the things
which are not seen are eternal." 2 Corinthians 4:16-18

> Providences are good and evil to us as they find or make
> us better or worse . . . . As God makes use of all the
> seasons of the year for the harvest, the frost and cold of
> winter, as well as the heat of the summer; so doth He of
> fair and foul, pleasing and unpleasing providences . . .
> Winter providences kill the weeds of lusts [1 Pe.4:1-2],
> and summer providences ripen and mellow the fruits of

righteousness; when He afflicts, it is for our profit, to make us partakers of his holiness.[19]

"Now no chastening for the present seemeth to be joyous, but grievous: nevertheless afterward it yieldeth the peaceable fruit of righteousness unto them which are exercised thereby."

Hebrews 12:11

Testimony

A letter sent to a friend struggling with health issues by a Christian brother that Apostle Edwin discipled back in the nineties helps "put a face" on this. Actually, the two of us worked with him as a Gospel Team to put it together after he had been delivered from a freak skin disease that had him cringing when in the public eye and tormented throughout his nights. It haunted him on and off for about two and a half years (before and after he stepped into our lives), until he made contact with the blood of Jesus through faith and repentance and as a result was marvelously delivered and totally healed.

The "*great stumbling block*" preventing him from connecting these two links holding the golden key on the "prophet's chain," so to speak, was what he called his "*corrupt concept of love.*"

> . . . I was caught up in a false "gospel" that says "God does not want His children to suffer." . . . I felt that I was trying my best to get right with Him and He was rewarding my earnestness with sickness. Because of that lie, I grew more bitter and resentful with each passing day, until, at last, I got downright angry at God for not taking the shame and agony of my horrendous affliction away. I just couldn't see His hand in my sufferings. At that point, Satan had the advantage. But God, (in what I now understand as love), began to show me what I should have recognized all along. Slowly I began to hear what He was trying to tell me. He was revealing the ugly truth about the condition of my heart before Him and my urgent need to repent. ...Not what I wanted to believe about myself, but the bald face truth.[20]

"There is a generation that are pure in their own eyes, and yet is not washed from their filthiness."   Proverbs 30:12

What a battle this prodigal waged in his fight to return to our Father's House after years of backsliding for the second time!

> God was answering my prayers to come completely back to Him—and it wasn't easy. Part of what I was reaping was the fruit of my own backslidings. I had a lot of repenting to do, far more than I ever imagined, or wanted to believe.[21]

"Thine own wickedness shall correct thee, and thy backslidings shall reprove thee: know therefore and see that it is an evil thing and bitter, that thou hast forsaken the LORD thy God, and that my fear is not in thee, saith the Lord GOD of hosts."
                                        Jeremiah 2:19

> The last stronghold I dealt with in relationship to the rash was a deep bitterness harbored against God. . . . The whole ordeal was like science fiction. Like a Frankenstein film! My skin actually started bubbling up as I confronted the bitterness. It was poison to me, both body and soul. I was at a place I had never been, ready to break before God or harden my heart in rebellion. . . . At last my iron will broke before the Lord. . . . I then went on, in the Name of Jesus, to cast out a powerful demon of bitterness. Almost immediately, the rash began to subside. . . . All traces of it are now gone! Hallelujah![22]

The Lord sure had a way of getting his attention and chipping away at his vanity at the same time. It's one of the most remarkable miracles we've ever witnessed. Once he came through it, the Holy Spirit brought to his remembrance a vision he had received years earlier about himself and another believer. The message, however, applies to all of us that similarly take up Christ's Cross.

. . . A long time ago I had a vision. In it, I saw a blazing fire. We walked into it in our street clothes until we disappeared and when we came out on the other side we were together dressed in white robes. . . . Now I understand the significance. Those of us who faithfully holdfast to Jesus amidst the fires of refinement while here on earth will pass into eternity united with the Father and one another. That's after having had the spots, wrinkles and blemishes removed from our lives (Eph. 5:26-27). That's what the painful ordeals with my skin . . . have been all about. They've been about repentance and sanctification. ...About washing our robes in the "blood of the Lamb" (Rev. 7:14). They've been about the purification of the Remnant Church of the very Last Days. All this chastening has been about being prepared by fire for the appearance of the Lord (1 Pe. 1:7).[23]

"And one of the elders answered, saying unto me, What are these which are arrayed in white robes? and whence came they? And I said unto him, Sir, thou knowest. And he said to me, These are they which came out of great tribulation, and have washed their robes, and made them white in the blood of the Lamb."   Revelation 7:13-14

Thrilled by what he was seeing (and at the same time super concerned about his ailing friend), this brother went the extra mile, line-by-line, humbling down and using his own testimony of repentance and healing to reach out in love. This particular part of his letter had a heading on it that said: *"Our Early Beliefs About Sickness."*

I remember the many times we prayed for healing when we walked together. . . . Most of the time, in our ignorance, we just endured through our afflictions and blamed them on the devil. All the while, our faith in the Lord was being eroded. We wondered why we weren't experiencing healing power like the saints recorded in the Book of Acts. Where was the manifestation of the popularly quoted scripture: "Jesus Christ the same yesterday, and to day, and for ever" (Heb. 13:8)? Well, I've come to realize that the problem has not been God's inconsistency. It's been our unbelief and ignorance. We've lacked the faith and spiritual awareness to scripturally deal with what's actually going on. . . . With the church background we had, we generally believed that all a Christian needed to do if smitten by an illness was call upon the name of the Lord and He'd answer with a miraculous healing. No repentance. No earnest soul searching. No separation from the world. No forsaking of heretical doctrines. Just "believe and receive!" This easy believism, [rampant in some venues of modern "Christendom"], has gotten so out of hand that thousands upon thousands of sin ridden professing Christians flock to crusades hoping to throw down their crutches while the newest and most popular "healing evangelist" breezes through town pronouncing magical unqualified "blessings." The hitch, however, is that for most of us nothing happens. We leave church meetings and Home Bible Studies with the same maladies with which we came. And if we are healed somehow, the affliction can return later and sometimes in greater measure. Then our faith and trust in God's power weakens, sometimes to the point of "shipwreck" (1 Tim. 1:19). Finally, out of sheer desperation, we give up on God and turn to the world's system of doctors and medication for relief. Don't get me wrong. [I'm] not against instant healings [nor doctors]. [I] rejoice in the moving of God's mighty power however He chooses to express it. What [I] do abhor, however, is the profiteering and corruption that has been wrought through the carnal exploitation of God's wonderful gifts [and the effect it's had in turning people away from the most vital dimension of healing there is; namely, repentance and the inward work of the Cross].[24]

How many of us have been susceptible to the same mentality—looking for the "big show"—rather than a complete work of the Spirit, much like Naaman the leper in the days of Elisha the prophet?

". . . Naaman came with his horses and with his chariot, and stood at the door of the house of Elisha. And Elisha sent a messenger unto him, saying, Go and wash in Jordan seven times, and thy flesh shall come again to thee, and thou shalt be clean. But Naaman was wroth, and went away, and said, Behold, I thought, He will surely come out to me, and stand, and call on the name of the LORD his God, and strike his hand over the place, and recover the leper. Are not Abana and Pharpar, rivers of Damascus, better than all the waters of Israel? may I not wash in them, and be clean? So he turned and went away in a rage. And his servants came near, and spake unto him, and said, My father, if the prophet had bid thee do some great thing, wouldest thou not have done it? how much rather then, when he saith to thee, Wash, and be clean? Then went he down, and dipped himself seven times in Jordan, according to the saying of the man of God: and his flesh came again like unto the flesh of a little child, and he was clean."

2 Kings 5:9-14

Rather than humbling ourselves and washing *"seven times"* in Jordan's crimson tide, as he eventually did, we stand on the banks covered with leprosy from head to toe. Had not the servants of this valorous Syrian captain persuaded him to submit to this symbolic course of action signifying repentance, obedience and the healing of the whole man, he would have missed his blessing and returned to his homeland a bitter man eaten up by the disease from which he sought deliverance.

> . . . We need to know each other rather than look for and run after the "great men of faith and power" to lay hands upon us and magically deliver us from our ills. We retain them because we had not the courage, in the first place, to call for the elders of the fellowship [as the Word teaches] that they might anoint us with oil and pray the prayer of faith that we be healed and forgiven of our sins. (See Jam. 5:14-16). Somehow it seems easier to have faith

in an impressive personality, rather than the elder whom we see every day. It saves us from the embarrassment of having to reveal anything about our lives that we want to conceal safely, and yet be happily delivered from it![25]

The Promise of Good Health

Going all the way back to the Israelite Exodus from Egypt, God gave an astounding promise of perfect health and well being to a favored people. Receipt of that promise, however, was conditioned upon their willingness to demonstrate their supreme love for Him by conforming their lives in sweet surrender to His Will, His Word and His ways.

". . . If thou wilt diligently hearken to the voice of the LORD thy God, and wilt do that which is right in his sight, and wilt give ear to his commandments, and keep all his statutes, I will put none of these diseases upon thee, which I have brought upon the Egyptians: for I am the LORD that healeth thee."

Exodus 15:26

Failure to do so cut them off from this blessing and opened them up to a corresponding curse, or series of curses, instead. (See Deuteronomy 28 for a list of blessings and curses).

"But it shall come to pass, if thou wilt not hearken unto the voice of the LORD thy God, to observe to do all His commandments and his statutes which I command thee this day; that all these curses shall come upon thee, and overtake thee. . . . The LORD will smite thee with the botch of Egypt, and with the emerods, and with the scab, and with the itch, whereof thou canst not be healed. The LORD shall smite thee with madness, and blindness, and astonishment of heart: and thou shalt grope at noonday, as the blind gropeth in darkness, and thou shalt not prosper in thy ways: and thou shalt be only oppressed and spoiled evermore, and no man shall save thee."

Deuteronomy 28:15, 27-29

These curses, just like blessings, were then passed down to their children.

"... I the LORD thy God am a jealous God, visiting the iniquity of the fathers upon the children unto the third and fourth generation of them that hate me; and shewing mercy unto thousands of them that love me, and keep my commandments."
Exodus 20:5-6

This is one of the principles built into spiritual law that the Lord uses to motivate us (as parents) to walk uprightly; to repent daily; and to make restitution (if possible) when we fall short. When we walk righteously in obedience to God's Word and the guidance of His Holy Spirit, our children are covered. Still further, they are BLESSED with all kinds of unspeakable mercies and graces, including good health; unless (of course!) they are at an age of understanding, locked into rebellion and are willfully sinning themselves.

"O that there were such an heart in them, that they would fear me, and keep all my commandments always, that it might be well with them, and with their children for ever!"
Deuteronomy 5:29

Conversely, when we, as parents, do evil (and fail to thoroughly repent and amend), then our children suffer a corresponding curse. Our disobedience and impenitence register to God as "*hate,*" and as such, are severely judged. Such was the case with David in his famed fall into adultery.

"Wherefore hast thou despised the commandment of the LORD, to do evil in his sight? thou hast killed Uriah the Hittite with the sword, and hast taken his wife to be thy wife, and hast slain him with the sword of the children of Ammon. Now therefore the sword shall never depart from thine house; because thou hast despised me . . ."   2 Samuel 12:9-10a

Though David had committed adultery and murdered a man, God gets to the real issue of the offence: David despised God in his heart. . . . God equates despising His commandments with despising Himself as God.[26]

Here is an example of this precept played out in the life of Jehoram, an evil king of Judah that led God's people into sin. Not only was he diseased as a judgment for his transgressions and failure to repent, but his lineage suffered enormously, as did the tribe of Judah from whence he came.

"And there came a writing to him from Elijah the prophet, saying, Thus saith the LORD God of David thy father, Because thou hast not walked in the ways of Jehoshaphat thy father, nor in the ways of Asa king of Judah, but hast walked in the way of the kings of Israel, and hast made Judah and the inhabitants of Jerusalem to go a whoring, like to the whoredoms of the house of Ahab, and also hast slain thy brethren of thy father's house, which were better than thyself: behold, with a great plague will the LORD smite thy people, and thy children, and thy wives, and all thy goods: and thou shalt have great sickness by disease of thy bowels, until thy bowels fall out by reason of the sickness day by day."   2 Chronicles 21:12-14

Sin is no light matter (ever!), especially when operational in the lives of leaders, due to its leavening effects. It may seem "insignificant" in its embryonic stages, but in its full outworking over time it encourages others (including one's own family members) to likewise *"go a whoring"* from God and join in affinity with the world. Let's not forget, we teach by example.

"Neither as being lords over God's heritage, but being ensamples to the flock."   1 Peter 5:3

The Way Back into God's Favor

Despite the peril of reaping sin's wages, God did not leave His people without remedy. In former times, as now, once sin came to light, the way back into our Father's grace and loving favor was repentance and atonement *(Lev. 17:11)*. ...Animal sacrifice in days gone by *(Lev. 16:21-30)*. ...And the blood of

Jesus, the Lamb of God, at this present Hour *(Jn. 1:29, 36; 1 Jn. 1:7-9)*.

Knowing this, our Lord's disciples, being Jews, queried Him as to what the unrepented sin might be that had brought the curse of blindness upon the man He healed.

"And as Jesus passed by, he saw a man which was blind from his birth. And his disciples asked him, saying, Master, who did sin, this man, or his parents, that he was born blind?" John 9:1-2

In that unique circumstance we learn that the man's handicap was preordained for the express purpose of confirming Christ's Deity before the eyes of all the world.

"Jesus answered, Neither hath this man sinned, nor his parents: but that the works of God should be made manifest in him."
John 9:3

...Not that the blind man and/or his parents had no sin, for Scripture declares plainly (and repeatedly) that *"in many things we offend all"* *(Jam. 3:2)*.

". . . There is not a just man upon earth, that doeth good, and sinneth not."   Ecclesiastes 7:20; See also 1 Jn. 1:8; Rom. 3:23

But rather, that the blind man and his kin had no unrepented sin for which God was calling them to account. It all happened as a testimony of divine power showing that the Promised Messiah had just stepped onto the scene.

"Since the world began was it not heard that any man opened the eyes of one that was born blind."   John 9:32

"Who is like unto thee, O LORD, among the gods? Who is like thee, glorious in holiness, fearful in praises, doing wonders?"
Exodus 15:11

Hallelujah! He makes *"the lame to walk and the blind to see!"*

"And great multitudes came unto him, having with them those that were lame, blind, dumb, maimed, and many others, and cast them down at Jesus' feet; and he healed them: Insomuch that the multitude wondered, when they saw the dumb to speak, the maimed to be whole, the lame to walk, and the blind to see: and they glorified the God of Israel."   Matthew 15:30-31

Counter-Attack

The glory that rushed into our midst through the preaching of the Cross was like the noonday sun revealing its brilliance from behind the clouds; especially for nominally versed and sickly Christians that had tapped into "prayer chains" time and again in hopes of getting their "miracle," yet experiencing very little (if any) lasting results. Hearing raw Scripture trumpeted while an anointing was present kindled faith in the hearts of the hearers *(Lk. 6:17-19)*; and at the center of the flame was *"Jesus Christ, and Him crucified"* *(1 Cor. 2:2)*.

"For the preaching of the cross is to them that perish foolishness; but unto us which are saved it is the power of God."   1 Corinthians 1:18

It seemed as though everyone in range of even the mere resonance of those thundering words of divine authority was going to be "instantly" healed.

"So then faith cometh by hearing, and hearing by the word of God."   Romans 10:17

But another phenomenon on the complete opposite side of the spectrum occurred. Two young children were immediately hit with a *"spirit of infirmity"* *(Lk. 13:11)*. Satan launched an uncanny counterattack so as to mock the glory and efficacy in the blood of Jesus. You could sense his sinister voice echoing its blasphemies off the walls:

It's all a charade. Repentance will not lead you to the hem of Christ's garment. There is no liberty at His Cross. ...No power in His blood.

The spirit in the room quickly changed. The very place where faith had gained the ascendancy, doubt laid its chilling footprint. The enemy had some fodder and he was gonna run with it. Like a Nazi patrolling the streets of Germany during the Holocaust, he was demanding (and I mean *demanding!*) our "papers." He wanted hard-core visible on-the-spot "proof" that Jesus was with us to heal. The assault in the spirit was so fierce that it seemed to ferret out the "doubting Thomas" in us all.

"But Thomas, one of the twelve, called Didymus, was not with them when Jesus came. The other disciples therefore said unto him, We have seen the Lord. But he said unto them, Except I shall see in his hands the print of the nails, and put my finger into the print of the nails, and thrust my hand into his side, I will not believe. And after eight days again his disciples were within, and Thomas with them: then came Jesus, the doors being shut, and stood in the midst, and said, Peace be unto you. Then saith he to Thomas, Reach hither thy finger, and behold my hands; and reach hither thy hand, and thrust it into my side: and be not faithless, but believing. And Thomas answered and said unto him, my Lord and my God. Jesus saith unto him, Thomas, because thou hast seen me, thou hast believed: blessed are they that have not seen, and yet have believed."

John 20:24-29

It was a royal battle trying to get the authority of Christ and His *"Sure Word"* of promise back in our midst *(Ps. 19:7; 2 Pe. 1:19-21; 2 Cor. 1:20; Mt. 5:18; Isa. 55:11).* ...More than a battle! It was also a test. The authority of God's Word and the surety of a faith rightly placed were on the line. How long could we hold on to God's promises without caving in to unbelief; giving heed to the world's counsel; or succumbing to the devil's unabated efforts to remove us from our faith? If we couldn't make it then at our beginning, how were we ever going to be counted

among the overcomers that *"endure unto the End"* and thus are *"saved"* *(Mt. 24:13; Rev. 2:11)*?

"Here is the patience of the saints: here are they that keep the commandments of God, and the faith of Jesus."

Revelation 14:12

Satan meant the entire scenario for evil, but God used it for good as a "hands on" lesson to teach us how to walk by faith when circumstances contradict the promises upon which we stand. It was part of our preparation for the perilous days in which we now live. Left behind in that particular instance was a living testament to the power of the "old time" Gospel of the Cross in 20th Century America. Once the parents of the children met together at the Cross of Repentance, the healing of their two young children naturally followed in the wake. Hallelujah! There is *"healing in His wings"* *(Mal. 4:2)*.

He promised the children of Israel a land with rivers of milk and honey [Exo. 3:8]. But brought them for the space of forty years into a land where not only rivers of milk and honey were not, but where so much as a drop of water was not, to nurture them and to teach them as a father doth his son, and to do them good at the latter end, and that they might be strong in their spirit and souls to use his gifts and benefits godly and after His will.[27]

CHAPTER FIVE

The Just Shall Live by Faith

W ho among us listeners in those early years of our pilgrimage knew enough of Scripture to launch an adequate defense? We were rough around the edges, and "green" as green can be as far as spiritual combat goes. Yet, the spoken Word was being quickened in our spirits and as eager recruits we were ready to go forth with it in hand so as to take back the field.

God said so. We take Him at His Word. We believe. Period. "End of story."

"So shall I have wherewith to answer him that reproacheth me: for I trust in thy word."   Psalms 119:42

Christ First

At that impressionable time, the Spirit of God began to teach us what standing in faith is all about: namely, putting Christ first. It is about denying self and Satan and laying aside all thoughts and outward indicators that dispute against God's sovereignty and supremacy over everything—even natural law.

"And they feared exceedingly, and said one to another, What manner of man is this, that even the wind and the sea obey him?"   Mark 4:41

. . . The believer, by faith, looks not only at the things which, through the creation and government of God, exist in nature . . . but to the goodness and omnipotence of the Promiser, unto whom nature and all creatural power in heaven, earth and sea, nay death itself, must bow. Upon this ground the believer stands fast, even when, with Abraham, the father of the faithful, and with many of the pious, he is tried of God by things seemingly contradictory; for he is assured that God cannot lie.

Biblical faith is about resisting every doubt that challenges our Father's faithfulness, even in the face of the naturally impossible, to fulfill (in due time) His covenant promises in the lives of those that abide by its terms.

"Now faith is the substance of things hoped for, the evidence of things not seen." Hebrews 11:1

"Therefore we are always confident [come what may] . . . (For we walk by faith, not by sight:)." 2 Corinthians 5:6a, 7

It's about giving the Word of God its rightful place of honor and eminence, high above natural sense and reason — two "*counsellors*"[1] seated in the carnal nature that refuse to concede to the miracle working power of God. Rather than compelling believers to depend on Him, they lend themselves to fear, disobedience, self-reliance and dependency on the world.

"Because the carnal mind is enmity against God: for it is not subject to the law of God, neither indeed can be." Romans 8:7

If given place, the opposing angles that spring out of the carnal mind tie up our thought processes in objections and rob us of the child-like faith and simplicity necessary to lay hold of God's promises and follow His guidance.

"Verily I say unto you, Whosoever shall not receive the kingdom of God as a little child, he shall not enter therein." Mark 10:15

"Him that is weak in the faith receive ye, but not to doubtful disputations." Romans 14:1

"And my speech and my preaching was not with enticing words of man's wisdom, but in demonstration of the Spirit and

of power: that your faith should not stand in the wisdom of
men, but in the power of God."   1 Corinthians 2:4-5

> . . . Beware with a pure fear of God, beware every way,
> that no one set up his reason . . . as a head, and relapse
> into his old natural state. But much rather let the heart
> and conscience grow and increase according to the Word
> of God.   Tijs Jeuriaenss, Slain by fire, A.D. 1569[2]

> Lord, help me never to put reason over Truth.[3]

This is said not to downplay our responsibility as Christians
to exercise sound judgment and godly reason; but rather, to
elevate the need for our reasoning capacities to be animated by
faith and exercised in full submission to a conscience washed in
the blood of Jesus and brought captive to the Word of God.

> "Let this mind be in you, which was also in Christ Jesus."
>   Philippians 2:5

Only then is it reliable in its effect and virtuous in its nature.

> Where reason is thus the servant of . . . conscience, there
> will come an ever greater clarity of mind, [spiritually]
> discerning why what is right is also reasonable, and
> discerning how what is reasonable may best be
> performed [1 Cor. 2:13].[4]

> ". . . O ye of little faith, why reason ye among yourselves . . ."
>   Matthew 16:8

William Tyndale described the thought processes that
spring from the unregenerate man as fleshly "*wit*," meaning:

> . . . Wisdom and all that is in a man before the Spirit of
> God come, and whatsoever springeth not of the Spirit of
> God and of God's word.[5]

Its dominant bent is gain and self-preservation. Every weight and balance it presents is about removing risk, making room for pet sins and saving one's life in this transitory world.

The serpent's wisdom is to keep his head and those parts wherein his life resteth.[6]

Yet, Jesus taught us to "*lose*" our lives by putting everything on the line for His sake and the honor of God's Word.

"For whosoever will save his life shall lose it; but whosoever shall lose his life for my sake and the gospel's, the same shall save it. For what shall it profit a man, if he shall gain the whole world, and lose his own soul?   Mark 8:35-36

The subtle design of fleshly "*wit*" can always be tracked by following the trail of the thoughts affixed to it.

If we have an anxiety on our mind, or a difficult decision to be taken, [or an area of moral weakness that makes us vulnerable to deception] we may do well to let the [Holy] Spirit show us every associated thought; He will [then] draw up our thoughts like the drag-net, and clarify our mind, by preserving every thought which came from His inspiration, and by casting away every thought which came from unworthy motives.[7]

John Bunyan gave "wisdom" devoid of divine illumination a character and a name in his allegory, calling it (i.e. "him") "*Mr. Worldly Wiseman*" — the man (according to the storyline) sent by the devil from the city of "*Carnal Policy*" to lead us away from God; away from Christ's sacrificial blood; and away from His commandments. His counsel, said Bunyan, "*favoureth only the doctrine of this world.*"[8]

. . . (Therefore he always goes to the town of Morality to church); and partly because he loveth that doctrine best, for it saveth him best from the cross . . .[9]

Indeed, it is by the exploitation of man's wisdom that Satan introduces *"doctrines of devils"* to the world.

> Every religion, every university and almost every man hath a . . . [different doctrine]. Now whatsoever opinions every man findeth . . . that is his gospel and that only is true with him and that holdeth he all his life long, and every man to maintain . . . withal, corrupteth the scripture and fashioneth it after his own imagination as a potter doth his clay. . . . Now there is no other division or heresy save man's wisdom, and when man's foolish wisdom interpreteth scripture.[10]

The devil's objective, said Bunyan, is three-fold: to turn us *"out of the way . . . render the cross odious"* to us and set our *"feet in that way that leadeth unto the administration of death."*[11] When Corrie ten Boom yielded to this Tempter amidst her sufferings at Ravensbrück, the largest women's concentration camp in Nazi Germany during WWII, she said that the joy of the Lord went clean out of her life.

> . . . As the cold increased, so did the special temptation of concentration-camp life: the temptation to think only of oneself. It took a thousand cunning forms. I quickly discovered that when I maneuvered our way toward the middle of roll-call formation we had a little protection from the wind. I knew this was self-centered: when Betsie [Corrie's sister] and I stood in the center, someone else had to stand on the edge. How easy it was to give it other names! I was acting only for Betsie's sake. We were in an important ministry and must keep well. It was colder in Poland than in Holland; these Polish women probably were not feeling the chill the way we were. Selfishness had a life of its own. As I watched Mien's bag of yeast-compound disappear I began taking it from beneath the straw only after lights-out when others would not see and ask for some. Wasn't Betsie's health more important? (You see, God, she can do so much for them! . . .). And even if it wasn't right—it wasn't so very

wrong, was it? Not wrong like sadism and murder and the other monstrous evils we saw in Ravensbrück every day. Oh, this was the great ploy of Satan in that kingdom of his: to display such blatant evil that one could almost believe one's own secret sins didn't matter. . . . Was it coincidence that joy and power imperceptibly drained from my ministry? My prayers took on a mechanical ring. Even Bible reading was dull and lifeless. . . . I struggled on with worship and teaching that had ceased to be real.[12]

By the grace of God, however, Corrie identified the convincing arguments of the natural mind as "temptations," repented of the doorway through which they accessed her thought life, confessed her sins to the women with whom she was in fellowship, and as a result was restored to right standing with the Father. From that point onward, regardless of the cost or consequence, she determined to put fleshly *"disputations,"* no matter how plausible and "justifiable," out of her thoughts.

I told the truth about myself—my self-centeredness, my stinginess, my lack of love. That night real joy returned to my worship.[13]

Choices

Over and over throughout Scripture and history we see men and women of faith likewise putting away carnal reasonings (their own and that of others) and choosing instead to be led of the Holy Spirit and governed by the Word, Will and Love of God—even when compelled into suffering and death; and even when misunderstood by family and friends. *(Acts 21:10-14).*

. . . The gulf between his former goal and his present call grew wider and deeper. Many of his friends and family thought he was throwing his future to the wind by leaving the University of Edinburgh. It made no sense to them and seemed a very ill-advised move. . . . [Yet, he prayed thus:] 'Lord, how I praise Thee for this College, it has been four years of unique loveliness, and now I give it up because I believe I do so in answer to Thy call.'[14]

Having faith often means doing what others see as crazy. Something is wrong when our lives make sense to unbelievers.[15]

Patriarchs of Faith

When God told Abraham that Sarah would bare him a son though they were past child bearing years, he, *"being not weak in faith, . . . considered not his own body now dead"* (Rom. 4:19), but rather God that gave the promise.

"(As it is written, I have made thee a father of many nations,) before him whom he believed, even God, who quickeneth the dead, and calleth those things which be not as though they were. Who against hope believed in hope, that he might become the father of many nations, according to that which was spoken, So shall thy seed be. And being not weak in faith, he considered not his own body now dead, when he was about an hundred years old, neither yet the deadness of Sarah's womb: he staggered not at the promise of God through unbelief; but was strong in faith, giving glory to God; and being fully persuaded that, what he had promised, he was able also to perform."   Romans 4:17-21

Sure enough, after the test of this chosen couple's love and faith ran its course, they received the promise; though it was naturally impossible. ...And all to the glory and praise of the Faithful God in whom they had placed their trust!

"Through faith also Sara herself received strength to conceive seed, and was delivered of a child when she was past age, because she judged him faithful who had promised. Therefore sprang there even of one, and him as good as dead, so many as the stars of the sky in multitude, and as the sand which is by the sea shore innumerable."   Hebrews 11:11-12

Contrariwise, Zacharias, the father of John the Baptist, being *"weak in faith,"* allowed sense and reason to be his counselors, resulting in his disputation with an angel and subsequent chastening.

". . . The angel said unto him, Fear not, Zacharias: for thy prayer is heard; and thy wife Elisabeth shall bear thee a son, and thou shalt call his name John. And thou shalt have joy and gladness; and many shall rejoice at his birth. . . . And Zacharias said unto the angel, Whereby shall I know this? for I am an old man, and my wife well stricken in years. And the angel answering said unto him, I am Gabriel, that stand in the presence of God; and am sent to speak unto thee, and to shew thee these glad tidings. And, behold, thou shalt be dumb, and not able to speak, until the day that these things shall be performed, because thou believest not my words, which shall be fulfilled in their season."
Luke 1:13-14, 18-20

...So much to learn about our Father's wisdom in dealing with us as sons. In that single instance, Zacharias was given a sign to accomplish two ends: one, to strengthen his faith; and the other, to *"severely punish his unbelief."*[16] Truly our God is *"wonderful in counsel, and excellent in working"* *(Isa. 28:29).*

God loves [that] his children should believe his word, not dispute his power . . . . [In order to cultivate a faith such as this, he gives] his choicest mercies, and greatest salvations to his people, wherein He lays the scene of his providence so, that when He hath done, it may be said almighty power was here. And therefore God commonly puts down those means and second causes, which if they stood about His work, would blind and hinder the full prospect thereof in effecting the same, 2 Cor. i. 9. . . . Christ staid while Lazarus was dead, that He might draw the eyes of their faith more singly to look on his power, by raising his dead friend, rather than curing him, being sick, which would not have carried so full a conviction of almightiness with it. Yea, he suffers a contrary power many times to arise in that very juncture of time when he intends the mercy to his people, that He may rear up the more magnificent pillar of remembrance to His own power, in the ruin of that which contends with Him. Had God brought Israel out of Egypt in the time of those kings which knew Joseph . . . they might have had a friendly departure and an easy deliverance; but God reserves this for the reign of that proud Pharaoh, who shall cruelly oppress them . . . . And why must this be the time? but that God would bring them forth with a stretched out arm: the magnifying of His power was God's great design, Exod. ix. 16 [Exo. 9:16]: 'In very deed for this cause have I raised thee up, to show in thee my power, and that my name may be declared throughout the earth.'[17]

[God] will not work until all be past remedy and brought unto such a case, that men may see how that his hand, his power, his mercy, his goodness and truth hath wrought all together. He will let no man be partaker with him of his praise and glory.[18]

Thank God for all the overcomers that have gone before us against the impossible lighting our path. They received manifold blessings for their faith. Abraham and Sarah not only begat Isaac, but through their bloodline came Christ. Hallelujah! Now it's our turn to carry the Torch.

"Trust in the LORD with all thine heart; and lean not unto thine own understanding. In all thy ways acknowledge him, and he shall direct thy paths."   Proverbs 3:5-6

In this End-Time, amidst a sea of escalating troubles, our challenge is to believe and act on God's Word and in so doing *keep Christ first*. Let His preeminence be our credo ...our watchword ...our anchor ...our stance.

Paul knew by faith in that dismal sea-storm where all hope of being saved was taken away — that is, sense and reason being judges — [that] not a man should lose his life. [Hence, in opposition to the natural odds prohibiting such an outcome, he boldly declared:] 'Be of good cheer, for I believe God that it shall be even as it was told me,' xxvii. 25 [Acts 27:25].[19]

Clash of Kingdoms

The incident sited in the previous chapter from the "Scrapbook" of my foundational discipling rested in my thoughts for quite awhile. Along with those musings came a statement made by Thieleman J. van Braght in his chronicles gathered from the accounts and writings of Christian martyrs dating back to the first century and continuing up to the sixteenth.

Where God builds a temple, says the old proverb, there the devil builds another in opposition.[20]

In other words, whenever the Lord is doing something exceptional and it becomes a threat to the kingdom of darkness, the devil strikes back; and with a fury!

"And these are they by the way side, where the word is sown; but when they have heard, Satan cometh immediately, and taketh away the word that was sown in their hearts." Mark 4:15

You see this two-fold pattern repeated time and again from the Fall of Man to the catching away of the saints: God acts and Satan and his children strike back.

"And it came to pass in Iconium, that they went both together into the synagogue of the Jews, and so spake, that a great multitude both of the Jews and also of the Greeks believed. But the unbelieving Jews stirred up the Gentiles, and made their minds evil affected against the brethren."   Acts 14:1-2

Understood, O Lord. ...The devil hates the link that unites faith and the Cross, so when we put them together, he strikes back.

Why? ...Because that's where repentance meets mercy and his spiritual dominion is overthrown. That's where we touch the border of Christ's garment and are changed, delivered and healed by the power in His wonder-working blood. This arch-enemy of all righteousness was trying to unnerve me so as to silence the wonderful news!

Lord, strengthen me by Your grace to refuse all intimidation. Empower us, as Your people, to push back by faith with the Sword of Your Word unsheathed, in Jesus' name, amen.

"For whatsoever is born of God overcometh the world: and this is the victory that overcometh the world, even our faith."

1 John 5:4

Onward Christian Soldiers...

Fortified by the two-fold warning drawn from recollections of Satan's counterattack to Apostle Edwin's past preaching and the quote from *Martyrs Mirror* affirming such repercussions, I continued writing. My hands were on the keyboard, but my spirit was on the battlefield for the saints in Zimbabwe and for us. Here's another excerpt from "Faith, Our Alarm System" to give you a perspective of the two distinct battles going on simultaneously. What hypocrites we'd be if we didn't make our home at the Cross and beseech the Lord to make these life-changing principles that we so often express real in our lives!

Attitudes, core beliefs and example are contagious. We need to show by the choices we make and the way that we live (all the way up to the End) that we *really* do revere and trust God with *everything*. ...We must demonstrate by our dependence on God that He is good. ...That His Eternal Word is as powerful today as it was in days gone by. ...That He will always be there to succour us, cover us and meet our every need (not our selfish wants), no matter how impossible our circumstances may seem, as long as we maintain a penitent spirit and right standing with Him. And when we fall short (as we all do — Jam. 3:2), then we must speedily repent and come under the blood covering and blessings of our Lord Jesus Christ once again.[21]

Holding Fast To God's Promises Till the End

God forbid that in our latter years of service we weaken in the faith that once propelled us onto the water to meet Jesus. God save us from sinking into the same mire as a vast number of apostates that have lost their first love and initial zeal and in their latter years turned aside from the path of faith.

"For we are made partakers of Christ, if we hold the beginning of our confidence stedfast unto the end."   Hebrews 3:14

Asa, an exceptionally valiant and devout king in the early years of his reign, is a prime example of such a frightful fall from faith. At one time a host of Ethiopians went out against him and the only place he looked for deliverance was the Lord.

"And Asa cried unto the LORD his God, and said, LORD, it is nothing with thee to help, whether with many, or with them that have no power: help us, O LORD our God; for we rest on thee, and in thy name we go against this multitude. O LORD, thou art our God; let no man prevail against thee. So the LORD smote the Ethiopians before Asa, and before Judah; and the Ethiopians fled."   2 Chronicles 14:11-12

But towards the end of his reign when Baasha, the king of Israel came out against him and the people of Judah, he turned to man for his help and made an unholy alliance with the king of Syria in hopes of garnering strength for the fight. In so doing, he hardened his heart against God and his prophets; opened a breach that resulted in subsequent wars; and wound up laden with disease. His disobedience had such a dramatic effect on his character that he wound up imprisoning the prophet that tried to turn him from his sins and refused to seek the Lord in repentance for healing after his fall. He even went so far as to mistreat his subjects.

"And at that time Hanani the seer came to Asa king of Judah, and said unto him, Because thou hast relied on the king of Syria, and not relied on the LORD thy God, therefore is the host of the king of Syria escaped out of thine hand. Were not the Ethiopians and the Lubims a huge host, with very many chariots and horsemen? Yet, because thou didst rely on the LORD, he delivered them into thine hand. For the eyes of the LORD run to and fro throughout the whole earth, to shew himself strong in the behalf of them whose heart is perfect toward him. Herein thou hast done foolishly: therefore from henceforth thou shalt have wars. Then Asa was wroth with the seer, and put him in a prison house; for he was in a rage with him because of this thing. And Asa oppressed some of the people the same time. . . . And Asa in the thirty and ninth year of his reign was diseased in his feet, until his disease was exceeding great: yet in his disease he sought not to the LORD, but to the physicians."   2 Chronicles 16:7-10, 12

How far one falls when he departs from the path of faith!

Unbelief makes way for carnal policy and thus one sin after another. Unbelief has often led Christians to call in the help of the Lord's enemies [as did Asa] in their contests . . . and some who once shone brightly, have thus been covered with a dark cloud towards the end of their days.[22]

Let us (one-and-all) stand warned and strive to remain in company till the Last Day with "*just men made perfect*" because they repeatedly and consistently choose to "*live*" by the faith they received and professed *(Heb. 12:23; Rom. 1:17; Hab. 2:4)*.

"Now the just shall live by faith: but if any man draw back, my soul shall have no pleasure in him. But we are not of them who draw back unto perdition; but of them that believe to the saving of the soul."   Hebrews 10:38-39

CHAPTER SIX

Covenant Conditions Attached

L ooking for ways to bolster my faith, I dug out a special list I got off the Internet several years ago when trying to encourage another believer in the heat of a healing crisis of her own. It has thirty-one passages from Scripture which it "prescribes" as medicine. Truly, God's Word, heals *(Ps. 107:20)*.

"The centurion answered and said, Lord, I am not worthy that thou shouldest come under my roof: but speak the word only, and my servant shall be healed."   Matthew 8:8

But the assimilation of that glorious healing power requires cooperation from our end. Simply put: We've got to take the "medicine" to make the *"prayer of faith"* effectual *(Jam. 5:14-16)*.

. . . Whosoever will pray . . . with success must first become a covenanter with God, by accepting the terms upon which God in it offers to . . . [fulfill His promises].[1]

When you do your part, God will do His. You can't do His part, and He won't do yours. Yours is to act on His Word, and let His Word do the work.[2]

"So shall my word be that goeth forth out of my mouth: it shall not return unto me void, but it shall accomplish that which I please, and it shall prosper in the thing whereto I sent it."
Isaiah 55:11

Repentance

That amounts to meeting the conditions attached to the promises; beginning with repentance.

"If I regard iniquity in my heart, the Lord will not hear me."
                                                    Psalms 66:18

"For the eyes of the Lord are over the righteous, and his ears are open unto their prayers: but the face of the Lord is against them that do evil."   1 Peter 3:12

That means our turn from sin and Satan to Christ and His righteousness has got to be thorough, ongoing and enduring.

"O Ephraim, what shall I do unto thee? O Judah, what shall I do unto thee? for your goodness is as a morning cloud, and as the early dew it goeth away."   Hosea 6:4

...Not an occasional repentance over a glaring issue. ...Not a casual restitution when we "get caught " and our sins catch up with us. Not a verbal acknowledgement of guilt, without the appropriate amendment in the aftermath.

"He that covereth his sins shall not prosper: but whoso confesseth and forsaketh them shall have mercy."
                                                    Proverbs 28:13

But rather, a perpetual examination of our lives in the searching light of Scripture as illuminated by the Holy Ghost and propelled by a healthy dose of the fear of God (Jn. 16:8).

"By mercy and truth iniquity is purged: and by the fear of the LORD men depart from evil."   Proverbs 16:6

...A worthy repentance whose proper end is evidenced by authentic "fruit" (Mt. 3:8; 2 Cor. 7:10-11); and a commitment to battle unto death until the last vice and rogue thought are squarely underfoot (2 Cor. 10:5; Heb. 12:1-4; Eph. 4:22-32, 5:3-4).

"Wherefore lay apart ALL filthiness and superfluity of naughtiness, and receive with meekness the engrafted word, which is able to save your souls. But be ye doers of the word, and not hearers only, deceiving your own selves. For if any be a hearer of the word, and not a doer, he is like unto a man beholding his natural face in a glass: for he beholdeth himself, and goeth his way, and straightway forgetteth what manner of man he was. But whoso looketh into the perfect law of liberty, and continueth therein, he being not a forgetful hearer, but a doer of the work, this man shall be blessed in his deed."

James 1:21-25

Forgiveness

Iniquity is a huge word that takes in every offense against the Lord's holiness, including any failure on our part to manifest His "*Royal Law*" of Love towards others *(Jam. 2:8)*.

"If a man say, I love God, and hateth his brother, he is a liar: for he that loveth not his brother whom he hath seen, how can he love God whom he hath not seen? And this commandment have we from him, That he who loveth God love his brother also."

1 John 4:20-21

If we harbor *any* unforgiveness in our hearts for anyone, God won't forgive us, much less hearken to our cry.

"So likewise shall my heavenly Father do also unto you, if ye from your hearts forgive not every one his brother their trespasses."

Matthew 18:35

Those "*blessed*" to receive His mercy and pardon, with the healing attached, must be merciful themselves.

"Blessed are the merciful: for they shall obtain mercy."

Matthew 5:7

"And when ye stand praying, forgive, if ye have ought against any: that your Father also which is in heaven may forgive you your trespasses. But if ye do not forgive, neither will your Father which is in heaven forgive your trespasses."

Mark 11:25-26

"They rewarded me evil for good to the spoiling of my soul. But as for me, when they were sick, my clothing was sackcloth: I humbled my soul with fasting; and my prayer returned into mine own bosom. I behaved myself as though he had been my friend or brother: I bowed down heavily, as one that mourneth for his mother."   Psalm 35:12-14

And if we are aware of a brother or sister nursing an offense towards us and there is something we can do to reconcile the conflict without supporting sin in his/her life; or compromising our integrity or stance in the Lord; then we need to reach out in love. Otherwise, again, our prayers will not be heard.

"Therefore if thou bring thy gift to the altar, and there rememberest that thy brother hath ought against thee; leave there thy gift before the altar, and go thy way; first be reconciled to thy brother, and then come and offer thy gift."
                                                    Matthew 5:23-24

This includes the vigilant maintenance of peace between husbands and wives; real oneness in the Holy Ghost; not an unspoken agreement to leave issues of controversy alone.

"Likewise, ye wives, be in subjection to your own husbands; that, if any obey not the word, they also may without the word be won by the conversation of the wives; while they behold your chaste conversation coupled with fear. . . . Likewise, ye husbands, dwell with them according to knowledge, giving honour unto the wife, as unto the weaker vessel, and as being heirs together of the grace of life; that your prayers be not hindered."   1 Peter 3:1-2, 7

Right standing with God is a mandate for deliverance, too. If we want Satan "off our backs" and out of our thoughts, we've got to have *"clean hands, and a pure heart" (Ps. 24:4)*. We've also got to be single-minded and penitent; not comfortably settled in divided affections for both God and the world. Then, we are

commanded to *"resist the devil."* God has not promised to unconditionally swoop down and drive him away *(1 Pe. 5:8- 9).*

"Submit yourselves therefore to God. Resist the devil, and he will flee from you. Draw nigh to God, and he will draw nigh to you. Cleanse your hands, ye sinners; and purify your hearts, ye double minded"   James 4:7-8

We can't just "name and claim" God's promises, as the "Word of Faith" doctrine purports (whether it be for healing or any other blessing); though voicing the promises of God as our own is definitely important. We've also got to bring our lives into alignment with the "directions on the bottle" (so to speak) so that the medicinal properties of the promises become effectual. Example:

". . . If thou wilt diligently hearken to the voice of the Lord thy God, and wilt do that which is right in his sight, and wilt give ear to his commandments, and keep all his statutes, I will put none of these diseases upon thee, which I have brought upon the Egyptians: for I am the Lord that healeth thee." Exodus 15:26

Belief: The Grandfather Condition

The great condition under whose roof all other conditions abide is "belief."

"Jesus said unto him, If thou canst believe, all things are possible to him that believeth."   Mark 9:23

"Jesus saith unto her, Said I not unto thee, that, if [big 'IF'!] thou wouldest believe, thou shouldest see the glory of God?"
          John 11:40

"For unto us was the gospel preached, as well as unto them: but the word preached did not profit them, not being mixed with faith in them that heard it."   Hebrews 4:2

There are other conditions, as well. ...Lots of them! ...Conditions impossible to meet, if not for the grace of God; the power of the Holy Ghost; the Presence of Jesus within us; and the fountain of forgiveness in His redeeming blood. Not only conditions attached to the promise of good health, but also, to salvation itself.

"That if thou shalt confess with thy mouth the Lord Jesus, and shalt believe in thine heart that God hath raised him from the dead, thou shalt be saved. For with the heart man believeth unto righteousness; and with the mouth confession is made unto salvation."　　　　　　　　　　　　　　Romans 10:9-10

And let's not forget the necessary catalyst: love.

". . . Faith which worketh by love." Galatians 5:6b

Not "lip love" only, as poured out in worship towards the Father and the Son and voiced in our manifold expressions of affection towards our brethren; but actual *"charity,"* meaning the outworking of that passion by means of obedience and *"good works" (Tit. 2:14; 3:8, etc.).*

"Hereby perceive we the love of God, because he laid down his life for us: and we ought to lay down our lives for the brethren. But whoso hath this world's good, and seeth his brother have need, and shutteth up his bowels of compassion from him, how dwelleth the love of God in him? My little children, let us not love in word, neither in tongue; but in deed and in truth."
　　　　　　　　　　　　　　　　　　　　　　1 John 3:16-18

Obedience

Faith and obedience combined with repentance when we fall short open us up to receive all the *"benefits"* written into the Everlasting Covenant of salvation that Jesus signed in His blood *(Ps. 103:2-3).* These conditions are the links on the chain that held the "golden key" to healing and deliverance seen in the prophetic dream that launched this book.

"Elect according to the foreknowledge of God the Father, through sanctification of the Spirit, unto obedience and sprinkling of the blood of Jesus Christ: Grace unto you, and peace, be multiplied."   1 Peter 1:2

Belief void of obedience makes us no better than a devil. Like outward water baptism, without the corresponding internal baptism with the Holy Ghost and fire, it is *"as useless and vain as the seal on an empty letter."*[3]

"Thou believest that there is one God; thou doest well: the devils also believe, and tremble. But wilt thou know, O vain man, that faith without works is dead?"   James 2:19-20

The children of God are the children of obedience, as was the great patriarch Abraham, who was awarded the honorable title *"father of us all"* because of the faith he exercised *(Rom. 4:16).*

"For what saith the scripture? Abraham believed God, and it was counted unto him for righteousness."   Romans 4:3

But when was his faith *"counted unto him for righteousness"?* ...Not until *"he was tried"* *(Heb. 11:17-19).*

"Was not Abraham our father justified by works, when he had offered Isaac his son upon the altar? Seest thou how faith wrought with his works, and by works was faith made perfect? And the scripture was fulfilled which saith, Abraham believed God, and it was imputed unto him for righteousness: and he was called the Friend of God. Ye see then how that by works a man is justified, and not by faith only."   James 2:21-24

It was when Abraham willingly offered up Isaac upon the altar that he showed in very deed that his fear of God (like Job's) was both real and enduring; and that his love for God was a rapture of His Person — not a mere affinity for the wonderful blessings afforded to those that are heirs of His House *(Job 1:9-11).*

"And the angel of the Lord called unto Abraham out of heaven the second time, and said, By myself have I sworn, saith the Lord, for because thou hast done this thing, and hast not withheld thy son, thine only son: that in blessing I will bless thee, and in multiplying I will multiply thy seed as the stars of the heaven, and as the sand which is upon the sea shore; and thy seed shall possess the gate of his enemies; and in thy seed shall all the nations of the earth be blessed; because thou hast obeyed My voice."   Genesis 22:15-18

The Fear of God

This is where the fear of God comes into play. ...Cause and effect: The *"if-then"* principle.[4] It is woven into the very fabric of life.

> *If we do* something, i.e. repent, trust, delight, pray, and so on, *then* God will do something for us [2 Ch. 7:14; Ps. 37:4-5; Pro. 3:5-6; Phil. 4:4-7].[5]

> I will keep you in peace, but only when your mind is stayed upon Me. (Isa. 26:3). I will order the steps of the man who has made goodness his rule of life. (Psa. 37:23). I will give rest to those who come to Me (Matt. 11:28). . . . I will keep your soul from bitterness as you love your enemies. I will make you like a flourishing tree planted by the river of righteousness if you do not walk in the counsel of the ungodly. (Psa. 1:1-3). I aid you toward holiness, but I will never force anyone to keep My commandments. I have told you that they are good, and those who keep them are happy (Prov. 29:18). The choice is yours.[6]

The Word of God says: If you do (or don't do) such-and-such, then this will be the result. In other words, consequences:

God's Law of Righteous Judgment. This profound working is written into both natural and spiritual law.

"Be not deceived; God is not mocked: for whatsoever a man soweth, that shall he also reap. For he that soweth to his flesh shall of the flesh reap corruption; but he that soweth to the Spirit shall of the Spirit reap life everlasting."   Galatians 6:7-8

It is reflected in both blessings and curses, depending upon our response to the New Covenant. By this rule, every person on earth is judged *(Rom. 2:6-8)*. In Isaiah 58 it shows up as the "when-then" principle. That's the passage where the Lord reproves religious pretense and reveals the earnestness that is necessary for moving His hand with our prayers. He calls it His *"chosen"* fast. Basically, it's a check list of standards by which we are to measure our lives, coupled with a teaching on how to repent and change course if we are off track. It then goes on to show how we are to do everything from that turning point onward with integrity and love, as is well pleasing to the Lord.

"Is not this the fast that I have chosen? To loose the bands of wickedness, to undo the heavy burdens, and to let the oppressed go free, and that ye break every yoke? Is it not to deal thy bread to the hungry, and that thou bring the poor that are cast out to thy house? WHEN thou seest the naked, that thou cover him; and that thou hide not thyself from thine own flesh? THEN shall thy light break forth as the morning, and thine health shall spring forth speedily: and thy righteousness shall go before thee; the glory of the Lord shall be thy rereward. THEN shalt thou call, and the Lord shall answer; thou shalt cry, and He shall say, Here I am. IF thou take away from the midst of thee the yoke, the putting forth of the finger, and speaking vanity; and IF thou draw out thy soul to the hungry, and satisfy the afflicted soul; THEN shall thy light rise in obscurity, and thy darkness be as the noon day: and the Lord shall guide thee continually, and satisfy thy soul in drought, and make fat thy bones [no more bone disease and degeneration!]: and thou shalt be like a watered garden, and like a spring of water, whose waters fail not."   Isaiah 58:6-11

A much longer list of passages could be cited, each with particular (though similar) conditions attached *(Deu. 7:12-15)*. But we'll stop here so as to challenge YOU, our fellow Bereans, to do your homework, too.

"These [abiding in Berea] were more noble than those in Thessalonica, in that they received the word with all readiness of mind, and searched the scriptures daily, whether those things were so."   Acts 17:11

Suffice it to say, that if we're not getting answers to our prayers, we need to pull out the "condition list" and make a thorough perusal of our lives.

"Examine yourselves, whether ye be in the faith; prove your own selves. Know ye not your own selves, how that Jesus Christ is in you, except ye be reprobates?   2 Corinthians 13:5

If correction needs to be made, then we must repent and amend. If all is well with our souls, then *"having done all,"* we must *"stand"* in faith on God's Word, *"nothing doubting"* till victory comes *(Eph. 6:13; Acts 10: 20; Jam. 1:6-7)*.

CHAPTER SEVEN

The Spirit of Fear

"For God hath not given us the spirit of fear; but of power, and of love, and of a sound mind."   2 Timothy 1:7

Fiery Darts

As the trial of my faith waxed on, I became acutely aware of the patterns of thought that had been moving in and out of my mind day and night since the first bumps surfaced under my chin. These rogue cycles started with a diagnosis and ended with a threat. "*It could be this???*" Or, "*It could be that???*" And "*If this ...or that ...then...!!!*" Round and round I went swimming in circles like a dolphin in a tank. The darts flew so fast that it was like going to the moon and back in the blink of an eye.

This is hives! You're going to be covered from head to toe.

I can only imagine the expression on my face!?! Flashing before my eyes were images of the time a soul dear to our hearts hardened his heart against God and turned back to the world. The anguish I experienced was so great that it set off a severe head-to-toe outbreak of hives. The Lord used the ordeal to reveal the "take charge" attitude that I used to manifest in tough times. (Thank God for changing me at the Cross!) Though Apostle Edwin prayed for me at the outset of the trial, the healing didn't manifest till several days later after "*fasting and prayer*" (Mk. 9:29). Once some of the inward pain had been sorted out and I accepted what had taken place (entrusting my concerns about the eternal consequences of such acts to the Lord), I began owning up to my disposition, as well as to the fear at its root. The healing that followed was nothing short of miraculous. The swollen bumps started vanishing like clouds from the sky as soon as my sin came to light and repentance was born out. Gone (in the Name of Jesus) went every hive from my scalp, eyelids, armpits and even from their final resting place: the bottom of my feet. It's another "*notable miracle*" that God used to add wealth to my "faith account" *(Acts 4:16)*. When I need spiritual "currency" for "trading" in times of testing, I dip into "my savings" with David and use them as "earnest money" for taking on new challenges.

"David said moreover, The LORD that delivered me out of the paw of the lion, and out of the paw of the bear, he will deliver me out of the hand of this Philistine. And Saul said unto David, Go, and the LORD be with thee."   1 Samuel 17:37

Yet, in this instance, it was as though I was a spiritual pauper. The "*spirit of fear*" had plundered my account and robbed me (actually "*blinded*" me) from all recollections of the mercies and miracles wrapped up in that trial; leaving me only with awful memories of the severity of the hives.

"In whom the god of this world hath blinded the minds of them which believe not, lest the light of the glorious gospel of Christ, who is the image of God, should shine unto them."
2 Corinthians 4:4

Next came a series of other frightful imaginations—a whole parade of them. There was a sticking power with every thought and image. Each one was "*full of deadly poison*" *(Jam. 3:8)*. Flashing across my mind, for example, were the faces of people I've met that suffer from psoriasis. If you don't already know, that's a skin disease that erupts in the form of pink and white crusty lesions in the scalp and on other places of the body. It is very painful. Plus, it's appearance is intimidating. "*That's going to be you soon,*" Satan whispered sinisterly. "*Wait and see!*"

Divide and Conquer

Next, I noticed another fear moving in. I starting feeling afraid that the turmoil going on inside my heart was going to drive a wedge between my husband and I. It seemed like I was one person on the outside and another within; and it wasn't going to be long before my duplicity would come to light.

Edwin is a staunch enemy of fear and the unbelief at its root — unless it be the reverential fear of God. He is a champion for that! Knowing the fate of those subject to other fears, he is not going to sympathize with it. Rather, he is going to reprove it and then (in the Mighty Name of Jesus) assist whoever it is that wants help out from its iron grip.

"But the fearful, and unbelieving, and the abominable, and murderers, and whoremongers, and sorcerers, and idolaters, and all liars, shall have their part in the lake which burneth with fire and brimstone: which is the second death."

Revelation 21:8

WOW! The *"fearful,"* right there beside *"murderers"* and *"liars"* suffering the anguish of a hell that never ends!!!

Enduring Effects of Family Discord

When I was growing up stress usually resulted in family strife. So to this very day I have to purpose my heart not to perpetuate the sins of my forefathers by lashing out when things get tough. I've also got to resist the temptation to let the effects of those painful circumstances cause me to shrink back and become uneasy when pressures mount. It's remarkable how deeply these fears, like ruts in road, get entrenched in our souls. Even though my childhood is long gone and I am no longer living with a family that is estranged from Christ, I *still* have to remind myself from time to time that everything is alright. Arguments and discord are not going to erupt into a showdown. That's not to say that nothing of controversy will surface — especially in the heat of trials. That's when our mutual weaknesses have a tendency to rise and react upon each other. But when things come up, we don't "blow up." Just the opposite. We take them to the Lord in prayer and repent.

"Forbearing one another, and forgiving one another, if any man have a quarrel against any: even as Christ forgave you, so also do ye."   Colossians 3:13

We pursue whatever it is that causes conflict prayerfully and honestly, in love!, with the Word as our guide. We respectfully seek the Lord for resolution, in due order, with an intreatable spirit and He always comes through.

"Blessed are the peacemakers: for they shall be called the children of God."   Matthew 5:9

"Let us therefore, as many as be perfect, be thus minded: and if in any thing ye be otherwise minded, God shall reveal even this unto you."   Philippians 3:15

Hallelujah! I'm safe with my God-fearing husband and a cherished Remnant of fellow believers that share the same determined purpose to respond to everything and everyone, *"as to the Lord,"* in patience and love, with reverence and godly fear *(Col. 3:23)*. And when we fall short and get irritable, impatient, selfish or proud, we follow the example of the martyrs. We go straight to the Lord and to each other in repentance so as to speedily heal the breach. We don't let fears unnerve us ...withdraw within ourselves ...storm out the front door ...throw a fit ...manifest disapproval ...or threaten divorce.

> . . . In whatever I have at any time grieved you, forgive me for the Lord's sake, for I gladly forgive them everything, who have sinned against me, so that I hope that the Lord will forgive me everything; all my sins and weaknesses.   Christian Langedul, A.D. 1567
> Captured, tortured & set on fire by Catholic decree[1]

"Let all bitterness, and wrath, and anger, and clamour, and evil speaking, be put away from you, with all malice: and be ye kind one to another, tenderhearted, forgiving one another, even as God for Christ's sake hath forgiven you."   Ephesians 4:31-32

Delay of any kind will only widen the gulf and separate us from God and our brethren. It also gives Satan the upper hand.

"Be ye angry, and sin not: let not the sun go down upon your wrath: neither give place to the devil."   Ephesians 4:26-27

Everything that comes as a barrier between us and another, be it ever so small, comes as a barrier between us and God. We have found that where these barriers are not put right immediately, they get thicker and thicker until we find ourselves shut off from God and our brother by what seem to be veritable brick walls. Quite obviously, if we allow new life to come to us, it will have to manifest itself by a walk of oneness with God and our brother, with nothing in between.[2]

Plus, contention and division bring reproach on the name of our Lord. They put out the flame of the Holy Spirit and nullify any kind of effectual ministry that we might employ in hopes of bringing Christ to others. They actually scare people away!

Every one is afraid to dwell in a house haunted with evil spirits; and hath hell a worse than the spirit of division?[3]

Divide and conquer was the devil's strategy. His endgame was to prevent the message of faith and love from going out.

O labour for peace and unity [among yourselves], for others' sake. . . . [For there is] no more . . .[effectual] means to . . . [cultivate receptivity] and pave a way for their conversion [and growth] than to commend the truths and ways of God to them, by the amiableness of your love and unity. . . . This is the cumin-seed that would draw souls, like doves, to the window. . . . O Christians, agree together and your number will increase [Acts 2:46-47].[4]

Outside and Inside — Two Different Worlds

The "long and the short" of all this is that amidst the rigors of writing, coupled with the devil's unabated bombardments, I gradually began to yield to his seductions and lies. A *"spirit of fear"* was gaining ground and beginning to take hold, in spite of the long history of healings in our outreach and personal lives.

"There were they in great fear, where no fear was . . ."
Psalms 53:5a

All this was going on at the very same time that I was working on a letter whose subject was faith! Amazing!!! ...So much to see in all this! How many professing Christians live this double-life? ...Talking up a show about faith, but not actually walking in it? It's the bane of the lukewarm "church;" hearing the Word without heeding it; thinking you're on the mount of transfiguration with Jesus; until (when brought to the Touchstone) you crash *(Jam. 1:22-24).*

"Therefore whosoever heareth these sayings of mine, and doeth them, I will liken him unto a wise man, which built his house upon a rock: and the rain descended, and the floods came, and the winds blew, and beat upon that house; and it fell not: for it was founded upon a rock. And every one that heareth these sayings of mine, and doeth them not, shall be likened unto a foolish man, which built his house upon the sand: and the rain descended, and the floods came, and the winds blew, and beat upon that house; and it fell: and great was the fall of it."
Matthew 7:24-27

. . . We've conditioned ourselves to hear messages without responding. Sermons have become Christian entertainment. We go to church to hear a well-developed sermon and a convicting thought. We've trained ourselves to believe that if we're convicted, our job is done. If you're just hearing the Word and not actually doing something with it, you're deceiving yourself [Jam. 1:22]. . . . [We don't think through this duplicity] because we've developed a habit of listening to the Word of God and not obeying it.[5]

"And they come unto thee as the people cometh, and they sit before thee as my people, and they hear thy words, but they will not do them: for with their mouth they shew much love, but their heart goeth after their covetousness. And, lo, thou art unto them as a very lovely song of one that hath a pleasant voice, and can play well on an instrument: for they hear thy words, but they do them not."   Ezekiel 33:31-32

Elephant Ears

The footprints of fear were everywhere. It was causing me to grow huge elephant ears. I became a "sponge" for news of every bodily hazard imaginable. Actually, "health scares" are a major strategy at the heart of the Beast System's Propaganda Machine.

Years ago, for example, we reached out with the Gospel to a woman raised in an impotent form of "Christianity." But like many others, she had become disillusioned and wound up turning to Buddhism. Though she didn't have the discernment to detect the demonic underbelly of that particular deception, she did pick-up on the danger of exposure to radio and TV. She listened with discretion to both so as to shield herself from the constant barrage of unsettling health warnings with detailed descriptions of the symptoms that accompany a seemingly endless variety of dangerous and debilitating diseases. Such a broad brush is used in the diagnoses that one thing or another, like bait on the end of a fishing line, has the potential for "snagging" listeners and sending them straight to the doctor or local pharmacy frantic for a cure, or even a promised preventative. "*I just tune out,*" she said. Sounds biblical *(Pro. 4:14-15; Eph. 5:11a)*. Christians would be wise to apply similar safeguards so as to prevent undue exposure to a seemingly endless stream of provocative reports talking up the perils of virus variants and promoting accelerated government control and mandatory vaccination as the only viable defense. The spirit of fear is contagious!

"And the officers shall speak further unto the people, and they shall say, What man is there that is fearful and fainthearted? Let him go and return unto his house, lest his brethren's heart faint as well as his heart."   Deuteronomy 20:8

A Pandemic of Fear

This deadly evil stops at no boundaries EXCEPT faith in God's Word and the blood of Jesus Christ. Here's an American public servant telling of its masterful use in subduing a great number of our citizens *"just four months"* into the present pandemic. Back then, he saw the "handwriting on the wall."

In less than four months, our government successfully instilled fear in a majority of the population in America — fear so powerful and binding that it allows them to control . . . what people eat, where they go, who they see, and even purchasing toilet paper. But you know what's the most dangerous and terrifying part of all this manipulation??? People, for the most part, are not afraid of the government who removes their freedom. They're afraid of their neighbors, family and friends, and they hate those who won't comply! It's absolutely terrifying! So many people don't question government about any of this, because the Government god "knows best." They're willing to surrender their critical thinking skills and independence and just swallow the narrative of the "experts" and give up without thinking, without a fight. You know what's coming next? "It's just a vaccine. Come on. It's for the greater good." Wait until you're told you can't enter any store or business without proof of the COVID-19 vaccine. Wait until you can't go to public events or get on a plane without proof of receiving the vaccine. ...To everyone that doesn't believe this is possible, let me say: "Just wait." Do you understand that government successfully dictated to people when they were allowed to be outside, where they were allowed to go and how their children would be educated? That actually happened over a period of just four months in a country whose foundational Constitutional precepts define government as "by the people ...of the people ...and for the people" — not God over the people. Yet a majority of the population [smitten with fear] follow blindly because they are "told to do so." You're kidding yourself if you think this behavior won't be repeated with a vaccine or whatever the next step is.[6]

One year later, this headline appeared in the news heralding European front runners. The emphasis belongs to the journalist:

[French president] Macron announced a full-blown authoritarian measure that takes France off the tourist list. He has made vaccinations MANDATORY for caregivers, store clerks, waitresses, and all other workers "in contact with the public" with no exceptions for health or religion. On top of that, he has made it also MANDATORY to have his Gates-inspired health pass to enter all restaurants, cafes, theaters, and cinemas. In other words, without a vaccination, you are not even allowed to go to the store and buy anything.[7]

A similar strategy was used during WWII to create an informant state. Then, as now, Satan used the spirit of fear to create suspicion amidst the German people; thus severing their bonds with each other; and binding them to the Reich instead.

The basic right of true community of peoples has been abrogated [cancelled] by the systematic undermining of trust among men. There is no more terrible judgment of a community of peoples than the admission, which we all must make, that not one of us any longer feels safe from his neighbors, no father from his own sons.
Professor Kurt Huber, Pronounced guilty of high treason
In a kangaroo court and executed, Nazi Germany, 1943[8]

It's a sign of the times that is sure to test the faith and fidelity of us all — especially as shakings increase and perils of one sort or another press in from every side.

"Trust ye not in a friend, put ye not confidence in a guide: keep the doors of thy mouth from her that lieth in thy bosom. For the son dishonoureth the father, the daughter riseth up against her mother, the daughter in law against her mother in law; a man's enemies are the men of his own house."   Micah 7:5-6

"And there shall be signs in the sun, and in the moon, and in the stars; and upon the earth distress of nations, with perplexity; the sea and the waves roaring; men's hearts failing them for fear, and for looking after those things which are coming on the earth: for the powers of heaven shall be shaken."
                                                          Luke 21:25-26

Not only did the devil use the spirit of fear to divide family and friends during the Holocaust; but also, to recast the Jews as scapegoats ordained to bear the burden for the evils of the day; thus providing the Nazi regime with a narrative to justify the annihilation of God's chosen people and the persecution of everyone opposed to Hitler's dictatorship as the cure.

Anti-Semitism was the magic formula which [Hitler] . . . used to explain all social ills and gain the support of the politically disorientated petty bourgeoisie. Anti-Semitism was the means by which he smashed the legal system, established the dictatorship and implicated the German people in his crimes. . . . . Nazi propaganda had succeeded in popularizing the absurd theory that all Jews were to blame for everything, any undesirable trend of thought or any opposition at all had only to be described as being under Jewish influence to justify the elimination and the physical persecution of its supporters.[9]

Similarly, those today who choose not to be vaccinated; or, who publish views other than "take the vaccine" (especially if those views emanate from the belief that mandated vaccination verification is a harbinger of the prophesied Mark of the Beast) are being characterized as kooks; censored on media venues; accused of being self-serving "spreaders"; and represented to be a threat to our survival as a people. Still further, so called "anti-vaxers" are being assigned the blame for the long continuance of the pandemic; leaving no supposed alternative for curtailment other than punitive measures designed to coerce subservience. The infrastructure is already in place.

Those who do not accept these measures will be confined in detention camps or placed under house arrest, and all their assets will be confiscated.[10]

...And daily news broadcasts reveal increasingly aggressive manifestations of its outworking.

Australians have racked up so many fines for violating their governments' draconian COVID-19 mandates that the state of Queensland is now threatening drastic action against those who haven't paid up, including the loss of their bank accounts, homes, or driver's licenses.[11]

If those that have chosen to abstain (whether their reason be compromised health, moral conviction or religious belief) would just *"go along, to get along,"* (so goes the narrative), *"health and harmony could be recovered and we could return to a semblance of 'normality.'"*

Prepare to be persecuted for not taking the vaccine. By this time next year our lives could be drastically different. When Hitler made his move on Austria, his propaganda ministers convinced the Austrian people that the Jews had contracted a deadly disease and as such were a health threat and needed to be separated from the rest of the population. By "flooding the zone" with continuous messaging, the Austrian people finally turned against the Jews–even though they had generally not been an anti-Semitic people. Something similar could happen in the US and elsewhere under the Covid narrative if the public becomes convinced through persistent propaganda that the unvaccinated are a threat to their well-being. In fact, this has already begun.[12]

Christians Getting Swept Up in the Deception

Fearful of being categorized as "malefactors..." Fearful of being perceived as "unloving." ...Fearful of falling victim to disease. ...And fearful of suffering punitive measures like demonization and round-ups, increasing numbers of professing Christians are casting off whatever faith they had; accepting the new narrative; and succumbing to the tide of tyranny.

"And such as do wickedly against the covenant shall he [the Antichrist] corrupt by flatteries: but the people that do know their God shall be strong, and do exploits."   Daniel 11:32

> I cannot tell you how grieved I am that Americans are throwing away their God-given freedoms in response to a godless, socialist, Covid narrative that has intoxicated its naïve and gullible followers. Christians are much to blame, as many have fallen for the deception—having surrendered to the continuous hype and pressure. Also, too many American Christians have counted on a pre-tribulation rapture to get us out of here before persecution begins and, as a result, have not stood against evil the way they should. Consequently, we are moving swiftly toward Satan's final deception. We are not yet in the Tribulation period, and the Antichrist is not yet visibly in power; but we're getting close.[13]

Major church denominations, for example, are now carrying the water for the masterminds behind the creation of a One World Beast System by promoting accelerated government mandates, rather than the freedom of conscience once enshrined by the American Constitution; especially when it comes to our responsibility as Christians to make sound moral choices based upon our faith; and to evaluate the content of the substances injected into our bodies so as to refuse anything that could produce harmful side effects; or still worse, serve as a platform for Mark of the Beast technology. We must be careful. Our bodies are members of Christ! We are not our own. We belong to God (1 Cor. 6:15-20)!

"Know ye not that ye are the temple of God, and that the Spirit of God dwelleth in you? If any man defile the temple of God, him shall God destroy; for the temple of God is holy, which temple ye are."   1 Corinthians 3:16-17

"What? know ye not that your body is the temple of the Holy Ghost which is in you, which ye have of God, and ye are not your own? For ye are bought with a price: therefore glorify God in your body, and in your spirit, which are God's."
                                                                1 Corinthians 6:19-20

Some are even showing their earnest by requiring vaccine verification for church assembly and missionary approval; and going so far as to shun those that have chosen not to receive shots and boosters.

We are living at a time when many Christians are allowing "perceived compassion" to override discernment and common sense. Some of these "compassionate" Christians who are pushing the vaccine are becoming forceful against fellow believers who are rejecting it. This trend leads me to conclude that much of the persecution against Christ followers who stand firm will come from professing Christians who've been lured into embracing the Progressive Socialist narrative. The fact is, a growing division is taking place among Christians not just over the Covid vaccines but over other socialist impositions relating to our health, economy, environment, education, religious matters, etc. Families are being split, as are churches; but this is just the beginning.[14]

"All these are the beginning of sorrows. Then shall they deliver you up to be afflicted, and shall kill you: and ye shall be hated of all nations for my name's sake. And then shall many be offended, and shall betray one another, and shall hate one another."   Matthew 24:8-10

"For I am come to set a man at variance against his father, and the daughter against her mother, and the daughter in law against her mother in law. And a man's foes shall be they of his own household. He that loveth father or mother more than me is not worthy of me: and he that loveth son or daughter more than me is not worthy of me. And he that taketh not his cross, and followeth after me, is not worthy of me. He that findeth his life shall lose it: and he that loseth his life for my sake shall find it."   Matthew 10:35-39

Thank God for His faith-filled Remnant pushing back against this Oppressor and using the present upheaval as an occasion—not to shrink back in fear—but rather, to take the Gospel to the world. *"None of these diseases"* is a promise to the upright *(Exo. 15:26).*

"Behold, I give unto you power to tread on serpents and scorpions, and over all the power of the enemy: and nothing shall by any means hurt you."   Luke 10:19

We must hold fast to God's promises—remembering always that Jesus stepped right into the lives of lepers and he wasn't harmed by making contact. Rather, they were healed!

"And it came to pass, when he was in a certain city, behold a man full of leprosy: who seeing Jesus fell on his face, and besought him, saying, Lord, if thou wilt, thou canst make me clean. And he put forth his hand, and *touched him,* saying, I will: be thou clean. And immediately the leprosy departed from him."   Luke 5:12-13

Look! People worldwide have been in caves hiding from an invisible microscopic creature. [Should we, as believers, be hiding with them?] How many souls can be brought to the Lord if we [rightly] respond [in faith] to the [crisis]? This is the opportunity to take the Gospel far and yonder trusting all the while that God will take care of us. It is not the time to be afraid, for Jesus said: "Lo, I am with you to the end of the world."[15]

Pestilence — Another Inroad to Incite Fear

"For nation shall rise against nation, and kingdom against kingdom: and there shall be famines, and pestilences, and earthquakes, in divers places."   Matthew 24:7

The spirit of fear continued unabated to pound away at my faith. This time it wormed in from another angle, but always with the objective of unnerving me in regards to good health. Out on one of my daily prayer and praise walks, for instance, I ran into a gal who told me that her husband had taken a picture of a rabbit in the grass. After blowing it up, he noticed a tick attached to the small creature and it was bloated with blood.

Ticks, I gasped, *That means Lyme Disease?!!*

My zeal for taking prayer walks on the beautiful hillside trails that wind through the grass suddenly chilled.

I guess I'll no longer be doing that!

Edwin and I understand wisdom and caution. We don't want to step out onto the water unless we are confident that it is the Lord that is bidding us to *"come" (Mt. 14:25-33)*. Recklessly taking fire to our bosoms under the auspices of "faith" is a foolhardy, presumptuous and potentially dangerous thing to do *(Pro. 6:27-28)*. It's also a mockery to God; something He definitely will not honor *(Num. 14:40-45)*.

". . . It is said, Thou shalt not tempt the Lord thy God."
Luke 4:9-12; Deuteronomy 6:16

But this wasn't wisdom or godly caution. It was the devil using the instrumentality of fear to worm his way into my mind, so as to gain the mastery over particular facets of my life. I struck back, as did the Lord in His wilderness testing, with:

"It is written . . ." Luke 4:4, 8, 10

Here's one of the torpedoes I launched. It's excellent for fending off such attacks.

"Surely he shall deliver thee from the snare of the fowler, and from the noisome pestilence."   Psalm 91:3

Quickly, however, Satan countered by enticing me to identify in an unholy way with the struggles of a young woman camped nearby that had been exposed for a long time to black mold. It had adversely affected her autoimmune system. ...So much so, that the hair on her head, as well as her eyelashes and eyebrows, had all fallen out. Our hearts went out to her. We reached out in love with the Gospel; but sadly, she showed no interest in seeking remedy in Jesus. Sad. This was her hour of visitation.

While making our bed after spending time with her, I saw some flakes of black colored soot near the window. Immediately the devil seized the occasion to create another charge. Here we go again...

Black mold, he hissed emphatically! *That's the problem. That's what you are suffering: you are seeing the first telltale signs of its ravaging effects. It could get worse before it gets better — IF it gets better.*

Poisonous Reptiles

Next came several encounters with other people in the area who vehemently warned about rattlesnakes — "*lots of them,*" they said, stressing the point with comments like: "*They are NOT friendly.*" Why should that send an inordinate shudder into my gut?! Edwin and I have spent a big chunk of our lives in desert regions and the Lord has always (without fail) kept us safe from reptiles. That's not to say we haven't seen venomous snakes directly in our path. We have! ...Big ones. But by God's grace, we've never been attacked.

We mentioned this in *Purified, Made White and Tried,* another testimonial book,[16] but it's worthy of acknowledgement here, too. In his earlier years, when the Lord was cultivating Edwin's faith in some really special ways, he was stung by a scorpion. But just like the Apostle Paul when the ship he was on capsized and he escaped to the island of Melita, Edwin shook it off in the Name of Jesus and suffered no ill effects; attesting to the supremacy of our great God.

"And when Paul had gathered a bundle of sticks, and laid them on the fire, there came a viper out of the heat, and fastened on his hand. And when the barbarians saw the venomous beast hang on his hand, they said among themselves, No doubt this man is a murderer, whom, though he hath escaped the sea, yet vengeance suffereth not to live. And he shook off the beast into the fire, and felt no harm. Howbeit they looked when he should have swollen, or fallen down dead suddenly: but after they had looked a great while, and saw no harm come to him, they changed their minds, and said that he was a god."

Acts 28:3-6; See also Mark 16:17-18

What a wonderful heritage we share!

". . . Great is our God above all gods!" 2 Chronicles 2:5b

Scare Tactics

I am reminded of the account of King Sennacherib's attack on the Israelites during the reign of King Hezekiah. Threatened by the growing courage and strength of the Jews, this Assyrian monarch sent his servants into their midst so as to "*affright*" God's people and knock them off the Rock of their faith. Sennacherib's strategy was to flaunt his past successes and use them as a tool of intimidation, all the while attacking the integrity of God's chosen leader, blaspheming God Himself, and exalting the power of his "*gods*" over the Almighty. It's a lot like the kind of stuff that the devil hurls at us. There we stand (or should I say bow in complete brokenness, need and humility) at the foot of the Cross, trusting God for mercy and miracles; and out from the shadows we hear voices attempting to sow doubt, puff the power of the world, and seduce us to compare our lives to the modus operandi of people functioning outside the realm of a truly biblical Cross-centered life of faith.

"After this did Sennacherib king of Assyria send his servants to Jerusalem . . . unto Hezekiah king of Judah, and unto all Judah that were at Jerusalem, saying, Thus saith Sennacherib king of Assyria, Whereon do ye trust, that ye abide in the siege in Jerusalem? Doth not Hezekiah persuade you to give over yourselves to die by famine and by thirst, saying, The LORD our God shall deliver us out of the hand of the king of Assyria? . . . Now therefore let not Hezekiah deceive you, nor persuade you on this manner, neither yet believe him: for no god of any nation or kingdom was able to deliver his people out of mine hand, and out of the hand of my fathers: how much less shall your God deliver you out of mine hand? And his servants spake yet more against the Lord God, and against his servant Hezekiah. He wrote also letters to rail on the Lord God of Israel, and to speak against Him, saying, As the gods of the nations of other lands have not delivered their people out of mine hand, so shall not the God of Hezekiah deliver His people out of mine hand. Then they cried with a loud voice in the Jews' speech unto the people of Jerusalem that were on the wall, to affright them, and to trouble them; that they might take the city."   2 Chronicles 32:9-11, 15-18

Under a guise of wisdom and support the devil similarly attempts to creep into our lives hoping to entice us to remove our trust from Christ and turn to the world for remedy instead; thus deceiving us to create the very thing we seek to avoid; and worst of all, to side-step the glorious wholeness of body and soul that God intends to work into our lives amidst our trials.

Our fear commonly meets us at that door by which we think to run from it.[17]

This is why we, personally, are so careful about the preservation of wholehearted reliance on God regarding every facet of our lives and ministry.

"Woe to them that go down to Egypt for help; and stay on horses, and trust in chariots, because they are many; and in horsemen, because they are very strong; but they look not unto the Holy One of Israel, neither seek the Lord!"   Isaiah 31:1

We don't want *anything* to jeopardize our favor and standing with the Lord. One faithless misstep can create the very circumstance we seek to avoid.

"The fear of the wicked, it shall come upon him . . ."
Proverbs 10:24

Nehemiah is another one of the patriarchs that withstood the encroachment of fear, and with an intensity rarely witnessed in our day. This outstanding leader knew what it means "to keep one's eye on the ball." Not once did he allow repeated railings from the enemy to remove him from his obedience to God. ...Not false accusations about vainglorious motivations. ...Not fiery darts threatening failure. ...Not concerns about how he and the Jewish people would be viewed by unbelievers. ...Not even fear about potential threats on his life. It's all there in Nehemiah 6:1-14: a very worthy read!

"For they all made us afraid, saying, Their hands shall be weakened from the work, that it be not done. Now therefore, O God, strengthen my hands."   Nehemiah 6:9

Fearlings

There is an allegorical figure in Hannah Hurnard's "one in a million" classic well worth bringing to remembrance when it comes to our struggles, as Christians, to conquer the ghosts of fear. Her name, Miss *"Much Afraid,"* rightly defines her disposition. In the story, this precious, but pitiful, character incessantly struggled to escape the grip of *"Craven Fear,"* the *"cousin"* that her *"Fearling Family"* insisted she marry.

Hannah, being a *"fearling"* herself in real life before the Lord laid claim to her and turned her into an overcomer, well understood the torment and oppression brought to bear by the *"spirit of fear"* (2 Tim. 1:7). She suffered terribly under its domination; so much so, that it isolated her from just about everyone outside of her immediate family.

In order to reveal its operation to readers, she sets forth a telling scenario. First, she tells of a breathtaking view given to "*Much-Afraid*" of the mountains leading up to the "*High Places*" of Victory in Christ Jesus. Awestruck, she falls to her knees in worship. But all of a sudden, when faced with the challenge of traversing the steep and narrow path to get there, she panics. Shaken by the potential dangers, she refuses to take the path, even with the loving support of the two companions assigned by the "*Shepherd*" to accompany her safely to the heights.

Here's a clip from the book. I'll pick it up at a juncture of relevance, when "*Craven Fear*" emerges out of seemingly nowhere in mocking glee:

> Ha, ha! My dear cousin, we meet again at last! . . . Take a look at the precipice before you . . . Won't you feel lovely up there! Just look where I'm pointing, Much- Afraid. See there, halfway up, where that dizzy little ledge breaks right off and you have to jump across the chasm on to that bit of rock. . . . Picture yourself jumping that . . . and finding yourself hanging over space, clutching a bit of slippery rock which you can't hold on to another minute. Just imagine those ugly, knife-like rocks at the foot of the precipice, waiting to receive and mangle you to pieces as your strength gives out, and you plunge down on them. Doesn't that give you a lovely felling, Much-Afraid? Just take time to picture it. That's only one of many such broken places on the track, and the higher you go, you dear little fool, the farther you will have to fall. Well, take your choice. Either you must go up there, where you know that you can't, but will end in a mangled heap at the bottom, or you must come back and live with me and be my little slave ever afterward.[18]

Fear: A Perilous Evil

Fear is nothing to take lightly. It's one of the primary instrumentalities presently being used by the devil to condition people from all walks of life for subservience to the coming

Antichrist. It leads to the world ...Christ-denial ...abandonment of the Flock ...and eventually damnation if not addressed in repentance at the Cross and then withstood by faith (to our last breath if need be) till Christ appears in the clouds (*Mt. 26:73-75; Jn. 12:42-43; Rev. 21:8*).

Remember what happened to King Saul when he allowed the *"spirit of fear"* to move him into disobedience? *(See 1 Sam. 13:5-13)*. That misstep put an end to his reign.

"And Samuel said to Saul, Thou hast done foolishly: thou hast not kept the commandment of the Lord thy God, which He commanded thee: for now would the LORD have established thy kingdom upon Israel for ever."   1 Samuel 13:13

But that's only half the story. God's pronouncement regarding the eternal consequence of his rebellion carries far more serious significance.

"But my mercy shall not depart away from him, as I took it from Saul, whom I put away before thee."   2 Samuel 7:15

Thank God for leading Edwin and I (and our brothers and sisters around the world) out onto the battlefield now amidst a myriad of trials (health related as well as others) so as to teach us how to recognize and "war" against this foreboding enemy. United with Christ and with one another at His Cross (come what may, persecution or peril), our faith will remain strong.

"God is our refuge and strength, a very present help in trouble. Therefore will not we fear, though the earth be removed, and though the mountains be carried into the midst of the sea; though the waters thereof roar and be troubled, though the mountains shake with the swelling thereof. Selah. There is a river, the streams whereof shall make glad the city of God, the holy place of the tabernacles of the most High. God is in the midst of her; she shall not be moved: God shall help her, and that right early."   Psalm 46:1-5

CHAPTER EIGHT

Spiritual Warfare

A s the waves of fear rolled in, the Spirit of the Lord began to stir within me, causing me to *"come to myself,"* like the prodigal when he woke up to the fact he was in a pig-pen, not the bounty and blessing of his father's house *(Lk. 15:17).*

". . . When the enemy shall come in like a flood, the Spirit of the LORD shall lift up a standard against him." Isaiah 59:19b

> *Wait a minute, Jody! You better put an end to this, and in a HURRY, or Satan's gonna get the upper hand. No more unbelief. No more "ear given to fear." Put on your armour and fight.*

"Fight the good fight of faith, lay hold on eternal life, whereunto thou art also called, and hast professed a good profession before many witnesses." 1 Timothy 6:12

"Above all, taking the shield of faith, wherewith ye shall be able to quench all the fiery darts of the wicked." Ephesians 6:16

That's one thing about sin, of whatever sort it may be: it's a tyrant, especially when paired with an evil spirit like fear, lust, unforgiveness or resentment. It is an unruly evil that wars in our *"flesh"* — meaning in the self-centered, unregenerated nature passed on to us from Adam *(Rom. 5:12, 19)*; a nature subject to temptation which receives its influence and disposition from Satan, the *"father"* of lies, the *"prince"* of this *"present evil world"* *(Jn. 8:44; 16:11).*

"And you hath he quickened, who were dead in trespasses and sins; wherein in time past ye walked according to the course of

116

this world, according to the prince of the power of the air, the spirit that now worketh in the children of disobedience: among whom also we all had our conversation in times past in the lusts of our flesh, fulfilling the desires of the flesh and of the mind; and were by nature the children of wrath, even as others."   Ephesians 2:1-3

"Let no man say when he is tempted, I am tempted of God: for God cannot be tempted with evil, neither tempteth he any man: but every man is tempted, when he is drawn away of his own lust, and enticed. Then when lust hath conceived, it bringeth forth sin: and sin, when it is finished, bringeth forth death."
                                                      James 1:13-15

The martyrs called the flesh our most *"inveterate enemy"* — one in contention with the Spirit within us from the first day of conversion to the last day of our lives when our earthly course ends and God calls us off the field.

"For the flesh lusteth against the Spirit, and the Spirit against the flesh: and these are contrary the one to the other: so that ye cannot do the things that ye would."   Galatians 5:17

. . . Our faith is tried in many ways, and besides by the daily conflict that never ceases; for it is a lasting conflict; the Spirit wars against the flesh, and the flesh against the Spirit. Gal. 5:17. Herein I find myself troubled the most; my own sinful flesh was my most inveterate enemy, which has cost me many a bitter tear. Satan thereby sought to sift me as wheat; but now falling, now stumbling, I have come thus far through the grace of God; for I always struggled up hard by the grace of the Lord. But what was it, I would so fain have been perfect, but this weak flesh was always in the way; which must now suffer, and I hope to offer it up as a burnt sacrifice.
Jan Wouterss, Tortured & consumed by fire, A.D. 1572[1]

William Gurnall, a 17th Century Puritan preacher, likened the struggle that took place in Rebekah's womb when pregnant with Esau and Jacob, to the struggle that goes on within our own bosom on a daily basis. In so doing, he punctured the popular myth that Christ's finished work at Calvary ended our warfare against sin. *(See Gen. 25:21-23)*. Just the opposite is true.

> Thou mistakest the state of a Christian in this life; when one is made a Christian, he is not presently called to triumph over his slain enemies, but carried into the field to meet and fight them. The state of grace is the commencing of a war against sin, not the ending of it . . . . Take comfort in this, that thou art a wrestler; this struggling within thee, if upon the right ground, and to the right end, doth evidence there are two nations within thee, two contrary natures; the one from earth, earthly; and the other from heaven, heavenly . . .[2]

Christian or pagan; new babe in the Lord, or "long-timer;" once sin is obeyed (whether it be unbelief, rebellion, selfish demanding, lust or a thousand other things), its servant the snared soul becomes.

"Jesus answered them, Verily, verily, I say unto you, Whosoever committeth sin is the servant of sin."   John 8:34

Speaking to believers Paul said:

"Know ye not, that to whom ye yield yourselves servants to obey, his servants ye are to whom ye obey; whether of sin unto death, or of obedience unto righteousness?"   Romans 6:16

"Therefore, brethren, we are debtors, not to the flesh, to live after the flesh. For if ye live after the flesh, ye shall die: but if ye through the Spirit do mortify the deeds of the body, ye shall live."   Romans 8:12-13

Whether a person at one point in life received Christ or not, if that individual continues onward in the practice of sin; or becomes entangled again once delivered and settles back into it *(2 Pe. 2:20-21)*, rather than walking in repentance and daily waging a relentless *"fight of faith"* against it *(Eph. 4:22-24; 6:12)*; then both alike shall experience the Second Death *(Eze. 18:20-24; 1 Cor. 6:9-10)*.

"For this ye know, that no whoremonger, nor unclean person, nor covetous man, who is an idolater, hath any inheritance in the kingdom of Christ and of God. Let no man deceive you with vain words [or doctrines of devils like 'Unconditional Eternal Security']: for because of these things cometh the wrath of God upon the children of disobedience."   Ephesians 5:5-6

Enemy Penetration

Immediately, I went back to the basics of spiritual warfare, knowing that once a believer opens the faucet of sin by giving the preeminence to the flesh, his spiritual "hedge" of protection is broken, and the devil's lies piggy-back in through the opening like the continual haranguing of a contentious women.

You cannot risk giving your thoughts free-rein. They will never choose the right path until you bridle them . . . by your own disciplined will. You are master of your own house. You do not have to invite into your mind the foul birds of evil thoughts and allow them to nest there and bring forth their young.[3]

Trying to corral the chaos at that point and put it under heel can be like trying to bridle a cyclone in full swing.

"A continual dropping in a very rainy day and a contentious woman are alike. Whosoever hideth her hideth the wind . . ."
Proverbs 27:15-16a

At the beginning sin always comes disguised as liberty. Its lure is the seductive freedom which it promises from the trammels of conscience and the authority of law. But every man who ever yet accepted sin's offer of a free, unfettered life, discovered the cheat. Free to do the evil thing, to indulge the baser moods [the sensual appetites and egotistical demands]—so men begin, but they end not free to stop, bound as slaves to the thing they were free to do.[4]

All of Satan's temptations and seemingly plausible arguments are aimed at sin's door. If he can get us to succumb to this "Delilah," then he has succeeded in gaining the ascendency and robbing us of our power and privilege with God.

"For this cause, when I could no longer forbear, I sent to know your faith, lest by some means the Tempter have tempted you, and our labour be in vain."   1 Thessalonians 3:5

Hence, the Apostle Paul's warning in his renowned chapter on spiritual warfare:

"For we wrestle not [only] against flesh and blood, but against principalities, against powers, against the rulers of the darkness of this world, against spiritual wickedness in high places."
                                        Ephesians 6:12

In other words, our battle for righteousness is not only with the remaining sin still *"warring"* against the Spirit for mastery over our souls (i.e. the *"old"* man against the *"new"* — *Rom. 7:23; 13:13-14; Eph. 4:22-24; Col. 3:9-10; 1 Pe. 2:11*); but also, against the devil and a huge host of very real and ruthless evil forces. Simply put, we fight a domestic enemy within, (meaning the old adamic nature); and a foreign enemy from without (meaning, the devil and his hosts). Once the two strike hands, legal ground is given to the devil. A *"covenant with death"* is made and there is trouble *(Isa. 28:17-18)*.

You are [now] resolved on your way, the devil hath got your hearts, and him ye will obey [Jn. 8:44] . . .[5]

The Christian wrestles not with his naked corruptions, but with Satan in them. Were there no devil, yet we should have our hands full, in resisting the corruptions in our own hearts; but the access of this enemy makes the battle more terrible, because he heads them who is a captain so skilful and experienced. Our sin is the engine, Satan is the engineer; lust is the bait, Satan the angler. When a soul is enticed by his own lust, he is said to be tempted, Ja. i. 14, because both Satan and our own lust concur to the completing [of] the sin.[6]

The only way to break the conspiratorial bond is by repentance and a commitment to spiritual warfare against both sin and Satan, sparing no cost.

"That ye put off concerning the former conversation the old man, which is corrupt according to the deceitful lusts; and be renewed in the spirit of your mind; and that ye put on the new man, which after God is created in righteousness and true holiness."   Ephesians 4:22-24

> . . . The ground [i.e. the inroad of sin] — and the cause or causes of it — when revealed, must be [acknowledged in repentance and] taken back from the deceiving spirits, by the rejection, or refusal of these points upon which ground has been given, until the ground given has passed away; for ground which admits the evil spirit is the ground that keeps him in . . . [power].[7]

> While speaking with the disciples one day, Jesus said, . . . ["I will not talk much with you: for the prince of this world cometh, and hath nothing in Me"]. (John 14:30) Jesus revealed within this one statement the reason He was able to . . . ["stand against the wiles of the devil," Eph. 6:10-18]. He said the ruler of this world had nothing in His life that was outside of the Father's will. There was no sin, rebellion, or secret habits. Satan did not have a "hook" in Jesus. There was absolutely nothing in Jesus which the devil had legal grounds to use against Him. This is the place of refuge for the believer. . . . The sinful nature may want to befriend unclean spirits, but by habitual acts of the will, the man can choose to remain in

fellowship with God by being obedient to Him [and repenting and amending when he falls short]; and as he does, the devil has nothing in him [1 Jn. 1:9].[8]

"Thou hast proved mine heart; thou hast visited me in the night; thou hast tried me, and shalt find nothing; I am purposed that my mouth shall not transgress."   Psalms 17:3

He is safe within the *"house"* (so to speak), protected by the blood of Christ, our Passover *(1 Cor. 5:7)*; in like manner as the Israelites were kept safe by the blood of a passover lamb splashed on their homes when the Destroyer passed through Egypt killing the firstborn males (but sparing their own) on the evening prior to their Exodus.

"And ye shall take a bunch of hyssop, and dip it in the blood that is in the bason, and strike the lintel and the two side posts with the blood that is in the bason; and none of you shall go out at the door of his house until the morning. For the LORD will pass through to smite the Egyptians; and when he seeth the blood upon the lintel, and on the two side posts, the LORD will pass over the door, and will not suffer the destroyer to come in unto your houses to smite you."   Exodus 12:22-23

Probing for Weakness

Ponder the subtlety wherewith Delilah conquered the mighty Samson. Satan led her to his *"Achilles Heel"*[9] and she pressed ...and pressed ...and pressed until (at last) Israel's conqueror gave up his secret and as a result was overcome.

"With her much fair speech she caused him to yield, with the flattering of her lips she forced him."   Proverbs 7:21

"And it came to pass, when she pressed him daily with her words, and urged him, so that his soul was vexed unto death; that he told her all his heart, and said unto her, There hath not come a razor upon mine head; for I have been a Nazarite unto God from my mother's womb: if I be shaven, then my strength will go from me, and I shall become weak, and be like any other man. And when Delilah saw that he had told her all his heart, she sent and called for the lords of the Philistines, saying, Come up this once, for he hath shewed me all his heart. Then the lords of the Philistines came up unto her, and brought money in their hand. And she made him sleep upon her knees; and she called for a man, and she caused him to shave off the seven locks of his head; and she began to afflict him, and his strength went from him. And she said, The Philistines be upon thee, Samson. And he awoke out of his sleep, and said, I will go out as at other times before, and shake myself. And he wist not that the LORD was departed from him. But the Philistines took him, and put out his eyes, and brought him down to Gaza, and bound him with fetters of brass; and he did grind in the prison house."   Judges 16:16-21

Once Samson's consecration with God was broken by the shearing of his hair, the Lord left him and he was as *"weak"* as *"any other man"* in the hands of an overpowering foe. It was only after his hair grew back that his strength returned. But at that point the defeat of the Philistines cost him his life *(Jdg. 16:22-30)*. Even so, we suffer the loss of God's mighty power in our warfare against sin and Satan when we violate our consecration with the Lord through disobedience. Once that breach occurs, the only way to close the gap and recover the strength of the Holy Ghost, is to have our "hair grow back" (so to speak) by virtue of sincere repentance and reconciliation to the Father through the blood of Jesus and a commitment to go and *"sin no more"* *(Jn. 5:14)*. Then, once again, we are safe within the Passover House, washed in the blood of the Lamb. We have *"gone up into the gaps . . . made up the hedge"* and are now ready *"to stand in the battle"* *(Eze. 13:5)*. Praise God!

The Good Fight of Faith

Deeply sobered and humbled by the battle in operation, I strapped on the *"helmet of salvation"* and renewed my repentance regarding all entertainment that I had been giving to the sin of unbelief and the spirit of fear reinforcing it *(Eph.*

6:17). Then, I resolved to put out of my mind, *in the Mighty Name of Jesus,* every thought that rose up in opposition to the Gospel of Christ and the promises allotted to the upright.

"(For the weapons of our warfare are not carnal, but mighty through God to the pulling down of strong holds;) casting down imaginations, and every high thing that exalteth itself against the knowledge of God, and bringing into captivity every thought to the obedience of Christ; and having in a readiness to revenge all disobedience, when your obedience is fulfilled."   2 Corinthians 10:4-6

When I say *"the upright"* I don't mean the inherently perfect. No one on the planet fits that profile *(Rom. 3:10).* I mean penitent believers that are sincerely trying to please God. ...Believers that mourn over (rather than take pleasure in) the weakness of their flesh; and as a result, continually call upon God for deliverance from *"the sin which doth so easily beset us"* *(Heb. 12:1).* Fighting posture for them (for us!) is on our knees.

> I also discover so many shortcomings in me, and that there is so much yet to die unto; I have to commit all to the Lord, with an humble heart, and trembling, contrite spirit, asking Him for grace, and not for justice. I feel that the more I humble myself, the more the mighty God works in me, and pours His grace into me. . . . What shall we render unto Him, my dear sister, but a penitent and contrite heart, and a broken spirit, with love and great gratitude, there rests the Spirit of the Lord, says David.
> Maeyken de Korte, Executed by Sword, A. D. 1559[10]

Cleansed by the blood of Jesus and as a result abiding under the Spirit of the Lord, we can then confidently step out onto the battlefield like Samson with a full head of hair in expectation of victory. Then, and only then, can it be said:

". . . Greater is He [Christ] that is in you, than he [Satan] that is in the world."   1 John 4:4b

Marching Orders

Here is a list of marching orders (in addition to 1 Tim. 6:12; Eph. 6:12, 16; 2 Cor. 10:2-4; 1 Jn. 4:4; and 1 Pe. 1:13 previously listed in this chapter) that the Lord used to lead me in triumph.

"Thou therefore endure hardness, as a good soldier of Jesus Christ. No man that warreth entangleth himself with the affairs of this life; that he may please him who hath chosen him to be a soldier."   2 Timothy 2:3-4

"Be sober, be vigilant; because your adversary the devil, as a roaring lion, walketh about, seeking whom he may devour: whom resist stedfast in the faith, knowing that the same afflictions are accomplished in your brethren that are in the world. But the God of all grace, who hath called us unto his eternal glory by Christ Jesus, *after* that ye have suffered a while, make you perfect, stablish, strengthen, settle you. To him be glory and dominion for ever and ever. Amen."   1 Peter 5:8-11

"Wherefore gird up the loins of your mind, be sober, and hope to the end for the grace that is to be brought unto you at the revelation of Jesus Christ."   1 Peter 1:13

Taken together, these passages thundered warnings, offered perspectives, announced promises and ultimately required action. May they never become so commonplace in our hearing that they lose their impact; their definition; or their application.

1) As born again Christians, we are confronting a ferocious enemy! His appetite is for our utter destruction. Let that reality burn out every trace of lightheartedness that would cause us to approach any area of our lives casually.

2) Our survival is hinged on sobriety and vigilance. Get off guard; compromise with sin; get out of rhythm with the Holy Spirit; draw back in fear; or launch out presumptuously and we will be defeated at a minimum and

utterly ravaged and eventually damned at a maximum; if the devil has full sway.

3) The resistance we put up can't be half hearted. It has got to be founded in absolute surrender to Christ and consistent and unwavering faith. When Paul talks about *"bringing into captivity every thought to the obedience of Christ"* he's talking about the total crucifixion of all lawlessness in our affections and thoughts, as well as in our behavior *(2 Cor. 10:5)*. All vain imaginations ...hidden lusts ...harbored grievances ...and worldly aspirations that are not in alignment with God's will for our lives have got to be relinquished at the Cross. There can be no compromise on any issue. It is a breach.

4) Combat with the devil is to be expected. It is not exclusive to an elite core of chosen believers, but rather a necessary and glorious part of the "sifting" and sanctification of us all *(Lk. 22:31-32; Mt. 3:11-12; Dan. 12:10, etc.)*.

5) Civilian life is over. We are now spiritual soldiers for Christ. Our brothers and sisters throughout the world are undergoing challenges that similarly test them to the quick. Hence, we are to take comfort and inspiration from their examples, rather than trying to circumvent the suffering associated with travail and triumph. United in the love of God we can overcome. Our warfare is all about pleasing Him. What a happy thought! We are in this TOGETHER, cheering each other on every opportunity we get *(1 Sam. 23:15-16; 2 Tim. 1:16-18; Rom. 16:1-4)*.

6) The God of all grace promises to be with us. That's the most blessed part of it all!!! He promises to be with us through "thick and through thin" and if we get into the flow, He will use the afflictions that befall us to purify our hearts, fortify our faith and bring us safely to the Great Day of our Bridegroom's appearance in the clouds *(Tit. 2:13-14)*.

CHAPTER NINE

Don't Be in Such a Hurry

There is one key word in the passage from 1 Peter 5 quoted in the previous chapter that needs to be considered on its own merit. That word is *"after."* Here's the sentence from whence it is plucked for review:

"But the God of all grace, who hath called us unto his eternal glory by Christ Jesus, *after* that ye have suffered a while, make you perfect, stablish, strengthen, settle you."   1 Peter 5:10

We don't want to make the mistake of trying to get *through* our trials in the most expeditious way possible; thus, praying *"amiss"* for quick deliverance as our first priority *(Jam. 4:3)*; rather than *thorough* deliverance and the total restoration of our lives to Christ in preparation for His appearance as the actual *"prize."*

"Not as though I had already attained, either were already perfect: but I follow after, if that I may apprehend that for which also I am apprehended of Christ Jesus. Brethren, I count not myself to have apprehended: but this one thing I do, forgetting those things which are behind, and reaching forth unto those things which are before, I press toward the mark for the prize of the high calling of God in Christ Jesus."

Philippians 3:12-14

The interim period of waiting from the outset of our trials to their divinely designated outplay is when we are brought into more intimate union with the Lord and our faith, in His faithfulness, grows. It's the wondrous Way of the Cross.

Many times . . . gradual recovery brings about a learning to trust in the Lord and to continue in *constant* dependence upon Him. God is often educating His child to the increasing exercise of faith and to continuance of communion with Himself.[1]

It's also when our corruption surfaces and we have the opportunity to repent and exercise our will against it; thus putting it to death in the Mighty Name of Jesus. You know you're on the right path when all that is yet carnal within you screams out for relief *(1 Pe. 4:1)*. What a glorious time of restoration this can be IF we seek the Lord with all our hearts and worship Him throughout.

If after long waiting . . . it be as thou complainest [and there be no answer nor remedy from God], inquire whether that which hinders be not found in thyself. . . . [Then, continue to wait with a bent towards repentance] till the [obstacle be revealed and the] passage be [made] free between Christ, thy head, and thee . . .[2]

In miraculous ways He then comes in and does His most exquisite work of sanctification in our lives; revealing pockets of darkness (and possibly even suppressed trauma and/or generational curses passed down through bloodlines); breaking down self-will; compelling us to the altar of repentance; strengthening our faith; renewing our minds; untangling us from Satan's intricately woven web of lies; preparing us for ministry; and removing from us all potential stumbling blocks that could trip us up in future days of tribulation and cause us to deny Christ, withdraw from our brethren and fall away.

With these redemptive purposes in view, the Apostle James counseled us to consider temptation, in whatever form it takes, as both a blessing and a joy.

"My brethren, count it all JOY when ye fall into divers temptations; knowing this, that the trying of your faith worketh patience. But let patience have her perfect work, that ye may be perfect and entire, wanting nothing."   James 1:2-4

"Blessed is the man that endureth temptation: for when he is tried, he shall receive the crown of life, which the Lord hath promised to them that love him."   James 1:12

> There is nothing that examines the heart more closely than ['hope deferred'—Prov. 13:12]. It teaches . . . [us] to discover, confess, and give up everything that hinders the coming of the blessing—everything that is not in accordance with the Father's will. It leads to closer fellowship with Him . . . . Complete surrender becomes possible under the covering of the blood and the Spirit. Christian! Give God time! He will perfect whatever concerns you [if you remain in the fight, faithful to the end—Jn. 8:31-32].[3]

Holding Fast to God's Purposes

Joy in the midst of suffering? That seems like an oxymoron. It actually is; but not to those of us that "*understand*" God's redemptive purposes for it.

"Many shall be purified, and made white, and tried; but the wicked shall do wickedly: and none of the wicked shall understand; but the wise shall understand."   Daniel 12:10

It makes perfect sense to the precious "few" that have been with Moses to Mt. Nebo, the highest peak in a mountain called Pisgah, and captured a glimpse of Christ and our promised Fatherland (*Mt. 7:13; Deu. 34:1-4*).

> . . . May the Lord through faith give you such a heart and vision, that you may with Moses and all the saints of God know what God has prepared for them that love Him; for the righteous shall live forever, for the Lord is their reward, and the care of them is with the Most High. Therefore shall they receive a glorious kingdom, and a beautiful crown from the Lord's hand, and they shall shine forth as the sun in the throne of heaven.
> Jacob de Roore, Burned to ashes by Catholic decree, 1569[4]

The Eyes of Faith

Indeed, vision and faith are foundational to endurance and fortitude.

He who has a Why to live for can bear almost any How.[5]

Remove the hope of future glory from our trials and our spirits fail.

"Where there is no vision, the people perish . . ." Proverbs 29:18

Renew it again, and our spirits soar...

To endure . . . [is] not to sink in our courage, or shrink from under the burden . . . but readily to offer our shoulder to it, and patiently carry it, looking with a cheerful eye at the reward . . . not to throw it off, but to have it taken off [in due season by the Father of mercy who allowed it for our good to be] . . . laid . . . on.[6]

. . . If the creature be able to elevate his mind and thoughts above his sufferings, by heavenly meditation on the great and precious promises, then . . . [he seeks not ready deliverance out of his trials, but the outworking of God's purposes through them]. Such a one's soul is in heaven, and a soul in heaven feels little what the flesh meets with on earth. Here is the most glorious prospect to be seen on this side heaven! When the soul stands upon this Pisgah [Deu. 34:1-4], . . . looking by an eye of faith, through the perspective of the promise, upon all the great and precious things laid up by a faithful God for him, it is easy to . . . [walk with patience through the most heated of trials]; but, alas! it is hard for us to get up thither, who are so short-breathed, and soon tired with a few steps up this mount of God. Oh, let us all cry out, as once David . . . . Lift us up to this high, holy hill . . . higher than all the surging waves that dash upon us from beneath . . .[7]

"From the end of the earth will I cry unto thee, when my heart is overwhelmed: lead me to the Rock that is higher than I."

Psalm 61:2

Premature deliverance, before our trials (in whatever form they take) have run their full course, circumvents God's highest purposes and can end in disaster.

> Before a chicken is hatched it is vital it is kept in the warm protection of the shell for 21 days. If you take the chick out of that environment one day too early, it will die. . . . There is always a purpose behind why God allows his children to go to prison. Perhaps it's so they can witness to the other prisoners, or perhaps God wants to develop more character in their lives. But if we use our own efforts to get them out of prison earlier than God intended, we can thwart His plans, and the believers may come out not as fully formed as God wanted them to be.[8]

Spiritual dwarfing is only half the danger. Circumvention of the Cross can put an end to our lives in Christ altogether.

"Cast not away therefore your confidence, which hath great recompence of reward. For ye have need of patience, that, after ye have done the will of God, ye might receive the promise."

Hebrews 10:35-36

Steve Gallagher learned this lesson well in his ministry to sex addicts. As a result, he too, renounced shortcuts and passionately preached going the full distance for Christ.

> Freedom Comes Slowly for a Reason . . . . God deals with man in His own timing. He knows when each person is prepared for the next step in the journey to freedom. The person dealing with sexual sin can often see no further than that seemingly insurmountable sin in his life. He wants to be freed of his sin and the suffering associated with it. Yet God sees the man's heart and his entire

future. He knows there are many deeply-rooted issues which must be exposed and subsequently dealt with. God is often more concerned about exposing and expelling the underlying issues of the heart than He is about the outward sin [and the suffering it begets] with which the person struggles. Since the man is looking for help, the Lord is able to use this critical period of his life to uncover areas which are aiding and abetting his unremitting addiction to sex.[9]

Hallelujah! God, in His great wisdom, knows exactly how to set us free and establish us in holiness so that we never again return to the bondages from which we are delivered. Come what may, renewed in Spirit and continuing day by day in obedience to His Word, our lives will be hid with Christ in God.

". . . If ye continue in my word, then are ye my disciples indeed; and ye shall know the truth, and the truth shall make you free. [And] . . . If the Son therefore shall make you free, ye shall be free indeed."   John 8:31-32, 36

"Stand fast therefore in the liberty wherewith Christ hath made us free, and be not entangled again with the yoke of bondage."
                                             Galatians 5:1

Brother Yun was so right...

The way to have God's presence is by walking through hardship and suffering—the way of the Cross. . . . When faced with such trials, the key is not to run from them or fight them, but to embrace them as friends. When you do this you'll not fail to experience God's Presence and help.[10]

If anyone ever let patience have *"her perfect work,"* it is our Saviour—and not for His own sanctification—but rather, for ours *(Heb. 5:6-10)*! Praise His Holy name! His infinite meekness and humility in the face of vicarious suffering is an unspeakable inspiration to press on.

"Wherefore seeing we also are compassed about with so great a cloud of witnesses, let us lay aside every weight, and the sin which doth so easily beset us, and let us run with patience the race that is set before us, looking unto Jesus the author and finisher of our faith; who for the joy that was set before him endured the cross, despising the shame, and is set down at the right hand of the throne of God. For consider him that endured such contradiction of sinners against himself, lest ye be wearied and faint in your minds. Ye have not yet resisted unto blood, striving against sin."   Hebrews 12:2-4

CHAPTER TEN

Enough is Enough — Fighting
Back with the Word, Worship & Prayer

Getting a hold of my thoughts with the help of the Holy Spirit and the encouragement of my husband, I stepped up my discipline and launched a "no-nonsense" campaign against a barrage of "worst case scenario" images and lies that assailed my mind. The fiery darts were flying...

It's getting worse. ...It's spreading. It will never go away. ...Learn to live with it.

Up went the shield of faith and out from my lips went verse after verse.

God's Word is where every solution is found to every problem or issue that a man or woman faces. There is no place for help like the Word of God. All God's healing work begins with His Word.[1]

"He sent his word, and healed them, and delivered them from their destructions." Psalms 107:20

I kept answering back: *"It is written . . ."* Then, I would renounce all waywardness and self-will *"in Jesus' name"* ...state an appropriate Scripture ...plant my feet squarely upon it ...and ask the Lord to purge my life of all falsehood. *"Dear Father,"*...

Give me a clean heart like Jesus with the Law of Truth at its core.

"Then said I, Lo, I come: in the volume of the book it is written of me, I delight to do thy will, O my God: yea, thy law is within my heart." Psalms 40:7-8

The Word of God washes the mind as soap does the hands. The Word is like soap in that it is only effective when used.[2]

"Sanctify them through thy truth: thy word is truth."
John 17:17

"That he might sanctify and cleanse it with the washing of water by the word."   Ephesians 5:26

"Thy word have I hid in mine heart, that I might not sin against thee."   Psalms 119:11

In so doing, I underwent a beautiful baptism of faith.

"So then faith cometh by hearing, and hearing by the word of God."   Romans 10:17

Physicians tell us, we are never so subject to receive infection as when the spirits are low, and therefore the antidotes they give are all cordials. When the spirit is low through unbelief, every threatening . . . makes a sad impression. Let thy faith but take a deep draught of the promises, and thy courage will rise.[3]

"The spirit of a man will sustain his infirmity; but a wounded spirit who can bear?"   Proverbs 18:14

My respect for Scripture soared and I received strength to drive away the lies that I had only been able to keep "at bay."

"Neither have I gone back from the commandment of his lips; I have esteemed the words of his mouth more than my necessary food."   Job 23:12

"Thy words were found, and I did eat them; and thy word was unto me the joy and rejoicing of mine heart: for I am called by thy name, O LORD God of hosts."   Jeremiah 15:16

No question about it: God's Word is *"quick"* (alive), and it is *"powerful"* (*Heb. 4:12*)! It virtually lives and breathes if we pursue it with fervor in our time of need. Corrie ten Boom tells how she watched the light of it leap from *"face to face"* as her sister Betsie read from its pages in the confines of Ravensbrück:

> . . . From morning till lights-out, whenever we were not in ranks for roll call, our Bible was the center of an ever-widening circle of help and hope. Like waifs clustered around a blazing fire, we gathered about it, holding out our hearts to its warmth and light. The blacker the night around us grew, the brighter and truer . . . burned the Word of God. . . . Sometimes I would slip the Bible from its little sack with hands that shook, so mysterious had it become to me. It was new; it had just been written. I marveled sometimes that the ink was dry.[4]

God's Word is a virtual smorgasbord tailored to every need. It is an all out *"feast of fat things"* (*Isa. 25:6*)—not so much because His promises are so grand (though they are!!!)—but rather, because *He* (through the stripes of Jesus) is the dispenser of each and every one.

"Every good gift and every perfect gift is from above, and cometh down from the Father of lights, with whom is no variableness, neither shadow of turning."   James 1:17

"For I will restore health unto thee, and I will heal thee of thy wounds . . ."   Jeremiah 30:17a

The Love of My Life

In all this, the bent of my prayers changed. I began to crave deepened intimacy with my Healer, *more* than the healing He brings.

Day by day, Oh Dear Lord, Three things I pray,
To see Thee more clearly, To Love Thee more dearly,
Follow Thee more nearly, Day by day . . .[5]

"I said, LORD, be merciful unto me: heal my soul [*remove every barrier that separates me from Your love*]; for I have sinned against thee."   Psalms 41:4

"O God, thou art my God; early will I seek thee: my soul thirsteth for thee, my flesh longeth for thee in a dry and thirsty land, where no water is; to see thy power and thy glory, so as I have seen thee in the sanctuary. Because thy lovingkindness is better than life [*better than health ... better than every added blessing we could ever receive!*], my lips shall praise thee. Thus will I bless thee while I live: I will lift up my hands in thy name."
                                                           Psalm 63:1-4

This was no easy road. I battled. And when I got bottled up I prayed in my heavenly language.

"What is it then? I will pray with the spirit, and I will pray with the understanding also: I will sing with the spirit, and I will sing with the understanding also."   1 Corinthians 14:15

"Likewise the Spirit also helpeth our infirmities: for we know not what we should pray for as we ought: but the Spirit itself maketh intercession for us with groanings which cannot be uttered. And he that searcheth the hearts knoweth what is the mind of the Spirit, because he maketh intercession for the saints according to the will of God."   Romans 8:26-27

When that form of travail subsided, I fought out from under the oppression by simply adoring the Lord for who He is and the beauty of His Person.

"Give unto the LORD the glory due unto his name; worship the LORD in the beauty of holiness."   Psalms 29:2

Praise & Thanksgiving

Echoing in my spirit were words spoken into my life by my husband. ...Words that he had embraced long before we ever met. ...Words that he received from a young college student who stepped in and out of his life like *"angels unawares"* in the early stages of his walk with Jesus *(Heb. 13:2)*.

> PRAISE ME, O MY PEOPLE, PRAISE ME. Praise Me out of a heart full of love. Praise Me for every blessing and every victory. Yea, and Praise Me when the most difficult thing to do is to Praise. This is the victory that overcometh the world, even your faith, and praise is the voice of faith. It is faith rejoicing for victories . . . in advance. The song of praise is made of the very fabric of things hoped for. It becomes an evidence of unseen things. It is the raw material in My hands from which I fashion your victories. Give it to Me. Give Me much, give to Me often. I dwell in the midst of the praises of My people. I dwell there because I am happiest there, and just as surely as ye make Me happy with your praising, ye shall make the enemy most unhappy. He has no power . . . [to overcome the stance of] a praising Christian. He cannot stand against a praising Church. This is [one of] the most powerful weapons you can use against him. So praise is like a two-edged sword, the one side bringing health to your own spirit and the other side cutting down the enemy.[6]

Over and over again I spoke the wonderful Name of Jesus: the name of the One that's higher than any other *(Isa. 9:6; Eph. 1:20-22)*. ...The name that makes demons tremble and flee *(Jam. 2:19)*; that makes the lame to walk and the blind to see *(Acts 16:18; 3:6, 11-16; Mk. 16:17-18)*. ...The name with the power to bend every knee *(Phil. 2:9-11)*. ...The only *"name under heaven given among men whereby we must be saved (Acts 4:12)*. I whispered it often. I emulated the example set by Ignatius when led away to the coliseum where he was devoured by lions. Those conversant with him testified that he *"frequently repeated the name of Jesus."*[7] I, too, proclaimed it aloud. And I spoke it with the meditations of my heart.

...Jesus! Jesus, Jesus. "My Lord and My God" (Jn. 20:28).

I also took my eyes off myself and my own little universe of concerns and lifted up petitions for my husband ...the fellow Cross-bearers with whom we walk ...and the saints at large. Plus, as Apostle Edwin and I often do, I interceded for a great outpouring of the Holy Spirit and a renewal of the Cross in the Church. The more I gave to others, the more our precious Jesus gave the *"fulness"* of Himself to me, *"grace for grace"* (*Jn. 1:16*).

"Give, and it shall be given unto you; good measure, pressed down, and shaken together, and running over . . ."   Luke 6:38a

It was a cherished time of reflection on our pilgrimage together and the supernatural ways God has met our needs and kept us covered in one "death, burial and resurrection" type "Cross-experience" after another.

"I will remember the works of the LORD: surely I will remember thy wonders of old. I will meditate also of all thy work, and talk of thy doings."   Psalm 77:11-12

How about the time we were bottomed out in the boondocks on a remote desert road with a car full of youth and no tools in the trunk. ...Huge oversight! Out we jumped side-by-side on the ground digging under the frame. Edwin conducted the whole event like a Sunday service awaiting the melody of the choir. No sunken spirits here. Time to sing! *"Lord, we need a wrench."* And there it was protruding from the sand to the left of the driver's side door. *"It's gotta be a half inch,"* Edwin exclaimed. ...And it was! Amazing! ...Right beside us reflecting off the sun! No time wasted. Smiles on all faces. The fan belt was put back in place and off we went.

Hallelujah! As it was then when our thoughts zeroed in on victory and our praises began to ascend, so again in my present trial: Paul's exhortation to the Philippians was in full exercise.

"Be careful for nothing; but in every thing by prayer and supplication with thanksgiving let your requests be made known unto God. And the peace of God, which passeth all understanding, shall keep your hearts and minds through Christ Jesus. Finally, brethren, whatsoever things are true, whatsoever things are honest, whatsoever things are just, whatsoever things are pure, whatsoever things are lovely, whatsoever things are of good report; if there be any virtue, and if there be any praise, think on these things."

Philippians 4:6-8

My Heavenly Father's own thoughts became incredibly "*precious*" to me.

"How precious also are thy thoughts unto me, O God! how great is the sum of them! If I should count them, they are more in number than the sand: when I awake, I am still with thee."

Psalm 139:17-18

The lyrics of an old traditional song came to mind:

Count your blessings, name them one by one . . .[8]

Thanksgiving has a wondrous way of lightening the heart and opening us up to a spirit of worship. And it's not just supposed to be voiced when we gather in a crop of answered prayer; but rather, from the moment we step out in faith on a promise, till the berries come to fruition on the trees *(2 Ch. 20:20-24)*.

May be, Christian, thou art upon a sick-bed, and some reviving thou hast, though far from thy former health — O bless God for this little lift of thy head from thy pillow.... knowing [there is] no way . . . better to engage God in the continuance and enlargement of his mercy, than by a praiseful entertainment thereof at its first approach.[9]

Praise is a profound discipline that helped Jordan Rubin turn his "*frown*" upside down and set his feet on the road to recovery from Crohn's Disease.

When I went to California to live with the man who taught me the first principles of how to eat foods from the Bible, he forced me to examine my negative thinking. Basically, he gave me no choice. I stayed in his home, and we studied the Bible in family meetings every day. He would not tolerate any negativity. I used to sit in the meetings wearing a frown, which had become a regular part of my wardrobe for two years. He eventually made me sit in another room because he didn't want his kids to learn that negative demeanor from me! His tough standards of conduct amounted to a rough boot camp for my soul. . . . I remember thinking as I left the bathroom one time, *I may have a stomachache in ten minutes, but right now I am fine.* . . . . It was a valuable lesson in learning how to live a moment-to-moment life of thanksgiving. . . . The impact of this change . . . was a huge factor in my healing. I believe that faith [and thanksgiving] . . . based on God's Word, are vital keys to recovering and maintaining health.[10]

Indeed, thanksgiving is a powerful weapon in the arsenal of Christian conquerors. It cultivates patience, and at the same time crucifies self-pity, discontent, despair and negativity. In a word, it sets believers up "on High."

"A merry heart doeth good like a medicine: but a broken spirit drieth the bones."   Proverbs 17:22

Whenever I *"put on the garment of praise"* the *"spirit of heaviness,"* would move away like a dark oppressive cloud and the peace of God would envelope me as a faithful *"keep[er]"* (Phil. 4:6-7; Isa 61:3).

"But thou art holy, O thou that inhabitest the praises of Israel."   Psalms 22:3

Praise Me. This I ask of thee in times when it seemeth indescribably difficult to do. I ask it of thee in love that is stern at this point because I know unequivocally that it is your only hope for survival. Distress of soul and grief of heart can only bring on destruction of body. Joy alone is a healer, and ye can have it in the darkest hour if ye will force thy soul to rise to Me in worship and adoration.[11]

Psalm 91 tells all!

"Because thou hast made the LORD, which is my refuge, even the most High, thy habitation; there shall no evil befall thee, neither shall any plague come nigh thy dwelling."

Psalm 91:9-10

Ponder the previously quoted Psalm in its entirety. ...Better yet, embrace it. It's awesome!

Man has contemplated the power of faith and of prayer, but only rarely have I revealed to men this far greater power of praise. For by prayer and faith doors are opened, but by praise and worship, great dynamos of power are set in motion, as when a switch is thrown and an electric power plant such as Niagara is thrown into operation. Praying for specifics is like requesting light for individual houses in various scattered places, while worshipping and praise flood the whole area with available current.[12]

Intruder

When the Apostle Paul said: "*We wrestle . . .*" he meant exactly that *(Eph. 6:12)*. Wrestlers cannot let up, lest in a split second they are laid flat. On one occasion, no sooner had I taken a moment of rest from aggressive combat, thanksgiving and reflections on past triumphs that a new rogue thought forced its way in:

Okay. If you get bit by a rattlesnake, what are you going to do? Are you going to take Oreganol? Are you going to take it; or,

are you going to trust in God for divine healing without any outside props? What are you going to do?[a]

"*Do?!!!!*" All of a sudden "Faith's Alarm System" went off like a high pitched siren in the dark of night. The red and white warning lights were flashing. The Holy Spirit came to my aide. There I was planning out a response to a venomous snakebite that hadn't even occurred.

This is insane! Or, as the Word says, unsound (2 Tim. 1:7). Is this who I am — a defeated and fearful wimp — still subject to the fears prophesied to follow my unbelieving and disobedient Jewish kin in the Latter Days?!

"And upon them that are left alive of you I will send a faintness into their hearts in the lands of their enemies; and the sound of a shaken leaf shall chase them; and they shall flee, as fleeing from a sword; and they shall fall when none pursueth. And they shall fall one upon another, as it were before a sword, when none pursueth: and ye shall have no power to stand before your enemies." Leviticus 26:36-37

Gone with the wind at a mere suggestion of danger were my recollections of the Lord's miracle working power throughout our wilderness years. That's when our Saviour profoundly and repeatedly revealed Himself to us as "*the God that doest wonders*" (Ps. 77:14). Through all kinds of severe persecutions and distress—and I mean severe!—(i.e. guns, kidnapping, break-ins, media defamation, court appearances, etc.), Apostle Edwin and I have most often been, over the long term, the most stable amongst the believers with whom we've walked. Yet now, when confronted with a proportionally small issue, I am a deflated balloon. I'm like a man captive to lust that "*by means of a whorish woman . . . is brought to a piece of bread*" (Pro. 6:26).

---

[a] Oreganol is a natural oil derived from the hyssop plant. It acts as an anti-venom and natural antibiotic. It is of the same species used in the application of blood to the doorpost and lintel at Passover. We keep a 1 ounce bottle in our emergency kit.

"Behold, thou hast instructed many, and thou hast strengthened the weak hands. Thy words have upholden him that was falling, and thou hast strengthened the feeble knees. But now it is come upon thee, and thou faintest; it toucheth thee, and thou art troubled."   Job 4:3-5

Think about Jimmy Swaggart at the peak of his ministry when he was taking the Gospel to the nations and huge numbers of people were being born again and baptized in the Holy Ghost through his outreach. Yet, even he was brought under; not by outward foes, but by his own uncrucified lusts.

Oh brethren, there is no bottom to all this, no matter who we are or how far we've come. If we give the devil a millimeter (any credibility whatsoever to his suggestions) he'll take a kilometer! He'll bring us right back to hell.

"Lest Satan should get an advantage of us: for we are not ignorant of his devices."   2 Corinthians 2:11

Timely Rebuke

At this juncture of our story it seems that nothing could be more appropriate for inserting than a clip from "Give Faith a Meal"—the message that we were preparing to send with our ten page epistle to our brethren in Zimbabwe. The exhortation that I supported Edwin in meting out to them was now at our doorstep, challenging me *(Mt. 7:1)*! Like Bishop Raymore so often reminds us: *"We meet at the Cross."* Amen and amen!

Who will say that man is genuinely thankful to his friend for a past kindness that nourishes an ill opinion of him for the future, and dares not trust him when he needs him again? . . . O how sad is this, that after God had entertained a soul many a time at his table with choice mercies and deliverances, [that] not a bit of them all should be left [in his grateful recollections] to give faith a meal; thereby to keep the heart from fainting, when God comes not so fast to deliver as we desire! He is the most thankful man that ponders up the mercies of God in his memory, and can feed his faith with the thoughts of what God hath done for him, so as to walk in the strength thereof in his present straights. . . . He that distrusts God, after former experience, is like the foolish builder, Mat. xii [Mat. 7] — he rears his monument for past mercies on the sand, which the next tide of affliction washeth away.[13]

Thank you, Brother Gurnall, for your kind reproof.

"Let the righteous smite me; it shall be a kindness: and let him reprove me; it shall be an excellent oil, which shall not break my head . . ."   Psalm 141:5a

And thank you, Brother Chambers, for confirming Gurnall's word and reminding me of the VALUE of today's trials. They are an indispensible part of our preparation for ministry to others amidst troublesome times like these (2 Cor. 1:3-4).

God expects His children to be so confident in Him that in any crisis they are the reliable ones. Our trust in God is up to a certain point, then we go back to the elementary panic prayers of those who do not know God. We get to our wit's end, showing that we have not the slightest confidence in Him and His government of the world; He seems to be asleep, and we see nothing but breakers ahead. "O ye of little faith!" What a pang that must have shot through the disciples — "Missed it again!" And what a pang will go through us when we suddenly realize that we might have produced downright joy in the heart of Jesus by remaining absolutely confident in Him, no matter what was ahead. There are stages in life when there is no storm, no crisis, when we do our human best; it is when a crisis arises that we instantly reveal upon whom we rely. If we have been learning to worship God and to trust Him, the crisis will reveal that we will go to the breaking point and not break in our confidence in Him.[14]

CHAPTER ELEVEN

To the Cross I Flee

I became filled with indignation and chagrin.

I've been following Jesus for over four decades. I am married to a devout church leader, who, in the truest sense of the word is "a man full of faith and of the Holy Ghost" (Acts 6:5). We've personally experienced and been part of one healing miracle after another; and yet I'm getting wobbly-kneed over mythical ponderings of events that haven't even transpired!

Thank God for His chastisements and providences *(1 Cor. 11:32; Heb. 12)*. They have a wondrous way of showing us whether our lives are securely *"hid with Christ in God"* (Col. 3:3); or, more faith-building and refinement needs to be done. At the *"breaking point"* I was just about to fold. Sobering!

These stubborn blemishes are like hidden fault lines in areas prone to seismic activity. All it takes is a minor temblor and "boom!" the roads and bridges of our lives start falling down. Deep down in my heart I knew that this "Goliath of Fear" had not yet been vanquished. But I still chose to leave it dormant once the storms of testing passed. Plus, I recoiled in cowardice each time I was called out onto the field to confront it.

Truly, my sins were stacked up. I was not only guilty of fear, but of the "effeminacy" (meaning cowardice) that springs from it. Though some may sympathize with that kind of paralysis, God assigns it the same judgment as the most abominable of other offences. It's sandwiched between adultery and sodomy.

"Know ye not that the unrighteous shall not inherit the kingdom of God? Be not deceived: neither fornicators, nor idolaters, nor adulterers, nor effeminate, nor abusers of themselves with mankind, nor thieves, nor covetous, nor drunkards, nor revilers, nor extortioners, shall inherit the kingdom of God."   1 Corinthians 6:9-10

Had I been consumed like David with zeal for the honor of the Great God of Israel, rather than for saving myself from the Cross of suffering, I would have risen up in the name of the Lord long ago; cut off its head; and taken its sword *(1 Sam. 17)*.

I'm gonna need to humble myself, tell Edwin about all this traffic in my soul at an appropriate time, and solicit his prayers.

Sharing comes of a willingness to be absolutely honest about oneself; it is a sign that the long attempt to compromise is over . . . an evidence that the soul really means what it says. Directly we are honest with God, with ourselves and with other people . . .[1]

But first I must get honest (no more hiding!) and seek the face of my Lord. I must begin with Him.

. . . Our walk in the light is first and foremost with the Lord Jesus. It is with Him first that we must get things settled and it is His cleansing and victory that must first be obtained. Then when God guides us to open our hearts with others, we come to them with far more of a testimony than a confession (except where that is specifically due) and we praise God together.[2]

Opening up with trusted brethren is a priceless blessing and integral part of healing *(Jam. 5:13-16)*; but it is never to be a substitute for our confession to God and our intimacy with Him. Only God, through Christ, has the power to forgive and cleanse our *"scarlet"* sins and make us *"white as snow" (Isa. 1:18)*.

"I acknowledged my sin unto thee, and mine iniquity have I not hid. I said, I will confess my transgressions unto the Lord; and thou forgavest the iniquity of my sin. Selah."   Psalm 32:5

Gravity of Repentance

I can't begin to express the gravity of approaching our Holy God as a penitent in hopes of being reconciled to Him through the life blood of His only Begotten Son, Jesus. Our hearts must be sincere, fully resolved that by His divine empowerment we are ready to put away the sins that bind us. We must also be willing to acknowledge in totality our waywardness and in so doing to justify our worthy Lord God in His Fatherly dealings.

"We acknowledge, O LORD, our wickedness, and the iniquity of our fathers: for we have sinned against thee. Do not abhor us, for thy name's sake, do not disgrace the throne of thy glory: remember, break not thy covenant with us."   Jeremiah 14:20-21

My God-fearing husband, as an apostle of Jesus Christ, "drives home" the need for utter sincerity on this all important issue every day of our lives.

> *If you want your plea for mercy answered, Jody, and you don't want to invite God's wrath instead, you better "call upon" our Righteous Lord "in Truth."*

"The LORD is righteous in all his ways, and holy in all his works. The LORD is nigh unto all them that call upon him, to all that call upon him in truth."   Psalms 145:17-18

Nothing [is] more hateful to God or man than falsehood and treachery in treaties of peace . . . . O take heed of any hollowness of heart in thy inquiry for peace! When found out—as it must needs be, except God's eye fails Him, which is impossible—it will exceedingly harden the heart of God against thee.[3]

"Should we again break thy commandments . . . ? Wouldest not thou be angry with us till thou hadst consumed us, so that there should be no remnant nor escaping? O LORD God of Israel, thou art righteous: for we remain yet escaped, as it is this day:

behold, we are before thee in our trespasses: for we cannot stand before thee because of this."   Ezra 9:14-15

"What shall we say then? Shall we continue in sin, that grace may abound? God forbid."   Romans 6:1-2a

"But God shall wound the head of his enemies, and the hairy scalp of such an one as goeth on still in his trespasses."
                    Psalms 68:21

"For if we sin wilfully after that we have received the knowledge of the truth, there remaineth no more sacrifice for sins, but a certain fearful looking for of judgment and fiery indignation, which shall devour the adversaries. He that despised Moses' law died without mercy under two or three witnesses: of how much sorer punishment, suppose ye, shall he be thought worthy, who hath trodden under foot the Son of God, and hath counted the blood of the covenant, wherewith he was sanctified, an unholy thing, and hath done despite unto the Spirit of grace?"   Hebrews 10:26-29

Calvary: The New Testament Altar of Sacrifice

To understand the heinousness of sin and God's sentiments about it, we need look no further than the Cross of Christ.

> . . . Only the judgment of God upon sin will truly reveal its nature and presence. In other words, we can begin to understand how deceptive [and deadly] sin is by the judgment it incurs. The crucified Christ, therefore, saves us from any self-justifying lightness about our own condition.[4]

The penalty for sin is death (the Second Death) meaning the Final Judgment assigned to anyone and everyone (professing Christian or not) who does not believe in Jesus as the only Mediator between God and man; and manifest that belief by coming to Him in continuing brokenness with a wholehearted commitment to walk in repentance and "*fight the good fight of faith*" until the Last Day; when the "*law of sin*" working in our members is swallowed up in Life *(1 Cor. 15:54; Rev. 21:7-8).*

> It is by seeing the concern of the doctor, and the extreme measures prescribed, that the patient learns for the first time the gravity of the trouble from which he is suffering. . . . So, in like manner, Jesus says from the cross, "See here your own condition by the shame I had to undergo for you." If the moment the Holy One took our place and bore our sins He was condemned by the Father and left derelict in the hour of His sufferings, what must our true condition be to occasion so severe an act of judgment![5]

> Most of mankind is devoid of sin-consciousness. . . . We find it hard to acknowledge ourselves as sinners. We would rather consider sin only as a category, a thing apart from who and what we are as humans, a subject of theological discussion rather than an inherent part of the human condition. However, the truth about sin, as well as its consequences, is not found in what we think about sin, but rather upon what God tells us about sin and its consequences [and by the only possible means He provides for removing the penalty for it].[6]

"For the wages of sin is death; but the gift of God is eternal life through Jesus Christ our Lord."   Romans 6:23

"For there is one God, and one mediator between God and men, the man Christ Jesus; Who gave Himself a ransom for all, to be testified in due time."   1 Timothy 2:5-6

The Blood of Love

To cancel the judgment against us as sinners the blood of an innocent had to be shed *(Lev. 17:11).*

> ". . . And without shedding of blood is no remission."
> Hebrews 9:22b

Reconciliation to the Father was intentionally established in this way so that man would be forced to take a good hard look at the horror of his sin and the suffering it begets. Coming to grips with this reality [is] intended to [humble us and] inspire a complete change of heart and relinquishment of evil.[7]

...Not "any blood" needed to be shed, or even "*the blood of bulls and of goats,*" as sacrificed on the Day of Atonement according to Old Testament Law, though that be remarkable indeed *(Heb. 10:4)*. But the "*precious blood of Christ, as of a lamb without blemish and without spot*" *(1 Pe. 1:19b)*.

To create, God had but to speak, and it was done. But to redeem, He had to bleed. And He did so in the Person of His Son, Jesus Christ, whom He sent to take the place of death upon the cross which our sin had so richly deserved.[8]

"For Christ also hath once suffered for sins, the just for the unjust, that He might bring us to God, being put to death in the flesh, but quickened by the Spirit."   1 Peter 3:18

Jesus is the fulfillment of the Old Testament foreshadow of animal sacrifice as the only means by which our sins can be atoned.

[On the Day of Atonement], the acting high priest sacrificed a bull on behalf of his own sins and the sins of his family, followed by a goat for the rest of the people. He then brought the blood of atonement through a veil into the most sacred part of the Jewish Tabernacle ("the Holiest of All" Heb. 9:3), where stood the physical representation of the mercy seat of God.

"Then shall he kill the goat of the sin offering, that is for the people, and bring his blood within the vail, and do with that blood as he did with the blood of the bullock, and sprinkle it upon the mercy seat, and before the mercy seat."   Leviticus 16:15

. . . Only the high priest was allowed to enter the chamber within the veil; and only once per year, otherwise death ensued. After blood was sprinkled on the mercy seat, the high priest took another goat, laid his hands upon its head and confessed the sins of the people. The joint offering up of these animals signified not only the washing away of man's sins, but also the transfer of guilt to a scapegoat who bore the penalty.

"And Aaron shall lay both his hands upon the head of the live goat, and confess over him all the iniquities of the children of Israel, and all their transgressions in all their sins, putting them upon the head of the goat, and shall send him away by the hand of a fit man into the wilderness: And the goat shall bear upon him all their iniquities . . . . For on that day shall the priest make an atonement for you, to cleanse you, that ye may be clean from all your sins before the Lord."   Lev. 16:21-22a, 30[9]

Jesus of Nazareth was the sin offering, as well as the Scapegoat, chosen by the Father to be the Burden Bearer and the High Priest of all those that are willing to repent, believe on Him and surrender their lives in totality to His Lordship *(Isa. 53:4-6; Jn. 1:29; Acts 2:38).*

"Who his own self bare our sins in his own body on the tree, that we, being dead to sins, should live unto righteousness: by whose stripes ye were healed."   1 Peter 2:24

Under Old Testament Law, the Scapegoat was removed from the camp and released into the wilderness. Similarly, the carcasses of the animals sacrificed for sin were taken beyond the periphery of the camp and burned. Both places, outside the boundaries of blessing, were a horrific portrayal of eternal separation from God.

. . . Outside the camp was . . . the place of foreigners, lepers, criminals and sin-cursed refuse—a place to be avoided. Yet . . . it was to the spiritual counterpart of that place . . . that the Lord Jesus went forth, bearing His cross, that He might sanctify . . . [us] with His own blood.[10]

His bloody death secured for us, poor sinners, release from sin and peace with God, yet without doing any damage to our Father's justice.

"For He hath made him to be sin for us, who knew no sin; that we might be made the righteousness of God in him."

2 Corinthians 5:21

". . . God hath set [Him] forth to be a propitiation through faith in His blood, to declare His righteousness for the remission of sins that are past . . . that He might be just, and the justifier of him which believeth in Jesus."   Romans 3:25a-26b

Who among us can thank Him enough?!

"For the bodies of those beasts, whose blood is brought into the sanctuary by the high priest for sin, are burned without the camp. Wherefore Jesus also, that he might sanctify the people with his own blood, suffered without the gate."

Hebrews 13:11-12

The brutally abused figure that shocked onlookers in Isaiah's Messianic prophecy was not there because of any wrong He had committed, but rather, as a substitute for us!

"As many were astonied at thee; his visage was so marred more than any man, and his form more than the sons of men: so shall he sprinkle many nations; the kings shall shut their mouths at him: for that which had not been told them shall they see; and that which they had not heard shall they consider."

Isaiah 52:14-15

Jesus was hated and few cared.[11]

"He is despised and rejected of men; a man of sorrows, and acquainted with grief: and we hid as it were our faces from him; he was despised, and we esteemed him not."   Isaiah 53:3

It was our sins He bore and our sorrows that weighed Him down. People thought His troubles were punishment from God for His own sins, yet He was lashed and tortured for ours![12]

"Surely he hath borne our griefs, and carried our sorrows: yet we did esteem him stricken, smitten of God, and afflicted."
Isaiah 53:4

His own creatures cast him off, and even worse, crucified Him as a malefactor *(Lk. 23:32; Jn. 18:29-30)*. Painful as that was (and still is!), it cannot be compared to the excruciating rejection He suffered from the Father Himself when the just decree of His righteousness was *"taken away"* in our behalf.

"In his humiliation his judgment was taken away: and who shall declare his generation? For his life is taken from the earth."   Acts 8:33

No wonder darkness covered the entire land as a prelude to that horrific Event!

"Now from the sixth hour there was darkness over all the land unto the ninth hour. And about the ninth hour Jesus cried with a loud voice, saying, Eli, Eli, lama sabachthani? That is to say, My God, my God, why hast thou forsaken me?"
Matthew 27:45-46

. . . What [then] must God see us to be? It is plain that God was not forsaking the Son as the Son. He was forsaking the Son as us, whose likeness He was wearing.[13]

"For . . . God sending his own Son in the likeness of sinful flesh, and for sin, condemned sin in the flesh."   Romans 8:3b

So great is our Father's love to us-ward that He *"spared not his own Son, but delivered him up for us all." (Rom. 8:32).*

"For God so loved the world, that he gave his only begotten Son, that whosoever believeth in him should not perish, but have everlasting life."   John 3:16

"For scarcely for a righteous man will one die: yet peradventure for a good man some would even dare to die. But God commendeth his love toward us, in that, while we were yet sinners, Christ died for us."   Romans 5:7-8

"Yet it pleased the LORD to bruise him; he hath put him to grief . . . Thou shalt make his soul an offering for sin . . . . for he shall bear their iniquities. . . . He hath poured out his soul unto death: and he was numbered with the transgressors; and he bare the sin of many, and made intercession for the transgressors."   Isaiah 53:10a, 11b, 12b

Who can comprehend such Love?! A mere gaze into the heart of God — as it was so gloriously laid bare in the face of *"Christ crucified"* — should break us into a thousand little pieces and completely revolutionize our entire outlook on (and attitude towards) repentance *(I Cor. 1:23).*

> In the searching light of Christ we see sin . . . as a blow struck at love. It is not so much our concern as to what Christ will do to us [as a consequence of our breach of Covenant] but what we have done and are doing to Him. I used to be afraid that God might hurt me; but when I saw the Cross I saw how I had hurt God who wills me good and not evil.[14]

"Then said I, Woe is me! for I am undone; because I am a man of unclean lips, and I dwell in the midst of a people of unclean lips: for mine eyes have seen the King, the LORD of hosts."   Isaiah 6:5

If we are asked, "Where do we see Jesus as the truth?", we reply, "Supremely on the cross of Calvary." There in Him we see the whole naked truth about sin, man, and the God with whom each of us has to do. The very scene that reveals the richest and sweetest grace of God toward man also reveals the starkest truth as to what man is. If grace flows from Calvary, so does truth, for both "grace and truth came through Jesus Christ" (Jn. 1:17).[15]

Upon the Cross of Jesus
Mine eye at times can see
The very dying form of One
Who suffered there for me.
And from my stricken heart with tears
Two wonders I confess —
The wonders of redeeming love
And my unworthiness.[16]

A True Heart

Captured by the revelation of *"Love Divine,"*[17] let us deeply repent of all nonchalance in our attitude about sin and give ourselves wholeheartedly in surrender and amendment when we make our plea for mercy to the One who held nothing back in extending His forgiveness to us.

"Let us draw near with a true heart in full assurance of faith, having our hearts sprinkled from an evil conscience, and our bodies washed with pure water."   Hebrews 10:22

God forbid that we, like the tribe of Judah in days gone by, render anything less!

"And yet for all this her treacherous sister Judah hath not turned unto me with her whole heart, but feignedly, saith the LORD."   Jeremiah 3:10

Now, suppose that [a] doomed criminal were a filthy, unclean harlot, imprisoned for a crime, or for having

herself alone committed (if it were possible) all the
wickedness and sins ever perpetrated by the whole
world, for which she were condemned to the most
shameful death that could be devised; and the King
should send His only, beloved Son from His kingdom
and glory into great poverty, imprisonment, suffering
and an innocent death, in the stead of the unclean harlot,
who by all manner of contempt and evil-doing had
angered the King, and merited death a thousand times,
but is now nevertheless, out of grace, through the death
of the King's Son (on the condition of her amending)
reconciled to the King, made at peace with Him, liberated
from prison, and delivered from death, and remains alive
a partaker and heir of all the riches of the King; ought she
not to accept this great love and grace, love the King,
amend her ways, and be greatly afraid of vexing the King
any more all her life, who cleansed her, forgave all her
evil deeds, paid all her debts, espoused her as His
beloved queen, exalted her into His glory, and protected
her as Himself from all enemies? But if she should not
amend (according to her promise), should again anger
the King, and do worse than before, were this not great
ingratitude, worthy of sorer punishment than before?
Hereby we may prove ourselves, whether we that are
redeemed through the grace of God, also keep the
promise of amendment.   Valerius Schoolmaster,
Wrote 2 books in prison prior to martyrdom, A.D. 1568[18]

Jesus gave us bread to break and a cup to drink. But along
with that unspeakable gift, He gave the command to *remember*
Him.

". . . The Lord Jesus the same night in which he was betrayed
took bread: and when he had given thanks, he brake it, and
said, Take, eat: this is my body, which is broken for you: this do
in remembrance of me. After the same manner also he took the
cup, when he had supped, saying, This cup is the new
testament in my blood: this do ye, as oft as ye drink it, in
remembrance of me."   1 Corinthians 11:23b-25

Woe be unto us if we don't!

"For he that eateth and drinketh unworthily, eateth and drinketh damnation to himself, not discerning the Lord's body."
1 Corinthians 11:29

About Face

I'll never forget a conversation I had with Sheila, a Jewess in her mid-seventies, who seemed, at times, to be knocking on Heaven's Gate, yet was stumbled up because she was unwilling to enter through Christ as the Open Door *(1 Cor. 1:23; Jn. 10:7-9)*. It was inconceivable to her that someone would *"take a bullet"* (her words) in her behalf. In venting her disapproval of the rampant hypocrisy in "Christendom," she acted out a scenario that has stuck with us ever since.

Sheila is just under five feet tall. Yet you'd never know it, because she can be so demonstrative. *"Repentance,"* she said emphatically as she marched forward in a full strut before stopping and making a 180 degree about-face, *"is going one way, ...then, turning around and going in the opposite direction."* Pausing, she then punctuated her point by tilting her red head and casting a rear glance through her emerald green eyes over her shoulder while saying: *"...and not turning back."*

Without even realizing it she was using body language to preach a sermon on repentance straight out of the Scriptures. She was acting out a "to and fro" drama on change: of turning *"to"* God ..."*from*" sin, Satan and the world.

"For they themselves shew of us what manner of entering in we had unto you, and how ye turned to God from idols to serve the living and true God."   1 Thessalonians 1:9

...And not to turn from one to the other only (though that is a necessary beginning), but to turn with a commitment never to let anything get between us and our fidelity to the Lord and the glory of His Love again.

"Turn us again, O God, and cause Thy face to shine . . . . So will not we go back from thee . . ."   Psalms 80:19a, 18a

"Let him that stole steal no more: but rather let him labour, working with his hands the thing which is good, that he may have to give to him that needeth."   Ephesians 4:28

She was trying to tell us that the same merciful Lord who said to the paralytic:

". . . Son, be of good cheer; thy sins be forgiven thee."
Matthew 9:2b

...And to the impotent man by the pool of Bethesda:

". . . Rise, take up thy bed and walk." John 5:8b

...Also warned:

". . . Behold, thou art made whole: sin no more, lest a worse thing come unto thee."   John 5:14b

...A warning that echoed thereafter through the teachings of His apostles.

"For if after they have escaped the pollutions of the world through the knowledge of the Lord and Saviour Jesus Christ, they are again entangled therein, and overcome, the latter end is worse with them than the beginning. For it had been better for them not to have known the way of righteousness, than, after they have known it, to turn from the holy commandment delivered unto them. But it is happened unto them according to the true proverb, The dog is turned to his own vomit again; and the sow that was washed to her wallowing in the mire."
2 Peter 2:20-22

CHAPTER TWELVE

Praying with Resignation

Quieted by grace and the reverential fear of God, I began (again) to pray.

Dear God, have mercy on me! I embrace your chastening rod. Thank you for another much needed trial of faith to liberate me from all duplicity and establish at my core unwavering trust in Your promised love and care.

"They that trust in the LORD shall be as mount Zion, which cannot be removed, but abideth for ever."   Psalms 125:1

Please forgive me for this debilitating unbelief and grant unto me whatever is best for my salvation.

O what great grace is this, that the good God seeks my salvation, which salvation has been, and still is, the sole object of my seeking and praying, as I wrote to you before my imprisonment, to help me to pray, that the Lord would give and let come upon me what is [best] for my salvation . . . for His grace knows better than I what I need.   Jan Wouterss van Kuyck, Chose torture & fire Rather than expose the saints to harm, A.D. 1572[1]

Fortify my "mustard seed" faith and turn this liability into a strength (Mt. 17:20). Let this passage come alive in my life, in Jesus' name, amen:

"Who through faith subdued kingdoms, wrought righteousness, obtained promises, stopped the mouths of lions. Quenched the violence of fire, escaped the edge of the sword, *out of weakness were made strong*, waxed valiant in fight, turned

to flight the armies of the aliens. Women received their dead raised to life again: and others were tortured, not accepting deliverance; that they might obtain a better resurrection."

Hebrews 11:33-35

It took a lot of gumption for me to launch a prayer of that kind because, like Oswald Chambers and many others, I had (and still have!) great apprehensions about the potential trials that God might deem necessary to bring about the answer. Just the thought of encountering any kind of pressured circumstance that might awaken dormant feelings like helplessness that so often accompany fear intimidated me.

Perhaps I shall not be worthy [to shine cleanly as a true witness and light] until He has weaned me by some great sorrow. What the great sorrow will be, I do not know; perhaps it won't be at all.[2]

I wanted to open up and wholeheartedly pray these words...

"Judge me, O LORD; for I have walked in mine integrity: I have trusted also in the LORD; therefore I shall not slide. Examine me, O LORD, and prove me; try my reins and my heart."

Psalm 26:1-2

But I was extremely reticent.

There is an inherent unwillingness in man to make peace with the cross, and an unwillingness to recognize that the way of faith is the way of suffering. It is the prospect of suffering that intimidates us, more than the suffering itself. . . . Therefore we gird ourselves about with every kind of justification to safely distance ourselves from any possibility of that prospect.[3]

I knew God wanted all of me, yet I feared what complete surrender to Him would mean.[4]

I was afraid my sin would be found out and I'd be left to my own devices amidst overwhelming odds. The unbelief still dogging my life robbed me from embracing the verse that follows on the heels of the two preceding it. That verse describes the *"lovingkindness"* that dwells in the heart of my Judge. Had I kept that in view, there is a strong possibility I could have "steadied the ship" and more confidently joined the psalmist in his plea for sanctification.

"For thy lovingkindness is before mine eyes: and I have walked in thy truth."   Psalm 26:3

Yet ever so timidly, I did pray ...and pray ...and pray again.

"O LORD, correct me, but with judgment; not in thine anger, lest thou bring me to nothing."   Jeremiah 10:24

...Not *"vain repetitions, as the heathen do"* (Mt. 6:7). But rather, *"importunity"* springing from utter weakness and intermittent waves of despair *(Lk. 11:5-13)*. I was beseeching my Lord for strength in my soul.

"In the day when I cried thou answeredst me, and strengthenedst me with strength in my soul."   Psalms 138:3

The account of a father pleading with Jesus for the deliverance of his son became one of my mainstays.

"And they brought him [the son] unto him [Jesus]: and when he saw him, straightway the spirit tare him; and he fell on the ground, and wallowed foaming. And he asked his father, How long is it ago since this came unto him? And he said, Of a child. And ofttimes it hath cast him into the fire, and into the waters, to destroy him: but if thou canst do any thing, have compassion on us, and help us. Jesus said unto him, If thou canst believe, all things are possible to him that believeth. And straightway the father of the child cried out, and said with tears, Lord, *I believe; help thou mine unbelief.*"   Mark 9:20-24

Added to my prayer was a willingness to step out in faith on the Lord's answer to my plea by renewing my commitment to put an end to the slack in my thought life and in so doing put the devil to flight.

> Then the Shepherd . . . said, "Be strong, yea, be strong and fear not." Then He continued, "Much-Afraid, don't ever allow yourself to begin trying to picture what it will be like. Believe Me, when you get to the places which you dread you will find that they are as different as possible from what you have imagined . . . . I must warn you that I see your enemies lurking among the trees ahead, and if you ever let Craven Fear begin painting a picture on the screen of your imagination, you will walk with fear and trembling and agony, where no fear is."[5]

Companions in Tribulation

When insecurities and fears came back upon me I would reflect on the candor of a particular martyr whose honesty in a letter to his wife from prison has always ministered to me. The two of them greatly bemoaned their inability to say to the Lord, point blank: *"Thy Will be done"* in accord with His teaching on prayer because of their reticence to accept the inevitable sufferings attached to such resignation of heart; namely, separation from one another, imprisonment and ultimately martyrdom *(Lk. 11:2)*. A true inspiration they have been to me! Not only does this brother confess our common weakness in prayer due to self-preservation and an inherent aversion to pain; but also, our failure to recognize sin, "as sin," and as a result, unsparingly nail it to Christ's Cross. Thank you Brother and Sister Imbroeck. Your testimony, like the testimony of Abel, lives on *(Heb. 11:4)*!

> . . . We may with truth lament, that we are still very unfit; even as you write me, that you cannot pray well, even as I also, alas! am imperfect. Jam. 4:3. But the reason of it, in my opinion, is this, that we are not sufficiently displeased with ourselves, and also, that we do not

perceive the thorns that are in our flesh. May the Lord
have compassion upon us, and open the eyes of our
understanding, so that we may hate sin, even as God
Himself hates it; for then He takes pleasure in us . . .

Thomas van Imbroeck,
Beheaded for the Testimony of Jesus, A.D. 1558[6]

These beloved saints (and a precious "few" of "like Spirit"
from one generation to the next) truly possessed both the fear
of God and the love of God—two sister virtues essential for
producing the sweet spirit of meekness and surrender that our
Father cherishes in His own. I can't begin to express how much
comfort and courage I have drawn from their testimonies in my
times of crisis. When pushed to new thresholds of faith I visit
their chronicles and letters with the same earnest that I visit the
saints set forth in the Scriptures. Though they may not have
"attained" unto holiness in every area of their lives *(Phil. 3:12)*,
each one greatly bemoaned his/her weakness and followed
hard after heart-washing in sincere repentance, as evidenced by
their willingness to go all the way for Jesus; some even offering
up their own bodies as a living sacrifice in order to lay hold of
the Crown *(Rom. 12:1)*.

He was no 'church window' saint, that is the last thing he
would have desired to be—very real and human; not
faultless, but blameless, a true knight of God, obedient to
death, laying his 'Isaac' unquestioningly on the altar. To
such is given the Crown of Life.[7]

My Ever Present Lord

Every time I cried out to God in this manner our Faithful
Lord Jesus was there somehow, someway, to meet me at my
point of need, giving me just enough courage and grace to
carry on the fight. It was a cherished time of brokenness. In
addition to leading me into *Martyrs Mirror*, He graciously led
me to a variety of passages from the Bible and quality books
like *The Christian in Complete Armour* so as to *"give faith a meal."*
I also reflected back over the many, many times the Lord

brought Apostle Edwin and I into the valley of the shadow of death and then into unspeakable resurrection on the other side. Any time I EVER see my husband hit with an affliction of any kind, whether it be a bodily infirmity, "*tribulation, or distress, or persecution . . . or peril*" *(Rom. 8:35)*; or, he finds me to be in such straights, he heads directly to the altar, face pressed to the dust until the "*Sun of righteousness arise[s] with healing in His wings*" *(Mal. 4:2)*. Trekking off to Egypt without a thorough and enduring visitation to the Cross is out of the question for him.

Mark how lovely, praiseworthy and advantageous godly patience is, as Jeremiah testifies: "It is a precious thing to be patient, and to wait for the help of the Lord; Yea, that a man that is forsaken, be patient when something befalleth him; and puts his mouth in the dust, and wait for the help of the Lord, and give his cheek to the smiter, and suffer much reproach, for the Lord will not cast off forever." Lam. 3:26. . . . "An humble man will wait for the time which will bring him comfort . . ."

Hendrick Alewijns,
Tortured & Burned Alive by Catholic decree, A.D. 1569[8]

The Greatest of All Consolations

I can assuredly testify that our beloved Jesus, the "*Son of Righteousness*," does arise. ...And with such grand fanfare of rainbow colored feathers in His wings! Who can describe the richness in His comfort?! It brings healing to both soul and body. ...And quite often, in that order *(3 Jn. 1:2)*.

The pardon of sin and healing of sickness . . . are as closely united as the body and the soul. . . . Unbelief may attempt to separate these two gifts, but they are always united in Christ.[9]

To a sincere believer, there is no satisfactory consolation in any good thing that is independent from the solace that *first* comes as a result of sins atoned by the blood of Jesus; and

forgiveness administered personally to his soul by the
Comforter Himself *(Jn. 15:26)*.

"Blessed are they that mourn: for they shall be comforted."
Matthew 5:4

"Comfort ye, comfort ye my people, saith your God. Speak ye
comfortably to Jerusalem, and cry unto her, that her warfare is
accomplished, that her iniquity is pardoned: for she hath
received of the LORD's hand double for all her sins."
Isaiah 40:1- 2

Peace and reconciliation with God through the blood of
Jesus Christ exceed every other need we have; including our
most desperate need for healing and deliverance.

This truth is nowhere more evident or better
demonstrated than in the history of the paralytic. The
Lord Jesus begins by saying to him, [Son, be of good
cheer;] "Thy sins be forgiven thee," after which He adds,
"Arise and walk." [Mt. 9:2-8.][10]

'Son, be of good cheer, saith Christ, to the palsied man,
'thy sins be forgiven thee,' Matt. ix. 2. Not, Be of good
cheer, thy health is given thee, though that he had also;
but, thy 'sins are forgiven thee.' . . . This and no other
argument will stop the mouth of conscience, and bring
the creature to true peace with his own thoughts. . . .
This, and this only, will reach the poor man's heart, and
overrun it with a sudden ravishment of joy.[11]

CHAPTER THIRTEEN

The Awesome Power of Confession

At my first opportunity I opened up to Apostle Edwin and shared all the childish, faithless inward clamor and satanic traffic that I already confessed to the Lord. I was so ashamed.

> It is not difficult to confess to sin in general, for then we do not confess any sin in particular. It is very costly, however, to say these things in the presence even of an entirely loving human being whom we can trust, but as a matter of experience, it is extraordinarily effective in putting the knife to our sins. Almost every vital movement in Christian history has . . . [been set ablaze by the application of this fundamental Biblical] practice.[1]

After all these years and *still* Satan was able to get that much ground in my thoughts. Thank God for His mercy in bringing all this to the surface ...again. And thank God for such a compassionate (yet uncompromising) fellow Cross-bearer with whom I can bare my heart and seek remedy.

> Confession is an instinct of the soul. As sin is the symptom of spiritual sickness, so confession is the appointed means of recovery.[2]

> The story of the heart of Robert Burns — the unuttered sob in the poet's soul — is an example of how tragic life may become for want of sharing. Burns lamented that he could not pour out his inmost soul without reserve to any human being. He commenced a journal of his own mental history "as a substitute," he said, "for a confidential friend." He felt he must have "something" in which he could unbosom himself, "without peril of

having his confidence betrayed." We all need someone with whom we can be perfectly frank.[3]

I definitely needed to share! It was time to "pull the blanket" off my sin in the fear of God—not minimally, but thoroughly—leaving no stone unturned, lest that very stone be my undoing at a future time.

> . . . Beware of such dissimulation. For though a man cover himself before his fellows (with such fig leaves, made by him into an apron), so that his nakedness is not seen, yet God beholds his reins and can search the heart, and He knows the thoughts and intents of all men, and will also judge all works and purposes; also, all secrets and hidden things, whether they do good or evil. Therefore give diligence that in all your words and works, in all your walk and conversation, you practice simple sincerity, as becomes the children of God, and our calling demands. And if any among you be overtaken by a fall, let him confess it simply and truly, without dissimulation, just as it is, and let him not be ashamed to confess it, since he was not ashamed to commit it; else it might be to his sorrow. He that covereth his sins, it is written, shall not prosper, but whoso confesseth and forsaketh them shall have mercy. Prov. 28:13.
>
> Matthias Servaes, A.D. 1565
> Tortured & Slain by Sword by Catholic Decree[4]

...Skip confession as a step of obedience and faith on the path to liberty and you may very well miss your blessing—not only the blessing of sins forgiven, but also, the healing that is promised to follow in its wake.

"Is any sick among you? let him call for the elders of the church; and let them pray over him, anointing him with oil in the name of the Lord: and the prayer of faith shall save the sick, and the Lord shall raise him up; and if he have committed sins, they shall be forgiven him. Confess your faults one to another, and pray one for another, that ye may be healed. The effectual fervent prayer of a righteous man availeth much." James 5:14-16

Note how the Apostle James instructs us to confess our faults "*one to another.*" He does not tell us, as erroneously taught in Catholic doctrine, to confess to a "priest" that has purportedly been vested with special "*authority*" to forgive sins.[a] Scripture says: None but God can absolve us of our sins.

". . . Who can forgive sins but God only?" Mark 2:7b

Auricular confession is a satanic invention. It is a usurpation of the seat of Christ that sends those in pursuit of pardon to the confessional booth, rather than first to the Lord and then (when appropriate) to trusted brethren who would humbly hear a brother or sister's confession and then render wholehearted support and prayer. Scripture says: "*Bear ye one another's burdens*" (Gal. 6:2). How can we bear that which we know not of? ...And how can we help one another break free from sin's dominion if we don't even know there is a struggle going on?

Breakthrough to the Cross

Confession "*one to another*" is a key ingredient in the Biblical "prescription" for good health (*Jam. 5:14-16*). It's a very effectual "medicinal" because it hits pride (a major roadblock on the path to mercy) head-on and "blows the whistle" on sin and Satan.

[Confession] hurts, it cuts a man down, it is a dreadful blow to pride . . . the root of all sin. . . . In confession occurs the break-through to the Cross.[5]

. . . [Confession] is where the real power of . . . [sin] is broken and where the deliverance from it comes. This is

---

[a] "Only priests who have received the faculty of absolving from the authority of the Church can forgive sins in the name of Christ." 1994 Catechism of the Catholic Church, p. 374, #1495.

where the blood has its opportunity to be applied. This is God's biblical prescription.[6]

To stand there before a brother as a sinner is an ignominy that is almost unbearable. In the confession of concrete sins the old man dies a painful, shameful death before the eyes of a brother. Because this humiliation is so hard we continually scheme to evade confessing to a brother. Our eyes are so blinded that they no longer see the promise and the glory in such abasement.[7]

Confession gives us the opportunity to put our fear of God above the fear of "losing face" in the eyes of men. Plus, it has a wondrous way of breaking the bands of condemnation and putting us in contact with the mercy and forgiveness of God.

. . . Our desire for the good opinion of others makes us shrink from taking . . . [this course] . . . 'What will be thought of me,' we argue, 'if I confess to such internal rottenness?' We are all in desperate need of forgiveness; but we do not receive it because we are insanely anxious to keep up a good appearance. Our reluctance to confess is as marked as our longing for it. . . . Probably the greatest hindrance is fear of betrayal. So confession is not made and the transgression remains unforgiven.[8]

Though not always necessary (as is our confession to God), complete transparency in the company of fellow Crossbearers is extremely liberating — especially if demonic strongholds are entrenched in the soul; addictions are dominant; and/or deeply ingrained patterns of rebellion are cemented into our thoughts and dispositions.

It is not enough for a person to come to grips with his sin. He must come into the light with others. Darkness is the devil's domain. Those who refuse to come into the light about their sin are choosing to remain in darkness [whereas those who choose to come into the Light are sure to find grace in their time of need].[9]

...And not grace only, but also freedom; the sense of which is often difficult to embrace due to lingering clouds of doubt and condemnation; or, failure to wholeheartedly own up. But with the added confirmation of even just one trustworthy believer that cares enough to "hear out" our confession (and then help us to test its integrity in God's sight), the comfort of the Holy Ghost can become more tangible *(2 Cor. 2:7-11; Jn. 20:23).*

The open acknowledgment of weaknesses and sins has a remarkably liberating effect in most cases of troubled conscience, despondency over failure, fear of human opinions and the like. When a timid seeker after God breaks through the inhibitions of moral cowardice, there comes an inrush of divine life and light and he becomes conscious of being possessed and guided by a power not his own—the power of the Holy Spirit.[10]

Yea and amen: *"Sharing makes God's pardon real."*[11]

Who can give us the certainty that, in the confession and the forgiveness of our sins, we are not dealing with ourselves [i.e. indulging in self-absolution] but with the living God? [Often] God gives us this certainty through our brother.[12]

I confessed my sin to God for years. I mean I poured my heart out, begging for His forgiveness, but it was within weeks of starting to confess to another brother, that I obtained victory.[13]

Why should we not find it easier to go to a brother than to the holy God? . . . We must ask ourselves whether we have not often been deceiving ourselves with our confession of sin to God, whether we have not rather been confessing our sins to ourselves and also granting ourselves absolution. And is not the reason perhaps for our countless relapses and the feebleness of our Christian obedience to be found precisely in the fact we are living on self-forgiveness and not a real forgiveness.[14]

Help from the Lord

...No detours here. If we don't volitionally press into the Light when impressed by the Holy Spirit to do so, then the Lord's Law of Righteous Judgment is set in motion and He (in His mercy) often times grants assistance by uncovering our sins via some sort of unexpected providence.

". . . Be sure your sin will find you out." Numbers 32:23b

Exposure, whether by our own choice amidst our brethren (which is preferable); or, by events outside of our control orchestrated by the Lord; is one of His ways of establishing His fear in our hearts and incentivizing us in the aftermath of repentance to go and *"sin no more" (Jn. 5:14)*, lest we be put in the position to suffer the anguish of exposure again.

God has been known to bring public humiliation upon ... His children in order to get . . . [their] attention. . . . He is very patient and gentle with us, but He loves us too much to leave us in our sin. . . . At some point, . . . [our] secret life will be exposed to those around . . . [us].[15]

"For nothing is secret, that shall not be made manifest; neither any thing hid, that shall not be known and come abroad."
Luke 8:17

But let our confessions, when they are made, be delivered with discretion—not indiscriminately—lest in our zeal for release from the burden of sin and the blessings that follow, we inadvertently reproach Christ, or do harm in the lives of those with whom we confide. The guiding question must always be: *"Lord, what would you have me do?"* If impressed with a conviction to share, then we must ask: *"When is the appropriate time to do it?"*

We have not necessarily got to tell everybody everything about ourselves. The fundamental thing is our *attitude* of walking in the light . . . . Are we willing to be in the open with our brother . . . when God tells us to? That is the "armor of light" — true transparency. This may sometimes be humbling, but it will help us to a new reality with Christ. . . . We have become so used to the fact that God knows all about us that it does not seem to register with us, and we inevitably end by not knowing the truth about ourselves. But let a man begin to be absolutely honest about himself with but one other, as God guides him, and he will come to a knowledge of himself and his sins that he never had before, and he will begin to see more clearly than ever before where the redemption of Christ has got to be applied progressively to his life. This is the reason why James tells us to put ourselves under the discipline of "confessing our faults one to another."[16]

We Meet at the Cross

Like no other commandment in Scripture, confession puts us on an equal playing field with each other. There, at the Cross of Humiliation, we are united by our common need for God's mercy, no matter how "successful," prestigious or socially lauded we may (or may not) be. Rich and poor ...male and female ...black and white ...educated and unlearned, all rally there to be washed in the blood of the Lamb.

"For there is no respect of persons with God." Romans 2:11

Think about it! The Son of God suffered public crucifixion as an evil doer in our behalf.

Jesus did not die on a bed . . . . He died on a cross, and a cross was a punishment about which there was a peculiar disgrace, for it was reserved only for criminals. Indeed, there was a criminal on either side of Him, and everybody thought that He must be one also. They "esteemed him stricken,/smitten by God, and afflicted" (Isa. 53:4) because of something that He must have done, "as one from whom men hide their faces" (53:3). And the astonishing thing is that He . . . . did not say, as we would have done, "Please, oh please, do not think that I am here for anything I have done—I am here for other people's sins." Instead, He kept silent. He was willing to let them think He really was a criminal. He was willing to be "numbered with the transgressors" (Isa. 53:12) and to die as such, just because He saw that that was our place, and He was willing to take it for us.[17]

We would be a proud and ungrateful people if we were to expect His blessing, yet were unwilling to humble ourselves by virtue of confession in order to meet Him at the place of humiliation where He hung in our behalf.

The Cross of Jesus Christ destroys all pride [and pretense]. We cannot find the Cross of Jesus if we shrink from going to the place where it is to be found, namely, the public death of the sinner. . . . In the deep . . . pain of humiliation before a brother—which means before God—we experience the Cross of Jesus as our rescue and salvation. The old man dies, but it is God who has conquered him. Now we share in the resurrection of Christ and eternal life.[18]

With Whom Can I Confide?

That special, trust-*worthy* person with whom we become vulnerable (if we are so blessed to know one) does not need to be a husband, wife, family member, or even a church leader (though confession to anyone in that wholesome list can be appropriate and glorious). It can also be with other God-fearing Christians, as long as they are in right standing with the Lord and aware of their own ongoing need of mercy; for we all stand before the Judgment Seat of Christ *(Rom. 14:10; 2 Cor. 5:10).*

Not only does the onus rest on the person who is confessing, but just as much on the person who is hearing that confession. God puts as much requirement upon the one hearing the confession as on the one making the confession, and it is this kind of requirement that calls us to be serious before the Lord and to be walking rightly with Him.[19]

To whom shall we make confession? . . . Anybody who lives beneath the Cross and who has discerned in the Cross of Jesus the utter wickedness of all men and of his own heart will find there is no sin that can ever be alien to him.[20]

The holy martyrs experienced that kind of transparency and mutual succoring in the friendships they forged amidst enormous persecution and peril when the fires of testing caused their lingering blemishes to surface. It was soul love; heartfelt care that exceeds natural affinities; a divine bonding that is born in humility and centered in mutual passion for the honor and holiness of God *(2 Sam. 1:26)*. Faithful friends such as these will help us come into the knowledge of the Truth about ourselves, not help us to cover it up *(Pro. 27:6)*.

Do not seek for someone who will be sympathetic with your carnal flesh.[21]

Get some Christian friend, whom thou mayest trust above others, to be thy faithful monitor. O, that man hath a great help for . . . maintaining the power of godliness, that has an open-hearted friend that dare speak his heart to him! A stander-by sees more sometimes by a man, than the actor can do by himself, and is more fit to judge of his actions than he of his own. Sometimes self-love blinds us in our own cause, that we see not ourselves so bad as we are; and sometimes we are over-suspicious of the worst by ourselves, which makes us appear to ourselves worse than we are. Now, that thou mayest not deprive thyself of so great a help from thy friend, be sure to keep thy heart ready with meekness to receive, yea, with thankfulness embrace, a reproof from his mouth. Those that cannot bear plain dealing hurt themselves most; for by this they seldom hear the truth. He that hath not love enough to give a reproof seasonably to his brother, nor humility enough to bear a reproof from him, is not worthy to be called a Christian. . . . Truly it is one great reason why . . . falls . . . are so frequent in our days, and . . . recovery so rare or late, because few in these unloving times are to be found so faithful as to do this Christian office of reproof to their brethren.[22]

Although Edwin would never in a lifetime identify with the doubts and surmisings springing from the unbelief that I was bringing out (and doesn't hesitate to reprove me for entertaining a single iota of it — *Eph. 5:11*), he is well acquainted with his own weakness; and engages daily in aggressive combat to keep the flesh and the devil under heel, too. We all battle fears and a host of other evils, as well.

"I therefore so run, not as uncertainly; so fight I, not as one that beateth the air: but I keep under my body, and bring it into subjection: lest that by any means, when I have preached to others, I myself should be a castaway."   1 Corinthians 9:26-27

For that reason, he doesn't condescend to me in my weakness; but rather, he kneels down beside me and together we *"lift"* our eyes unto the Lord *"from whence cometh [our] help"* (Ps. 121:1).

"Who can have compassion on the ignorant, and on them that are out of the way; for that he himself also is compassed with infirmity."   Hebrews 5:2

Release from the Burden of Sin

Something absolutely divine transpires in the Spirit when we bring our sins to Light in the presence of trusted fellow Cross-bearers. It brings us out from the darkness where Satan dwells into the Light of God's Love where forgiveness, atonement, deliverance and healing are to be found.

. . . Thanks be to the God in heaven, who has given me poor weak servant an unwounded or uncondemned conscience (of which I acknowledge myself unworthy); for I never had greater joy on earth as long as I can remember, than I now have."

Matthias Servaes, A.D.1565[23]

It gives us added strength in our battle to defeat deeply ingrained patterns of sin by stripping away the mask that hides our true colors and making us accountable not only to God, but to our brethren, as well. Plus, it gives caring saints the opportunity to help bear our burden by exercising the gifts of the Spirit; shining even greater Light into our areas of need; upholding us in prayer; and supporting us in the renewal and regeneration that is to follow our confession.

[When] confession of sin is made in the presence of a [trustworthy] Christian brother, the last stronghold of self-justification is abandoned. The sinner surrenders; he gives up all his evil. He gives his heart to God, and he ... [embraces] the forgiveness of all his sin in the fellowship of Jesus Christ and his brother. The expressed, acknowledged sin . . . . has been revealed and judged as sin. . . . Now the fellowship . . . [supports him in his battle to mortify it altogether—Gal.6:2]. He is no longer alone with his evil for he has cast off his sin in confession and handed it over to God. It has been taken away from him. Now he stands [restored to God] in the fellowship of . . . [fellow penitents] who [like him] live by the grace of God in the Cross of Jesus Christ. . . . He can confess his sins and in this very act find fellowship for the first time. The sin concealed separated him from the fellowship, made all his apparent fellowship a sham; the sin confessed has helped him to find true fellowship with the brethren in Jesus Christ.[24]

Let it be said, once again, that confession amidst the assembly of the saints when appropriate is not a substitute for going first to the Father, based on Christ's finished work; but rather; a wondrous and fulfilling extension of it.

". . . If we walk in the light, as he is in the light, we have fellowship one with another, and the blood of Jesus Christ his Son cleanseth us from all sin. If we say that we have no sin, we deceive ourselves, and the truth is not in us. If we confess our sins, he is faithful and just to forgive us our sins, and to cleanse us from all unrighteousness."   1 John 1:6-9

Please Forgive Me...

Once I brought my sin out into the Light, I then besought our Father for forgiveness in the precious Name of Jesus. Next, I asked my husband to forgive me, being that everything about my persona (whether godly or defiled) affects him, too. And he received me, in love, with open arms. I also ask all my brothers and sisters in Christ to forgive me for being weak in the very faith that I so much desire to herald.

> I entreat everyone from the depth of my heart, and with tears, before God, to excuse my weakness kindly and in love. I deplore it before God and men, that I have not been more of a light, and that the talent which I have received has gained so little profit.   Wouter Denijs,
> Tortured and slain by fire with six others, A.D. 1569[25]

Dietrich Bonhoeffer, a leader of the Underground Church during the Nazi era, pointed out that "what we do" (or don't do, and who we are) in our private time when we're not together face-to-face, "*react[s] upon the community*" as a whole. In our solitude, he said, we can "*sunder and besmirch the fellowship*" or, we "*can strengthen and hallow it.*"[26] True!—even if we live on different continents and the wide open sea stands between us.

> . . . There is no sin in thought, word, or deed, no matter how personal or secret, that does not inflict injury upon the whole fellowship. An element of sickness gets into the body; perhaps nobody knows where it comes from or in what member it has lodged, but the body is infected. This is the proper metaphor for the Christian community. We are members of a body, not only when we choose to

be [or sit side-by-side], but in our whole existence. Every member serves the whole body, either to its health or to its destruction. This is not mere theory; it is spiritual reality. And the Christian community has often experienced its effects with disturbing clarity, sometimes destructively and sometimes fortunately.[27]

Recognizing our inter-connectedness, Edwin and I jointly pursue repentance when infirmity comes to light in either of our lives; or even in the lives of others in our corporate Body. *"Whether one member suffer, all the members suffer with it"* (1 Cor. 12:26). When Job was tried, his wife, friends, relatives and acquaintances were also brought to the Touchstone. Perhaps our struggles are adversely affecting the other; or, the Lord is calling us both to account? The observance of this practice grants occasion for the Holy Spirit to sweep through entire fellowships, leading every member to thorough purging and "higher ground."

Hand-in-hand, my husband and I prayed for deliverance, healing and renewal. The Lord answered handsomely by lifting up my sorrowful spirit with the sheer force of His love and by setting me upright in His comfort and favor.

"Humble yourselves in the sight of the Lord, and He shall lift you up."   James 4:10

Come into the fellowship of those who have overcome sins and problems similar to your own and who can witness to victory. The Divine very often comes to us through the human. That was why Christ was born in Bethlehem and took upon Him the form of a man that He might speak to us in human words and heal us with the touch of a human hand.[28]

It is a night that God lit up with a galaxy of tender mercies. It is MUCH to be remembered! Or, to put it in the familiar words spoken by my kinsmen at their annual Passover Celebration: *"It is a night to be much observed . . ."* (Exo. 12:42).

CHAPTER FOURTEEN

Living in the Light of Christ

There is no greater way to eradicate fear, foster faith and break free from condemnation than to respond swiftly and uncompromisingly in repentance and open confession to Holy Ghost conviction. Whether His reproof is administered directly to us from "*on High;*" or, via the loving counsel (and at times rebuke) of renewed church leaders and/or other caring Cross-bearers; it helps keep our "pipes" open — our connection with the Lord clear.

> Where sin has been faced and confessed and cast out, there the conscience is cleansed and purified to fulfil its proper task, and to listen in other matters to the guiding voice of God. There can then follow the faith which hears and obeys God's will, and which, living under authority, can itself speak and act with authority.[1]

Failure to respond in this manner to conviction results in the casting off of one's "*first faith*" and creates many feebleminded Christians *(1 Tim. 5:12)*. It is, in essence, spiritual suicide.

"Holding faith, and a good conscience; which some having put away concerning faith have made shipwreck."   1 Timothy 1:19

This is why the faithful saints that went before us preached so vehemently against half measures when it comes to sin.

> . . . By thy negligence . . . thou endangerest thy faith, which is kept in a good conscience, as the jewel in the cabinet . . . . A holy life, to faith, is as . . . clear air . . . to the eye. We can see farthest in a clear day. Thus faith sees farthest into the promise, when it looks through [a clear

conscience washed in the blood of Jesus and] a holy, well-ordered conversation. . . . If faith cannot see a pardon in the promise, then hope cannot look for salvation, [healing, deliverance or any other blessing. It is dead].[2]

Once convicted, we need to take our sin directly to the Lord without procrastination, lest the devil get in the mix, and we fall prey to self castigation and despair; or, we wind up sweeping it under the rug; or, rationalizing, justifying and ultimately accepting its presence. To combat these temptations, we've got to take an aggressive stance against it. Surround the house (so to speak). Call in your God-fearing brethren, if need be, with the same fervor as the woman in the parable of the Lost Coin. Then, together, *"light a candle"* ..."*sweep*" the chambers of your heart ...and *"seek diligently"* until the sin that is consigning you to chastisement, eroding your faith and robbing your peace with the Lord and His Church is found *(Lk. 15:8- 9)*.

Go, therefore, as a poor malefactor condemned to die would do, shut thyself up from all old flattering companions, that would still lullaby thy miserable soul in a senseless security — the cradle which the devil rocks souls in, to their utter destruction; let none of them come to thee, but send for those that dare be faithful to thee, and like Samuel, dare tell thee every word that God saith against thee, and conceal nothing; yea, read they doom with thy own eyes in the word and take thy condemnation from God's own mouth, and not man's [1 Sam. 3:15-19]. . . . Muse on it till it cleaves to thy soul like a drawing-plaster to a sore, and brings out the very core of thy [sin] . . . which hardened thy heart from all sense of thy condition . . . [Then, confess it and repent.][3]

Officer of Peace

We cannot overstate the significance of the previous exhortation. We must not allow ourselves to suppress the healthy operation of conscience, but rather, embrace it as the "officer of peace" and reconciliation that our Father intends for it to be.

> Conscience is God's sergeant He employs to arrest the sinner. . . . [It] is appointed to judge of a man's actions and state; whether good or bad, pardoned or unpardoned. If the state be good, then it is to acquit and comfort; if evil, then to accuse and condemn him.[4]

". . . Their conscience also bearing witness, and their thoughts the mean while accusing or else excusing . . ."   Romans 2:15

...Not a conscience bound by the ecumenical standards of the religious status quo; or by the traditions of our forefathers if they be out of alignment with the Bible; or by the pagan societies in which we live. ...But rather, a conscience first and foremost *"captive to the Word of God"*[5] and obedient to the still small voice of the Holy Spirit guiding us (in concert with Scripture) through all the unique circumstances, choices and challenges that arise in our daily lives.

> . . . All Christians are in duty bound to bow their whole heart, mind and soul under the obedience of Christ and the mind of the Holy Spirit expressed in the holy Scriptures, and to regulate and measure their whole faith and conversation according to the import thereof. . . . To this new law of Jesus Christ all decrees, councils and ordinances made contrary to it by men in the world, must give place; but all Christians must necessarily, as far as the faith is concerned, regulate and conduct themselves only in accordance with this blessed Gospel of Christ."[6]

God forbid that we dismiss the warrant (or deface the verdict) conscience brings from the Holy Spirit compelling us to carry our sins to Jesus and humble ourselves (when appropriate) before the brethren in confession. He is sent to us in Love. Thank the Lord for the strength (and persistence) of his repeated thunderings! A conscience enlivened by the Holy Ghost simply will not let the soul go free till self-justification ceases; authentic repentance is born out; and our faith is rightly placed in Christ's intercession and atonement *(Isa. 53:12; Rom. 8:33-34; Heb. 7:25; 1 Jn. 2:1-2).*

> Nothing can take off conscience from accusing but that which takes off God from threatening.[7]

"If God will not withdraw his anger, the proud helpers do stoop under him. How much less shall I answer him, and choose out my words to reason with him? Whom, though I were righteous, yet would I not answer, but I would make supplication to my judge."   Job 9:13-15

Then (and only then) authorization comes from our Father, signed in the blood of Jesus, endorsing our release.

"Therefore being justified by faith, we have peace with God through our Lord Jesus Christ."   Romans 5:1

Stand warned. Hidden sin left unconfessed for fear of losing esteem in the eyes of others (or, because of harbored idolatries or for any other reason) can put the soul outside the reach of conscience and sink the sinner into the abyss of unbelief and apostasy.

"Who being past feeling [beyond conviction] have given themselves over unto lasciviousness, to work all uncleanness with greediness."   Ephesians 4:19

"How can ye believe, which receive honour one of another, and seek not the honour that cometh from God only?"   John 5:44

This is why, in his ministry as a *"life-changer,"* Frank Buchman performed what came to be called *"the moral test"* in hopes of drawing people out of the shadows. From experience he learned that most sin is committed on the lowest level and must be brought to the Cross in confession for a *"lively hope"* of salvation to be born and nurtured in the soul *(1 Pe. 1:3)*. Buchman broke through the walls of pride and shame holding back some of the most needy and difficult to reach "sinners and saints" by being totally honest about his own inward struggles, and then patiently guiding them to the core issues in their lives that similarly needed to be laid bare.

A man can have no saving sense of the power of the Living Christ if that power has not saved him from the sin that, in his heart of hearts, he knows lives on, and that is festering and poisoning his spiritual life. It is the easiest way to argue with a man about his doubts, of which he may be half proud; it is the most difficult thing to evoke a confession of the sin of which he is altogether ashamed.[8]

One of the terrible and frightening aspects of sin is the unbelief it fosters. The more deeply entrenched the sin, the greater the darkness of unbelief.[9]

Faith in Action

From the very outset of His Gospel preaching, Jesus conditioned salvation on belief and sited our willingness to come into the light as a necessary evidence of that belief. Take, for example, the "crown jewel" of all passages in the Bible on the blessedness of belief in Jesus Christ as our Atonement.

"For God so loved the world, that he gave his only begotten Son, that whosoever believeth in him should not perish, but have everlasting life. For God sent not his Son into the world to condemn the world; but that the world through him might be saved. He that believeth on him is not condemned: but he that believeth not is condemned already, because he hath not believed in the name of the only begotten Son of God. And this is the condemnation, that light is come into the world, and men loved darkness rather than light, because their deeds were evil. For every one that doeth evil hateth the light, neither cometh to the light, lest his deeds should be reproved. But he that doeth

truth cometh to the light, that his deeds may be made manifest,
that they are wrought in God."   John 3:16-21

We might have thought that since it says "He that does
evil hates the light" it would have gone on to read "He
that does good comes to the light." Surely the opposite of
doing evil is doing good! But that is not the contrast here.
What God says is, he that does truth comes to the light.
The alternative that God presents to our doing evil is not
doing good, but doing truth; that is, honesty with regard
to our evil. He does not want in the first place our efforts
to do good where we have done evil, to try to be kind
where we have been unkind, to be friendly where we
have been critical. We could do all that without any
repentance for what has been there already, and without
any cleansing and peace in our hearts. What God asks
first of all is truth, that is, plain truthful repentance and
frank confession of the sin that has been committed. That
will take us to the cross of Jesus for pardon, and, where
necessary, to the other whom we may have wronged, for
his forgiveness, too. In that place of humble truthfulness
about ourselves we shall find peace with God and man,
for there we shall find Jesus afresh and lay hold as never
before on His finished work for our sin upon the cross.
Simple honesty, that is "doing truth" about our sins will
put us right with God and man through the blood of
Christ, where all the "doing good" in the world will not.[10]

Contrary to what is taught in many denominations, such
transparency is not something that we are commanded to
manifest one time only at the waters of baptism when we
openly confess our *"sins that are past"* and make the lifetime
commitment to *"walk in newness of life" (Rom. 3:25; 6:3-4)*; but
also, a spirit of repentance that we are to walk in every day of
our lives *(1 Jn. 1:7-9, 2:1)*.

No matter how long we have been Christians, nor how
mature we think we have become, Calvary has
something fresh to show us of sin today. For sin is like an

octopus. Its tentacles are everywhere. It has a thousand lives and a thousand shapes, and by perpetually changing its shape it eludes capture. If we are to see sin in all of its subtle shapes and forms, and prove the power of Jesus to save us from it, we need to pray daily: Keep me broken, keep me watching, at the cross where Thou hast died. For only there do we know our need as sinners, and therefore of Jesus.[11]

It is here, and here alone, broken at the Cross of Repentance and Confession, with our hearts *"sprinkled from an evil conscience"* by the blood of Jesus, that the faith we profess with our mouths can be securely held *(Heb. 10:22-23)*.

"Holding the mystery of the faith in a pure conscience."
1 Timothy 3:9

"O house of Jacob, come ye, and let us walk in the light of the LORD."   Isaiah 2:5

CHAPTER FIFTEEN

Abraham's Faith Steps

In a very special way the Lord used my beige turtleneck sweater to bring these powerful precepts that I knew in theory (and had worked so wondrously in times past) to the fore. Oh, how I loved that sweater. It was like an old friend. I had it during the peak of this trial, but finally let it go because it had become so tattered. We bought it at a second hand store. It was always a bit short and over time it had gotten stretched out. But on chilly mornings it was great for snuggling up.

Before "'calling it a day" on one of the nights that the battle raged on, Apostle Edwin laid it out on the table right beside his clothes so when we got up we could get an edge and dive directly into the Word. He was exceptionally tired and I still had a few chores to wrap up, so we read a Psalm, he crawled into bed, we said our prayers and I finished up. He spoke many blessings over me that evening, including a renewed blessing for my healing. Just before climbing up to our loft-like bed and curling up beside my sleeping husband, however, I walked over to my stack of clothes, picked up my sweater and returned it to the shelf.

Better not wear this. It will rub on your neck and exacerbate the irritation, possibly even make it spread.

Silence.

Where did that kind of thinking come from? I wondered. *Was that God's wisdom "from above," or was it "earthly, sensual, devilish" (Jam. 3:15b)? Was it grounded in faith? Or, fear?*

Thirty minutes hadn't passed since such wonderful blessings had been pronounced over my life and there I was planning how to respond the next morning to unanswered prayer. I should have been finding ways to round up five loaves and two fishes and trusting God for His supernatural multiplication to meet the need at hand — NOT behaving like the doubtful disciples when they counseled our miracle working Saviour to send the multitudes that flocked to see Him away so as to buy victuals on their own *(Mt. 14:13-21)*.

Unbelief — The Culprit — Cornered Again

"Caught" — again! Plain as day. The rat was cornered. Unbelief was on display. Fear got a foot in. My sin found me out *(Num. 32:23)*!

"And he said unto them, Why are ye troubled? and why do thoughts arise in your hearts?"   Luke 24:38

Hard times are coming. Persecution is going to be merciless. In many places it's already sheer madness. I cannot allow myself to be tossed to and fro on any issue — fear or any other.

"A little leaven leaveneth the whole lump." Galatians 5:9

It will unmoor me from Christ and eventually sink the whole ship, calling into question the integrity and soundness of my entire Christian life.

"But let him ask in faith, nothing wavering. For he that wavereth is like a wave of the sea driven with the wind and tossed. For let not that man think that he shall receive any thing of the Lord. A double minded man is unstable in all his ways."
                                                        James 1:6-8

"Wherefore when we could no longer forbear, we thought it good to be left at Athens alone; and sent Timotheus, our brother, and minister of God, and our fellowlabourer in the gospel of Christ, to establish you, and to comfort you concerning your faith: that no man should be moved by these

afflictions: for yourselves know that we are appointed
thereunto."   1 Thessalonians 3:1-3

How can I pray with conviction for courage and healing in
the lives of my brothers and sisters with this underlying
wickedness within?

"And he did not many mighty works there because of their
unbelief."   Matthew 13:58

Stung with conviction, I paused ...and prayed.

*Lord God, You masterfully uncovered my heart. Unbelief is the
greatest of my lingering sins. Time and again it has cut me off
from the "root and fatness of the olive tree." But even now, I
know You can graff me back in again (Rom. 11:17-23). Forgive
me. I repent! Empower me now, by Your gracious Spirit, to
stand upright in heart on these feeble knees so as to receive the
healing Your Son purchased for all of His penitents at Calvary.*

"Wherefore lift up the hands which hang down, and the feeble
knees; and make straight paths for your feet, lest that which is
lame be turned out of the way; but let it rather be healed."
                                                    Hebrews 12:12-13

*Help me (side-by-side with my husband) to minister grace and
healing with greater confidence than ever to others who
likewise come to Thee on bended knee — in Jesus' name, amen.*

"And into whatsoever city ye enter, and they receive you, eat
such things as are set before you: and heal the sick that are
therein, and say unto them, The kingdom of God is come nigh
unto you."   Luke 10:8-9

Sneaking Around

Scripture says:

". . . Whatsoever is not of faith is sin." Romans 14:23b

If you read the passage from whence that verse was plucked you come to understand that behavior governed by faith is behavior that is acted out, *"as to the Lord"* (Col. 3:23-25; Heb. 11:6), with full conviction that God is pleased with it.

I had no such confidence. Just the opposite! Honestly, I felt kinda sneaky about what I did. ...Like I was doing something wrong. Most likely, I'm the only one that would have ever noticed. Notwithstanding, the Lord knew exactly what was going on and mightily rained His wrath down on my conscience, prompting repentance and an "about face" change of course. The words of Oswald Chambers come to mind: *"Trust"* in God, he pointed out, is not all that complex. It's simply doing *"the next thing."*[1] Or, as the Apostle Paul taught in his doctrine, it is walking in the *"steps of that faith of our father Abraham"* (Rom. 4:12).

> Jesus . . . said to . . . [the impotent man], "Do the impossible thing. Rise, take up thy bed, and walk." Jesus called on the man with the withered hand to do the impossible—to stretch forth his hand. The man did the impossible thing—he stretched out his hand, and it was made whole. And so with this impotent man—he began to rise, and he found the power of God moving within. He wrapped up his bed and began to walk off.[2]

Immediately, I walked back over to the shelf, picked up the sweater, returned it to my neatly piled stack of clothes, turned out the light and curled up beside my husband, having put fear to bed. Praise God! These seemingly "small" faith actions may not appear to be of much significance—but the truth is, they are the substance from which the Lord fashions our victories.

> When the angel smote Peter on the side, and bade him 'arise up quickly . . . and follow me,' he did not allow sense and reason to reply and cavil [raise objections] at the impossibility of the thing. How can I walk that am in fetters? Or to what purpose when an iron gate withstands us? But he riseth and his chains fall off—he

follows, and the iron gate officiously opens itself to them.[3]

Faith verses Presumption

I'm not talking about exercising what William Gurnall calls a *"saucy presumptuous faith,"*[4] void of the necessary working of the Cross to go with it, like the perversion we see in the "Word of Faith" Movement and other unscriptural religious sects. Rather, I'm referring to *"a living faith,"*[5] as described by the martyrs; *"the faith of Jesus" (Rev. 14:12).* ...Faith that prompts believers to take Christ at His Word and drop their nets into the deep when told to do so, even though they've been laboring all night at that very same spot and come up empty *(Lk. 5:4-10).* ...*"Holy faith"* that God rewards with double blessings *(Jude 1:20).* In that instance, for example, the Lord Jesus turned an otherwise unprofitable night of fishing into a success, while at the same time imparting a promise to make His disciples prolific fishers of men.

"Now when he had left speaking, He said unto Simon, Launch out into the deep, and let down your nets for a draught. And Simon answering said unto him, Master, we have toiled all the night, and have taken nothing: nevertheless at thy word I will let down the net. And when they had this done, they inclosed a great multitude of fishes: and their net brake. And they beckoned unto their partners, which were in the other ship, that they should come and help them. And they came, and filled both the ships, so that they began to sink. When Simon Peter saw it, he fell down at Jesus' knees, saying, Depart from me; for I am a sinful man, O Lord. For he was astonished, and all that were with him, at the draught of the fishes which they had taken: and so was also James, and John, the sons of Zebedee, which were partners with Simon. And Jesus said unto Simon, Fear not; from henceforth thou shalt catch men."   Luke 5:4-10

"Living faith" walks *"not by sight,"* meaning it operates on God's promises independently from natural impossibilities of attainment *(2 Cor. 5:7).* It is bold, but not reckless; cautious, but

not cowardly. It ventures out onto the water to meet Jesus *(Mt. 14:29)*, yet does not turn Christian liberty into a blank check to go forth "claiming" whatever impulse and desire dictate *(1 Tim. 6:5; Jude 1:4)*.

In that one "little" act of amendment I yielded to the governing authority of Scripture. I reckoned myself *"dead indeed to sin,"* and in so doing, I closed the door on the *"spirit of fear" (Rom. 6:11; 2 Tim. 1:7)*. I chose Christ as my Master, thus making way for my miracle. As soon as I did, something changed inside. Courage took the preeminence over cowardice, and as a result I spontaneously issued a declaration of war.

This gateway sin of unbelief that has long dominated my Jewish kinsmen is no longer going to rule in league with the devil as both Tempter and Tyrant over my life.

Like the American adage goes: *"The buck stops here."*[6]

"Likewise reckon ye also yourselves to be dead indeed unto sin, but alive unto God through Jesus Christ our Lord. Let not sin therefore reign in your mortal body, that ye should obey it in the lusts thereof. Neither yield ye your members as instruments of unrighteousness unto sin: but yield yourselves unto God, as those that are alive from the dead, and your members as instruments of righteousness unto God. For sin shall not have dominion over you: for ye are not under the law, but under grace."   Romans 6:11-14

". . . The law of the Spirit of life in Christ Jesus hath made me free from the law of sin and death."   Romans 8:2

Hallelujah! I was standing on the promises of God. I was following in the *"steps of that faith of our father Abraham" (Rom. 4:12)*.

Standing on the promises I cannot fail,
When the howling storms of doubt and fear assail,
By the living Word of God I shall prevail,
Standing on the promises of God.[7]

CHAPTER SIXTEEN

A Journey of Ever Increasing Faith

This brings me to another faith-building episode years earlier that I can't help but inject. ...Different situation, but the same pattern for moving God's hand, starting with faith in His promises and the acknowledgment of His sovereignty in all of our providences.

> Every event is the product of God's providence; not a sparrow, much less a saint, falls to the ground by poverty, sickness, persecution, &c. [etc.], but the hand of God is in it.[1]

...Then, soul searching and repentance. ....Compliance with Holy Spirit inspired *"steps of that faith of our father Abraham"* *(Rom. 4:12)*. ...Patient waiting ...And finally, the unleashing of God's mighty power—AFTER we have been thoroughly tried. "A, B, C." Simple in theory; but a struggle in its outworking.

This time the test came in the form of an abscessed tooth. My face swelled up like a balloon and it felt as though I had a fever. Apostle Edwin prayed for me (and with me), repeatedly. One eye was almost totally shut and I could barely open my mouth wide enough to slide in a spoonful of yogurt or oatmeal. Not that I was hungry *(Ps. 102:4)*! To the Cross I fled doing some serious repenting, beginning exactly where His rod touched down: my mouth!

Unsure of what the Lord was honing in on, I started asking Him to forgive me for all the unseemly meditations that had bubbled up from my heart and escaped through my now swollen lips into His ears and the ears of others *(Ps. 19:14)*. No more clinging to the flesh on any matter and thus defiling my witness of His grace: *"If the LORD be God, follow him"* *(1 Ki. 18:21)*.

"Either make the tree good, and his fruit good; or else make the tree corrupt, and his fruit corrupt: for the tree is known by his fruit. O generation of vipers, how can ye, being evil, speak good things? for out of the abundance of the heart the mouth speaketh. A good man out of the good treasure of the heart bringeth forth good things: and an evil man out of the evil treasure bringeth forth evil things."   Matthew 12:33-35

Sanctify my lips, O Lord, and create in me a clean heart from which the sweetness of Your loving Spirit may flow.

"She openeth her mouth with wisdom; and in her tongue is the law of kindness."   Proverbs 31:26

"And all bare him witness, and wondered at the gracious words which proceeded out of his mouth . . ."   Luke 4:22

Forgive me for all the "corrupt" communications, the cutting words, condescending comments, sarcasm, trivial babble, faithless confessions and "course jesting" that polluted my life before conversion and whatever is left of it that carries over into my present walk with You (Eph. 4:29; 5:4). Let nothing come forth from this cistern that does not reflect Your Person or bring Your Life to others, in Jesus' name, amen.

"Let your speech be alway with grace, seasoned with salt, that ye may know how ye ought to answer every man."
                    Colossians 4:6

Searching for Answers

One day, bucking the wind on a prayer walk, I used my thumb and index finger to force open my jaw so as to lift up the Name of Jesus in song.

"O Lord, open thou my lips; and my mouth shall shew forth thy praise."   Psalms 51:15

It's such a blessing to seek the Lord where He places His rod and then let His Spirit lead us from there so as to rightly interpret the reason for our afflictions and thereby avail from our Father's chastening.

"I applied mine heart to know, and to search, and to seek out wisdom, and the reason of things . . ."   Ecclesiastes 7:25

What better place to turn for insight than the Scriptures?

. . . I would like to thank William "Bud" Keith, who once told a sick, emaciated young man that "the answer to all of your health problems is found in the Bible."[2]

Example: Are you in pain? ...Seek the Lord.

"The troubles of my heart are enlarged: O bring thou me out of my distresses. Look upon mine affliction and my pain; and forgive all my sins."   Psalm 25:17-18

"*Troubles*" and "*distresses*" are challenges for us all and they are multiplying daily due to the times. But the question is: Are we responding in acceptance and praise and allowing them to drive us to the Cross? Or, is our faith wavering (and our vision waning); and as a result we are reverting to old patterns of complaining and self pity, like people of the world that don't understand God's grand purposes for our trials and their role in preparing us for glory?
Is the pain in a particular part of your body?

"He is chastened also with pain upon his bed, and the multitude of his bones with strong pain: so that his life abhorreth bread, and his soul dainty meat."   Job 33:19-20

"There is no soundness in my flesh because of thine anger; neither is there any rest in my bones because of my sin. For mine iniquities are gone over mine head: as an heavy burden they are too heavy for me. My wounds stink and are corrupt because of my foolishness. I am troubled; I am bowed down greatly; I go mourning all the day long. For my loins are filled with a loathsome disease: and there is no soundness in my flesh."   Psalm 38:3-7

Follow the verses that directly speak to your ailment and as you go the Holy Spirit will give you Light.

'Be sure your sin will find you out,' the Bible states [Num. 32:23]. One of the most common ways that hidden sin is revealed is through the maladies of the body.[3]

Is there an area of your life where you will not suffer yourself to be moved? ...Or, reproved?

"Why should ye be stricken any more? ye will revolt more and more: the whole head is sick, and the whole heart faint."
                                                                                                      Isaiah 1:5

...How about a stubborn streak in your character?

"Now be ye not stiffnecked, as your fathers were, but yield yourselves unto the LORD, and enter into his sanctuary, which he hath sanctified for ever: and serve the LORD your God, that the fierceness of his wrath may turn away from you."
                                                                                          2 Chronicles 30:8

...A grudge you are unwilling to relinquish and forgive?

More arthritis is brought about by resentments and ill-will than is caused by wrong diet. More asthma is caused by repressed fury than by pollen or cat fur. There was no illness in the body of Jesus because there was no sin in His soul.[4]

How is your disposition? Haughty? Arrogant? Proud?

"Moreover the LORD saith, Because the daughters of Zion are haughty, and walk with stretched forth necks and wanton eyes, walking and mincing as they go, and making a tinkling with their feet: Therefore the Lord will smite with a scab the crown of the head of the daughters of Zion, and the LORD will discover their secret parts."   Isaiah 3:16-17

Sorrow of Heart

Are you of a sorrowful spirit—suffering an emotional wounding equally as torturous (if not more so) than bodily injury or disease? ...Bound by depression? ...In a perpetual cycle of insecurity ...anxiety ...despair ...or discontent? Pray. Turn to the Lord Jesus. Let Him show you why and also the way out.

"Why art thou cast down, O my soul? And why art thou disquieted within me? Hope thou in God: for I shall yet praise him, Who is the health of my countenance, and my God."
                                                                Psalms 42:11

Entrust the Lord with your cares and be sure that waning faith   ...desires   turned   into   demands   (coveting)   ...vain imaginations ...harbored unforgiveness ...or failure to let go of things in the past are not at the root *(Phil. 3:13-14; Lk. 9:62).* As long as thorough repentance and amendment have been made for the sins of our past, then all lingering cycles of condemnation must be resisted and the Father's forgiveness through the blood of Jesus embraced instead. We cannot undo the damage done through our past offenses by wallowing in guilt. But we can certainly entrust ever failure into the hands of our Redeemer and make it our determined purpose to take the lessons learned into our present relationships and soul winning endeavors.

'Come unto Me,' it is written 'all ye that labor and are heavy laden, and I will give you rest.' (Matt. 11:28) Only when your mind is at rest can your body build health. Worry is an actively destructive force. Anxiety produces tension, and tension is the road to pain. Fear is devastating to the physical well-being of the body. Anger throws poison into the system that no anti-biotic ever can counteract. . . . How can I give you healing for your body whilst there is anxiety in thy mind? So long as there is dis-ease in thy thoughts, there shall be disease in thy body. Ye have need of many things, but one thing in particular ye must develop for thine own preservation, and that is an absolute confidence in My loving care.[5]

Disobedience of any kind is a doorway to sorrow of heart. It is a violation of our Love Covenant with Jesus and puts us outside of His loving favor.

"And if ye shall despise my statutes, or if your soul abhor my judgments, so that ye will not do all my commandments, but that ye break my covenant: I also will do this unto you; I will even . . . cause sorrow of heart . . ."   Leviticus 26:15-16

When King Saul disobeyed the commandment of the Lord, he suffered many sorrows. Not only did it cause the Spirit of the Lord to depart (which is sorrow enough!) but it also opened a breach for a tormenting evil spirit to come in and take its place — thus amplifying his grief *(Eph. 4:26-27; 1 Sam. 18:15-27).*

"But the Spirit of the LORD departed from Saul, and an evil spirit from the LORD troubled him."   1 Samuel 16:14

If you are suffering similar straits, we beseech you: Turn to the Lord. Invite the Holy Spirit to search your heart. Don't let the devil get in between you and your Lord. Acknowledge Him in all your ways. Renew your obedience to His Word and His still small voice — in everything — and His Spirit will heal your grieving heart and comfort you with His welcome Presence.

"If ye love me, keep my commandments. And I will pray the Father, and he shall give you another Comforter, that he may abide with you for ever."   John 14:15-16

"Quench not the Spirit" *(1 Th. 5:19).* Repent of all waywardness, independence and slack. Make a full turn from the sins of your forefathers and renounce the curses and plagues attached *(Rev. 18:4; Num.14:18).* Draw nigh unto God and He will draw nigh unto you *(Jam. 4:8).* Seal the breaches.

Use the authority we've been given in the Name of Jesus to *"cast out devils"* and then go on to keep Satan and his tormentors out by the ongoing exercise of acceptance and praise *(Acts 10:38; Mk. 6:12-13; 16:17-18)*.

"The Spirit of the Lord GOD is upon me; because the LORD hath anointed me to preach good tidings unto the meek; he hath sent me to bind up the brokenhearted, to proclaim liberty to the captives, and the opening of the prison to them that are bound; to proclaim the acceptable year of the LORD, and the day of vengeance of our God; to comfort all that mourn; to appoint unto them that mourn in Zion, to give unto them beauty for ashes, the oil of joy for mourning, the garment of praise for the spirit of heaviness; that they might be called trees of righteousness, the planting of the LORD, that he might be glorified."   Isaiah 61:1-3

Feeling Alone?

"My lovers and my friends stand aloof from my sore; and my kinsmen stand afar off."   Psalm 38:11

Perhaps you haven't recovered from the loss of a loved one; or let go of a ruptured relationship; or you've been so distracted by an unanswered desire for particular kinds of relationships (like those that spring from marriage and child bearing), that you've neglected to make Jesus your "all in all."

"For thy Maker is thine husband; the LORD of hosts is his name; and thy Redeemer the Holy One of Israel; The God of the whole earth shall he be called."   Isaiah 54:5

It is God's Will that some of his children should learn this deep union with himself through the perfect flowering of natural human love in marriage. For others it is equally his will that the same perfect union should be learned through the experience of learning to lay down completely this natural and instinctive desire for marriage and parenthood, and accept the circumstances of life which deny them this experience.[6]

Perhaps you are barren? If so, don't let the enemy cause you to "*fret.*"

"But unto Hannah he gave a worthy portion; for he loved Hannah: but the LORD had shut up her womb. And her adversary also provoked her sore, for to make her fret, because the LORD had shut up her womb."   1 Samuel 1:5-6

Appreciate your spouse and use the freedom you have from the duties of child rearing to win souls to Christ and disciple them with the same devotion as a parent towards his/her own offspring *(1 Sam. 1:8).*

"Sing, O barren, thou that didst not bear; break forth into singing, and cry aloud, thou that didst not travail with child: for more are the children of the desolate than the children of the married wife, saith the LORD."   Isaiah 54:1

Follow the Apostle Paul's example. He had no controversy with God about being either single or without natural children. ...No root of bitterness, self-pity or discontent. Rather, he saw in God's providence an advantage and used it as an occasion for preaching the Gospel and rearing spiritual children ready to meet the Lord at His appearing *(1 Cor. 7:8, 27-35).*

"My little children, of whom I travail in birth again until Christ be formed in you."   Galatians 4:19

"For though ye have ten thousand instructers in Christ, yet have ye not many fathers: for in Christ Jesus I have begotten you through the gospel."   1 Corinthians 4:15

Do likewise and you shall have peace. Get your eyes off yourself. Relinquish your plans and look for God's hand — His plan. ...His divine purposes for your life and do your utmost, day by day, to surrender wholeheartedly to that.

"When ye pray, say, Our Father which art in heaven, Hallowed be thy name. Thy kingdom come. Thy will be done, as in heaven, so in earth."   Luke 11:2

Repentance and Surrender

So many of our ailments on every level find their cure in repentance and absolute surrender to Christ.

"My son, give me thine heart . . ." Proverbs 23:26

...ALL of it!

The surrender of self must include every interest, [desire,] possession and relationship. If self is kept back from God, life will be a series of reluctances . . . . We try to be religious in patches while the great surrender has not been made. . . . The soul is irritated and divided against itself. Until we surrender, praying and waiting will avail nothing. We shall be disappointed and we must expect to be. Are we willing to make a full surrender? to yield ourselves absolutely to God? That is the great question. What God wants is not praising lips, nor reverence and prayers only — but ourselves . . . . The clear ringing challenge . . . is this: are you willing to let God run your life, or will you keep it in your own hands? Are you wanting to use God for your purposes or are you willing to let Him use you for His purposes? How much of prayer is an attempt to induce God to further our wishes instead of lifting our wishes into the range of His will![7]

Speak, Lord. Help us to discern Your voice through our unique dealings. Help us to accept our circumstances with thanksgiving ...to recognize your goodness in all of them ...and as a result to grow in faith, love and hope. Show us the error of our ways; the changes that need to be made in our affections ...temperament   ...lifestyle   ...thought   patterns   ...priorities

...aspirations ...relationships ...and activities. Grant us the vision and desire to be good students in your "Holy Spirit School of Affliction."

"He openeth also their ear to discipline, and commandeth that they return from iniquity."   Job 36:10

"It is good for me that I have been afflicted; that I might learn thy statutes."   Psalms 119:71

Natural versus Spiritual Solutions

The swelling in my mouth finally peaked, but at the very same time we were due for a trip to town. Before going we discussed the possibility of getting some Bee Propolis. It's a medicine straight from God's creation that is very effectual for knocking out infection if used aggressively and enlivened by His Spirit. We were undecided, living in expectation of a miracle that would eliminate the need.

Seeing me in such distress once we got to town, however, and knowing that our camp was a long way off, Edwin asked if before leaving I'd like to go to the local natural foods store to pick some up. He was in no wise pushing an alternative to patient waiting on God in a posture of repentance with no added assistance from outward options for remedy. He was simply letting me know that he was open to whatever means the Lord chose to move.

He was such a loving coach—helping me to walk on water, but not defining exactly how it was to be done. He was teaching me precepts and leaving the choices in my hands. I think it pained him more to see me in that condition, than for me to actually suffer the scourging of it at my Father's hand. Normally, I would have leapt at the idea. But God was at work drawing my attention to issues of greater concern instead.

Vanity

Immediately, I was reminded of an ugly reaction that triggered from within my heart a day or so earlier when Edwin suggested that we go over to the Motor Vehicle Division

(MVD) the next time we got to town so I could get my picture taken for my Driver's License Renewal. It was about to expire and time was running out. My ego was "up in arms."

But you said we could wait till the swelling went down!!!

Pure vanity!

Oh, God, forgive me in Jesus' name! It should be long dead.

This was my moment to tear down the idol. My need for purging from a tooth infection paled in comparison to my need for further deliverance from vanity and the ungodly fruit it begets. Can't put the horse before the cart. The first pimple I got in my adolescence was enough to make me beg to stay home from school. And as soon as I hit sixteen I was determined to have cosmetic surgery to change the shape of my *very* "Jewish nose." Need I say more? What a trap vain glory can be! It has thrown me into rejection perpetually and caused me, at times, to literally obsess negatively on my appearance.

Our merciful Father, by virtue of His divine providence, was again taking the axe to the root of the tree. Not only was I forced to face this giant by walking around town looking like I had been in a fist fight, or was a victim of domestic violence; but now He was requiring me to have a picture taken so as to crucify it altogether. He put in my heart another divinely inspired "*step of that faith of our father Abraham*" (just like He did when he compelled me to put my beige turtleneck sweater back on the shelf). ...A step that would ultimately pave the way to my healing—both body and soul *(Rom. 4:12)*. ...Not a "dead work" conceived in my own imagination; but rather, a lively step of faith born of His Fatherly engineering.

Love.... I said to Edwin. Please forgive me for rising up in disrespect the other day when you talked about going over to the MVD. I was out of order. What do you think about me making restitution today and we drive over there now?

Repentance & Faith Translated into Action

The truck was hopping! Edwin was *more* than ready to forgive me and to support me in taking the devil by the horns in the Mighty Name of Jesus. Oh what a day! The Lord rewarded that simple step of faith in a way that only He can.

After getting the picture taken, we went over to the grocery store. From the parking lot we caught a glimpse of a young man in his twenties trying to make some money standing out front playing what turned out to be a mandolin. Unusual sight. The manager of that particular market didn't allow that kind of thing and most street minstrels play guitar, not mandolin.

Pull $5 out of the wallet, Jody, and put it with a copy of "The Original Profound True Gospel of Jesus Christ."[a] Let's go over and share the Gospel and see if we can help him out."

A small crowd was gathered around, so I held up the booklet with the money sticking out and pointed to his open instrument case filled with coins asking with my eyes if we could toss it in. He gave a nod. Onward he played. But when he noticed we were about to leave, he called out: *"Wait!"* We had a lot to do, so Edwin went ahead into the store and I stood outside mingled amongst the people while the man in need finished the fiddling-type tune. The next thing I knew he was "heart and soul" into a familiar Gospel favorite:

Would you be free from the burden of sin?
There's power in the blood, power in the blood;
Would you o'er evil a victory win?
There is wonderful power in the blood.

Would you be free from your passion and pride?
There's power in the blood, power in the blood;

---

[a] A concise booklet we've written filled with Scripture and freely given in our outreach. It covers the basics of the Gospel of Christ and has been translated by brethren from various nations into their native tongues; (i.e. Portuguese, Shona, French, Chichewa & Luganda).

Come for a cleansing to Calvary's tide;
There's wonderful power in the blood.

There is power, power, wonder-working power
in the blood of the Lamb.
There is power, power, wonder-working power
in the precious blood of the Lamb.

Would you be whiter, much whiter than snow?
There's power in the blood, power in the blood.
Sin stains are lost in its life-giving flow;
There's wonderful power in the blood. [Chorus]

Would you do service for Jesus your King?
There's power in the blood, power in the blood;
Would you live daily His praises to sing?
There's wonderful power in His blood. [Chorus][8]

My hands reached for the clouds. Tears were streaming down my checks in buckets and I was singing with the young man at the top of my lungs amidst the onlookers. No problems then with opening my mouth! As soon as he was done, I rushed inside the store, running up and down the aisles looking for Edwin so as to bring him back outside. But when we made it to the entrance where the young man once stood, he was gone. ...Or was it a young man? Perhaps it was an angel???

Double Blessings!

Turned out he was very much flesh and blood. A little later in the day we bumped into him at the Post Office and learned that his name was Sam. He is a Christian that had come down from a northern part of a neighboring state in hopes of getting a new lease on life. He was a recovering addict with a job opportunity that separated him from his old stomping grounds, but had delayed commencement by two weeks. He feared returning to his former street life as a means of generating funds to cover his needs in the interim, and was trying to make ends meet in a wholesome way by exercising his gift in music. It was a "divine appointment." By God's grace we had the privilege of giving to him yet further, just as God had so profoundly used him to give to us. Double blessings! What a magnificent God we serve! When He is well pleased, He has unimaginable ways of letting us know and at the same time spreading His love around!

". . . Well done, good and faithful servant . . . enter thou into the JOY of thy Lord."   Matthew 25:23

From that time onward the swelling began its decline and overnight vanished completely. Plus, my ego shrunk and I was more guarded about the meditations of my heart and the words of my mouth. The physical healing (though absolutely glorious!) seemed so incidental in comparison to my freedom and the glory that Edwin and I shared in the favor of our Lord. Truly, His lovingkindness is *"better than life"* *(Ps. 63:3),* and every other blessing He adds to it. It was another faith-building experience with the Cross at its center that neither I, nor my husband, will soon forget.

The First ...The Best ...The Greatest Physician

Andrew Murray wrote an excellent treatise on divine healing after being miraculously cured of a throat affliction that almost ended his ministry as a preacher. In it he acknowledged the vocation of doctors. At the same time, however, he extolled Jesus as our actual Healer and pointed to direct access to Him as the preferred path to wholeness.

A large number of . . . [doctors] seek truly to do, with love and compassion, all they are able to alleviate the evils and sufferings which burden humanity as a result of sin. . . . Nevertheless it is Jesus Himself who is always the first, the best, the greatest Physician. Jesus heals diseases in which earthly physicians can do nothing, for the Father gave Him this power when He charged Him with the work of redemption. Jesus, in taking upon Him our human body, delivered [us not only from disease, but also] from the dominion of sin and Satan.[9]

Murray was impacted by this fundamental truth the hard way. At one point in his journey towards health he turned to the medical world, but even there his prayer was turned away. Like the woman in the New Testament who exhausted all her resources on doctors, he too, *"was nothing bettered, but grew worse,"* until the faith he manifested at the Cross of Repentance put Him in direct contact with the healing *"virtue"* of Christ. There, he not only received cure from his disease, but also, the greater blessing of *"peace"* from our forgiving God.

"And a certain woman, which had an issue of blood twelve years, and had suffered many things of many physicians, and had spent all that she had, and was nothing bettered, but rather grew worse, when she had heard of Jesus, came in the press behind, and touched his garment. For she said, If I may touch but his clothes, I shall be whole. And straightway the fountain of her blood was dried up; and she felt in her body that she was healed of that plague. And Jesus, immediately knowing in himself that virtue had gone out of him, turned him about in the press, and said, Who touched my clothes? And his disciples said unto him, thou seest the multitude thronging thee, and sayest thou, Who touched me? And He looked round about to see her that had done this thing. But the woman fearing and trembling, knowing what was done in her, came and fell down before him, and told him all the truth. And he said unto her, Daughter, thy faith hath made thee whole; go in peace, and be whole of thy plague.   Mark 5:25-34

Like the Queen of Sheba when she came from the *"uttermost parts of the earth to hear the wisdom of Solomon"* and wound up telling him *"all that was in her heart"* (Mt. 12:42; 1 Ki. 10:2); even so, this precious soul pressed through a crowd so as to make contact with Jesus, a *"greater than Solomon,"* and wound up telling Him *"all the truth."* May our defenses dissolve in His Presence, too.

In his book, Murray compared the benefits of divine healing administered directly to a believer through his/her faith in the blood of Jesus, with healing received through medical treatment and *"remedies which are found in the natural world."* It is so important to understand his message, lest in our rush for relief, we miss the blessing wrapped up inside our Father's chastening rod.

> The difference between these two modes of healing is very marked. . . . When it is Jesus only to whom the sick person applies for healing, he learns to reckon no longer upon remedies, but to put himself into direct relation with His love and His almightiness. In order to obtain such healing, he must commence by confessing and renouncing his sins, and exercising a living faith. Then healing will come directly from the Lord . . . and it thus becomes a blessing for the soul as well as for the body....
> The healing which is wrought by our Lord Jesus brings with it and leaves behind it *more* real blessing than the healing which is obtained through physicians. . . . [Similarly, believers that opt for natural remedies often times become] preoccupied . . . with the remedies which they use, much more than with what the Lord may be doing with them, and in such a case their healing will be more hurtful than beneficial.[10]

Why? Because rather than the Lord, as the ultimate Source of all blessing, being wholeheartedly trusted, recognized and adored as our "*Healer,*" we find ourselves exalting (and even preaching!) herbs and medications, therapies, protocols and practitioners (*Jam. 1:17; Exo. 15:26*).

"I taught Ephraim also to go, taking them by their arms; but they knew not that I healed them."   Hosea 11:3

Knowing our adamic propensity to rely on tangible remedies, we must be very careful so as not to become like the idolaters cited in Isaiah 44 who bowed down to trees, simply because of the benefits derived from their use.

"He burneth part thereof in the fire; with part thereof he eateth flesh; he roasteth roast, and is satisfied: yea, he warmeth himself, and saith, Aha, I am warm, I have seen the fire: and the residue thereof he maketh a god, even his graven image: he falleth down unto it, and worshippeth it, and prayeth unto it, and saith, Deliver me; for thou art my god."   Isaiah 44:16-17

Healing has been a misfortune to more persons than one. On a bed of sickness serious thoughts had taken possession, but from the time of his healing how often has a sick man been found anew far from the Lord! It is not thus when it is Jesus who heals. Healing is granted after confession of sin; therefore it brings the sufferer nearer to Jesus, and establishes a new link between him and the Lord, it causes him to experience His love and power, it begins within him a new life of faith and holiness.[11]

It's the glorious Way of the Cross, leading to none other than our Lord Jesus Christ.

Yea, and amen! You, Lord Jesus, and You First, are our "exceeding great reward" (Gen. 15:1)! Thank you, Father, for your unspeakable Gift of Love!

CHAPTER SEVENTEEN

He Turned Our Mourning into Dancing

The same undercurrent of fear and unbelief that caused me to shelve my beige turtleneck sweater caused me to do a similar thing years earlier when I was smitten with a fungal infection. It started on my toes and made its trek up as far as my ankles. At one point my left leg nearly doubled in size! It was another "Cross-experience" that God used to expose lingering unbelief and reinforce my faith.

Rebellion: A Hidden Reef

One particular afternoon the itching became so radical that I couldn't sit still. It felt like tiny bugs were burrowing in and eating up my flesh. I reached out to Apostle Edwin with an anguished cry for support and he assured me that so long as we sought the Lord at the Cross of Repentance everything was going to be alright. That same message of reassurance echoed over and over again. At one point, however, I said something in the anguish of my spirit like:

I'm not sure I'm going to be able to endure.

Whoops! I should have never made such a faithless statement, much less thought it. But, truth be told, the continuing agony, coupled with an endless stream of fiery darts, was ferreting out a subtle streak of rebellion that has risen up within me when I've reached new thresholds of suffering, tempting me to draw lines, as though such a miserable creature as I could countermand an Awesome God like ours. Capitalizing on this weakness, the devil was enticing me, as he did Esau, to grow weary amidst the chastening process, and as a result, abandon the Cross in exchange for what he promised would be immediate relief.

"Looking diligently lest any man fail of the grace of God; lest any root of bitterness springing up trouble you, and thereby many be defiled; lest there be any fornicator, or profane person, as Esau, who for one morsel of meat sold his birthright. For ye know how that afterward, when he would have inherited the blessing, he was rejected: for he found no place of repentance, though he sought it carefully with tears."   Hebrews 12:15-17

Thank the Lord for revealing this dangerous propensity in my life! Not only did I repent, but from that time forward I've been guarded against its subtle incursion, knowing it could resurface in future times of testing and rob me of my *"birthright."* God forbid!

We've witnessed the subtle influence of rebellion rise up repeatedly in the lives of others. Rather than hanging in there when trials pinnacle and deliverance is delayed; thereby letting *"patience have her perfect work"* breaking down self-will, purging away sin and building faith *(Jam. 1:4)*; they cave into the flesh at breakthrough time; give up the fight; fall back into natural reasonings; and turn to the world for respite. ...Taking their eyes off of Jesus and the extremity of suffering He endured to purchase our redemption, they become *"wearied and faint in [their] minds."* As a result, they miss the spiritual prosperity that God intends for those who endure through their trials till He brings them to an expected end *(Heb. 12:3, 11)*.

I am so grieved by that confession. It was an outright lie: direct blasphemy against the Word of God. I have since repented. In no uncertain terms, the Apostle Paul (who paid the price to speak with authority) preached no such doctrine. Instead, he taught (and lived out to the uttermost) the ultimate "can do" message to all who are willing to join him at the Cross.

"I know both how to be abased, and I know how to abound: every where and in all things I am instructed both to . . . abound and to suffer need. I can do all things through Christ which strengtheneth me."   Philippians 4:12- 13

A Brother Born for Adversity

That faithless confession on my part added *"sin to sin,"* not only separating me from God's grace, but tearing down my husband, as well *(Isa. 30:1)*. We were in this testing together and his concern for me was great. If I were to abandon the fight, where would that leave him? Plus, think of the weight on his shoulders, knowing his accountability before God for rendering sound oversight *(Heb. 13:17)*. ...And what about our testimony? There would be none.

I really wasn't being forthright. I was reaching for my husband's help, but my cry came out in a clumsy sort of a way. It would have been far better if I had simply said:

> *Love... I'm getting bombarded. Can I lean on you? Like Moses needed Aaron and Hur in the heat of the battle against the Amalekites, I could use your support to help me stay steady throughout the afternoon (Exo. 17:10-12).*

I look forward to the day that all my floundering and drama cease.

Let me pray for you, he responded.

Edwin was compassionate, but he did not coddle me; nurse self-pity; or come in like a "saviour," usurping the seat of Christ in my life by attempting to wage the *"good fight of faith"* for me, while I whimpered and complained *(1 Tim. 6:12)*. That would have only weakened me, left my sin intact and set me up for future stumbling. Instead, he came up alongside me, buttressing my stance with intercession and supporting me at the altar of repentance when I acknowledged my sins and cried out to the Lord for mercy. Truly, *"The Law of Christ"* is brought to its fulfillment when we *"bear . . . one another's burdens"* *(Gal. 6:2)*; but we each must deny self and carry our own Cross if we are to be counted as Christ's disciples *(Lk. 9:23)*.

But the torment returns every five minutes, I retorted.

Alright. ...So I'll pray with you every five minutes.

Precious! ...*Can* do!

"Charity never faileth . . ." 1 Corinthians 13:8a

"A friend loveth at all times, and a brother is born for adversity."   Proverbs 17:17

"Two are better than one; because they have a good reward for their labour. For if they fall, the one will lift up his fellow: but woe to him that is alone when he falleth; for he hath not another to help him up. Again, if two lie together, then they have heat: but how can one be warm alone? And if one prevail against him, two shall withstand him; and a threefold cord is not quickly broken."   Ecclesiastes 4:9-12

An amazing miracle takes place when we bear one another's burdens. In that exchange of love we are reminded that we are not alone in our struggles. God is with us! When we are weak, He is strong. If we are unable to connect with fellow Cross-bearers to walk with us at such times, we can still garner encouragement knowing by faith that we are surrounded by a company of witnesses cheering us on *(Heb. 12:1)*.

Cry'in

Sensing an infilling of enormous consolation, I picked up Smith Wigglesworth's book on healing called *Ever Increasing Faith*, stretched out on the bed hoping to get some rest due to the long hours of wrestling, and returned to the place where I had it bookmarked. That tiny paperback was another one of the books in our treasure chest (in addition to the Bible) that the Lord used to keep me going throughout my trial.

Love... I said softly, trying to get Edwin's attention. *"I just read something I'd like to share."* After receiving his nod, I began:

If you are sure of your ground, if you are counting on the presence of the living Christ within, you can laugh when you see things getting worse.[1]

A smile came over his face; but a frown overshadowed mine. With tears rolling down my cheeks I said:

...I'm not laughing. I'm crying!

Oh what a special time of sanctification and faith building this was for both of us! Awesome isn't a big enough word. We were touching the face of Jesus. It's another account worthy of record in the *"book of the wars of the Lord"* *(Num. 21:14).*

"Then they that feared the LORD spake often one to another: and the LORD hearkened, and heard it, and a book of remembrance was written before him for them that feared the LORD, and that thought upon his name. And they shall be mine, saith the LORD of hosts, in that day when I make up my jewels; and I will spare them, as a man spareth his own son that serveth him."
                                        Malachi 3:16- 17

Unfettered Faith

With the comfort of my husband's encouragement, my eyes were lifted off my affliction and fastened once again on Jesus and the promises (and purposes!) of our Great God.

Yes, Lord. Just like Edwin says, the same God that made sunshine and rainbows, laughter and love, tornadoes and floods, can cure cancer and every other frightful disease imaginable "just as easily as the common cold."

In other words: Keep up the faith and don't limit God.

"Then said Martha unto Jesus, Lord, if thou hadst been here, my brother had not died. But I know, that even now, whatsoever thou wilt ask of God, God will give it thee."
                                        John 11:21-22

"How oft did they provoke him in the wilderness, and grieve him in the desert! Yea, they turned back and tempted God, and limited the Holy One of Israel. They remembered not his hand, nor the day when he delivered them from the enemy. How he had wrought his signs in Egypt, and his wonders in the field of Zoan."   Psalm 78:40-43

Whence is it that the poor Christian is so distressed with the present affliction that lies upon him, but because he museth more on his trouble, than on the promise? There is that in the promise which would recreate his spirit, if he could but fix his thoughts upon it. When the crying child once fastens on the teat, and begins to draw down the milk, then it leaves wrangling, and falls asleep at the breast. Thus the Christian ceaseth complaining of his affliction, when he gets hold on the promise, and hath the relish of its sweetness upon his heart. . . . Here is a Christian that will sing when another sighs; will be able to spend that time of his affliction in praising God, which others . . . (who think only upon what they suffer) too commonly bestow on fruitless complaints of their misery, which reflect dishonourably upon God himself. . . . When a swarm of bees dislodge themselves, they are all in confusion, flying here and there without any order, till at last they are hived again; then the uproar is at an end, and they fall to work peaceably as before. . . . So the Christian will find it with his own heart. God in the promise is the soul's hive. Let the Christian dislodge his thoughts thence, and presently they run riot, and fly up and down as in an affright at the apprehension of the present affliction or temptation that lies upon him, till he can recollect himself, and settle his heart again upon the promise, and then he recovers his former peace . . .[2]

Lead us Not into Temptation

One day while in the heat of the battle we were in town and I asked Edwin if it would be alright to buy some over-the-counter fungal cream. My skin was so radically infected that it seemed as though nothing I applied externally would have much effect. But, I was desperate. Funds were lean then, and it troubled my conscience to spend the money. Gas money was hard to come by and trips to town were limited.

What about our African brethren? Would this affect our ability to support them?

Edwin answered my question with his own:

Have you prayed about it?

Then, he encouraged me to respond to whatever I sensed to be the Lord's leading. I was unsure — well aware of the fact that this was a "test" and a shift in my faith from the Lord and His Cross to the world and its *"gods"* could invite judgment, rather than blessing, and magnify the suffering I hoped to relieve.

"And Ahaziah fell down through a lattice in his upper chamber that was in Samaria, and was sick: and he sent messengers, and said unto them, Go, enquire of Baalzebub the god of Ekron whether I shall recover of this disease. But the angel of the LORD said to Elijah the Tishbite, Arise, go up to meet the messengers of the king of Samaria, and say unto them, Is it not because there is not a God in Israel, that ye go to enquire of Baalzebub the god of Ekron? Now therefore thus saith the LORD, Thou shalt not come down from that bed on which thou art gone up, but shalt surely die . . ."   2 Kings 1:2-4a

God *"dealeth"* with believers *"as with sons,"* meaning He is very strict about where His children turn for remedy *(Heb. 12:7).* ...Very!

"And in the time of his distress did he [King Ahaz] trespass yet more against the LORD . . . . For he sacrificed unto the gods of Damascus, which smote him: and he said, Because the gods of the kings of Syria help them, therefore will I sacrifice to them, that they may help me. But they were the ruin of him, and of all Israel."   2 Chronicles 28:22a, 23

After a few moments of silence I was still of the inclination to try to find something. Edwin went with me into the pharmacy and then returned to our truck. I asked the pharmacist what he could recommend and he only confirmed how pathetically useless it would be unless I addressed the issue medically. Notwithstanding, I picked out a tiny tube of what was supposed to be one of the better products, went to the counter and paid. When I came out to the parking lot and showed Edwin what I bought I had no peace in my heart.

Do you think I did the wrong thing?

He didn't have an answer. He wasn't about to get in the way of God by making that decision for me. Not Edwin. It was time for the training wheels to come off my bicycle; not to tighten the bolts. His silence was like the nudge of a mamma bird thrusting her babes out of the nest to try out their wings. If he were to have allowed me to ride on his back, it is not likely that I would have dealt with the fears and ungodly thoughts that were assailing me with the aggression necessary to get free. I needed to learn for myself how to live and breadth faith.

Trepidation and excitement welled up inside as I pondered both the peril and glory of launching out into the open skies.

Don't be like a wave tossed to and fro. What do you want to do? We need to get going.

I reached for his hands and we prayed. "*The Spirit of the Lord*" then breathed renewed faith into my "*dry bones*" and I rose up from the grave of unbelief with resolve *(Eze. 37:1-6)*.

I think the Lord would have me to return it.

Okay. Go ahead.

A Power-Packed Step of Faith

In that one simple "*step of that faith of our father Abraham*" something broke in the spirit just like it did when I put my beige turtleneck sweater back on the shelf *(Rom. 4:12. ...*And just like it did when I chose to go get my picture taken at the MVD when my mouth was swollen up like a balloon, rather than look for relief at the natural foods store.

I was no longer looking at Jesus *"cross-eyed,"* as Smith Wigglesworth puts it; one eye upon Jesus and the other on some sort of alternative remedy. I gave up what Bishop Raymore calls: *"Plan B."* Like the impotent man at the pool of Bethesda, I took my rogue eye off the water hoping to receive my healing there, and fastened them both on Jesus instead. Fully focused I would then be tuned to His command to *"rise, take up [my] bed, and walk" (Jn. 5:1-17).*

> There they were, a great multitude of impotent folk, of blind, halt, withered, around the pool, waiting for the moving of the water. Did Jesus heal everybody? He left many around that pool unhealed. There were doubtless many who had their eyes on the pool and who had no eyes for Jesus. There are many today who have their confidence in things seen. If they would only get their eyes on God instead of on natural things, how quickly they would be helped.[3]

When we finally got back to our resting place, the only goods we had with us were groceries and camp supplies. Our Faithful Lord Jesus had answered my prayers:

"And lead us not into temptation; but deliver us from evil."
Luke 11:4b

The Mighty Name of Jesus

Edwin was super happy at that time, as he is now, to have me gliding with him on the wings of the Spirit. I can't be content leaning on his lion-like faith in my moments of crisis; though I can definitely rely on him for feedback and support whenever I need help. My primary focus, however, has got to be on Jesus, for it is in His name (and His *"Wonderful"* name only!) that any among us can ever be made whole *(Isa. 9:6).*

"Then Peter said, Silver and gold have I none; but such as I have give I thee: In the name of Jesus Christ of Nazareth rise up and walk. And he took him by the right hand, and lifted him up: and immediately his feet and ancle bones received strength. And he leaping up stood, and walked, and entered with them into the temple, walking, and leaping, and praising God."

Acts 3:6-8

"And as the lame man which was healed held Peter and John, all the people ran together unto them in the porch that is called Solomon's, greatly wondering. And when Peter saw it, he answered unto the people, Ye men of Israel, why marvel ye at this? or why look ye so earnestly on us, as though by our own power or holiness we had made this man to walk? The God of Abraham, and of Isaac, and of Jacob, the God of our fathers, hath glorified his Son Jesus; whom ye delivered up, and denied him in the presence of Pilate, when he was determined to let him go. But ye denied the Holy One and the Just, and desired a murderer to be granted unto you; and killed the Prince of life, whom God hath raised from the dead; whereof we are witnesses. And his name through faith in his name hath made this man strong, whom ye see and know: yea, the faith which is by him hath given him this perfect soundness in the presence of you all."

Acts 3:11-16

Godly Shepherding

Trustworthy shepherds, or even wise parents for that matter, (unlike hirelings propelled by selfish interests), are not to make the saints entrusted to their charge "dependents" upon their faith; thus amassing followers to themselves. Rather, they are charged to make disciples of Christ by cultivating a *"living faith"* in the lives of others; encouraging them to personally rely with all their hearts upon our Lord Jesus and His Sure Word.

"Remember them which have the rule over you, who have spoken unto you the word of God: whose faith follow, considering the end of their conversation."

Hebrews 13:7

Jesus is the "*Rock*" upon which we are to stand.

"My soul, wait thou only upon God; for my expectation is from him. He only is my rock and my salvation: he is my defence; I shall not be moved."   Psalm 62:5-6

They teach us to go "all out" now (while we still can!) like the five wise virgins so as to "*buy*" oil for our lamps. That way, when the Midnight Cry of the Bridegroom sounds, we'll be ready to run out and meet Him, rather than be left behind, with our "flame of faith" gone out.

"And at midnight there was a cry made, Behold, the bridegroom cometh; go ye out to meet him. Then all those virgins arose, and trimmed their lamps. And the foolish said unto the wise, Give us of your oil; for our lamps are gone out. But the wise answered, saying, Not so; lest there be not enough for us and you: but go ye rather to them that sell, and buy for yourselves. And while they went to buy, the bridegroom came; and they that were ready went in with him to the marriage: and the door was shut. Afterward came also the other virgins, saying, Lord, Lord, open to us. But he answered and said, Verily I say unto you, I know you not."   Matthew 25:6-12

Church leaders are called to be succorers, not surrogates. They stand side-by-side with us on the Battlefield, sharing in our sufferings and the victories that follow. But they don't climb into the seat of Christ, so as to take His place of preeminence in our lives.

"Not for that we have dominion over your faith, but are helpers of your joy: for by faith ye stand."   2 Corinthians 1:24

They do this first and foremost by example *(2 Th. 3:9; 1 Pe. 5:3; Phil 3:17; 4:9)*. ...Then, by giving us as much Light, coaching, counsel and "*precept upon precept; line upon line*" doctrine as possible *(Isa. 28:10)*; all the while challenging us to personally seek the Lord at His Cross in our time of need. As the martyrs so often remind us: The way into the Kingdom is narrow and the gate *"strait"* *(Mt. 7:13-14)*. ...So *"strait"* that the only way to get through it is single file.

> . . . Fire on the right hand, and on the left a deep water: and one only path between them both, even between the fire and the water, so small that there could but one man go there at once.[4]

Signs and Wonders

When we returned to our camp I started putting away our goods. In the process, I glanced down and caught a glimpse of my left leg. To my utter astonishment it had radically reduced in size. Edwin's face lit up! The Holy Spirit *"had led me in the right way to take"* and our Heavenly Father revealed His good pleasure with a miraculous token of mercy *(Gen. 24:48)*. Praise His holy name forever!

"But without faith it is impossible to please him: for he that cometh to God must believe that he is, and that he is a rewarder of them that diligently seek him."   Hebrews 11:6

"The LORD rewarded me according to my righteousness: according to the cleanness of my hands hath he recompensed me. For I have kept the ways of the LORD, and have not wickedly departed from my God. For all his judgments were before me: and as for his statutes, I did not depart from them. I was also upright before him, and have kept myself from mine iniquity. Therefore the LORD hath recompensed me according to my righteousness; according to my cleanness in his eye sight."   2 Samuel 22:21-25

"Blessed be God, which hath not turned away my prayer, nor his mercy from me."   Psalms 66:20

". . . All the promises of God in him [Christ Jesus] are yea, and in him Amen, unto the glory of God . . ."   2 Corinthians 1:20

Hallelujah! When we bring our lives into alignment with the Word and walk in the Light of the Cross, *"mercy and truth"* meet *"together,"* the blood of Jesus washes away our sins, and miracles happen *(Ps. 85:10; 1 Ki. 3:6; 1 Jn. 1:7-9).*

If You Lose Your Life, You Shall Find It—Luke 9:23

By the grace of God, the money that I almost squandered on ointment was turned into another kind of investment altogether: the purchase of spiritual gold *"tried in the fire"* and laid up for future sustenance amidst trials like the ones we've been describing; and still further, for the days that access to public health care, pharmaceuticals and the purchase of natural medicinals won't be an option anyway, because they'll be contingent on receiving the Mark of the Beast *(Rev. 3:18).* In fact, due to vaccine mandates, many so called "anti-vaxers" are already being shut out.

This was a wonderful *"exercise"* in *"godliness"* (1 Tim. 4:7-8). I "fasted" the world's remedy of relief and learned experientially that Jesus Himself is more than able to deliver a great feast to those that place their trust in Him.

"Then came the disciples to Jesus apart, and said, Why could not we cast him out? And Jesus said unto them, Because of your unbelief: for verily I say unto you, If ye have faith as a grain of mustard seed, ye shall say unto this mountain, Remove hence to yonder place; and it shall remove; and nothing shall be impossible unto you. Howbeit this kind goeth not out but by prayer and fasting."   Matthew 17:19-21

My mustard seed faith (cultivated by the Holy Spirit through abstinence) was becoming a tree into whose branches other *"birds of the air"* in need of the Master's touch would one day come and *"lodge"* (Mt. 13:31-32). Had I fainted and chosen a lower road for remedy, I would have played "truant" in the "Holy Spirit School of Blessing" and in so doing missed this divinely orchestrated "how-to lesson" on the ins-and-outs of living by faith *(Gal. 6:9).* But by God's grace (and His grace only!) the "Mt. Everest of Unbelief" was step-by-step being removed from my life.[5] The *"Author"* of our noble Christian faith, was doing more of His "finishing" work, just as He promised *(Heb. 12:2)*. All He needs is our cooperation.

"Wherefore, my beloved, as ye have always obeyed, not as in my presence only, but now much more in my absence, work out your own salvation with fear and trembling. For it is God which worketh in you both to will and to do of His good pleasure."   Philippians 2:12-13

Receiving freedom and healing in answer to prayer is generally not something that is done to you, a situation in which you are just a passive participant. Occasionally God works this way and simply heals or frees a person outright. He is certainly capable of this. But in my experience, He typically asks us to play an active role in the journey towards wholeness.[6]

Immediately, I started doing a jig. Our little camper was shaking (I'm not exaggerating!) and our hearts were leaping.

"Thou hast turned for me my mourning into dancing: thou hast put off my sackcloth, and girded me with gladness; to the end that my glory may sing praise to thee, and not be silent. O LORD my God, I will give thanks unto thee for ever."
                                        Psalm 30:11-12

Up shot our hands heavenwards in elation and praise.

"Who can utter the mighty acts of the LORD? who can shew forth all His praise?"   Psalms 106:2

On that grand day my husband and I were *"caught up into Paradise"* in anticipation of the complete healing of my feet and ankles, as well *(2 Cor. 12:4)*.

"Hope deferred maketh the heart sick: but when the desire cometh, it is a tree of life."   Proverbs 13:12

CHAPTER EIGHTEEN

Walking on Water with Jesus

Thrilled by what was taking place, Apostle Edwin went out and bought me a brand new pair of shoes; the same kind I already used for hiking, but on the rigid side because they had never been worn. Little did we know at the time (being that my feet were at the pinnacle of infection) that the Lord was going to use those shoes to uncover the root of my unbelief; and at the same time build up my faith by "bidding" me to come unto Him afresh walking on water.

"And when the disciples saw him walking on the sea, they were troubled, saying, It is a spirit; and they cried out for fear. But straightway Jesus spake unto them, saying, Be of good cheer; it is I; be not afraid. And Peter answered him and said, Lord, if it be thou, bid me come unto thee on the water. And he said, Come. And when Peter was come down out of the ship, he walked on the water, to go to Jesus. But when he saw the wind boisterous, he was afraid; and beginning to sink, he cried, saying, Lord, save me. And immediately Jesus stretched forth his hand, and caught him, and said unto him, O thou of little faith, wherefore didst thou doubt?"   Matthew 14:26-31

Surprise!

My feet were so swollen and sore at the time that the only way for me to squeeze into my "long-timers" was to stretch out the supple leather and leave the laces fanned open as far as possible. Handing the new shoes to me with a hopeful sparkle in his eyes, Edwin said something like:

Your old pair is worn out. These will work GREAT.

I cringed! Then, feigning a smile that was intended to signal appreciation, I thanked him and put the shoes carefully away, never removing them from the bag or the box. I also took the receipt and put it in a drawer, *just in case* there was a need to return them. There I was, years earlier, doing with the receipt exactly the same thing that I had done with my turtleneck sweater: "s*neaking around.*" I was playing the hypocrite; confessing faith with my lips, but acting on fear and unbelief. "*As silver tried in a furnace of earth,*" so the faith of every child of God is brought to the touchstone and "*purified*" in the crucible of divine providence multiple times *(Ps. 12:6).* It takes so much for every one of us to come out of a world steeped in unbelief, where the reflex response to bodily ills is to seek remedy in doctors, pharmacies and/or natural cures, rather than first and foremost in God and His Word. ...And then, letting the Holy Spirit lead us from there in exactly how to address our infirmities in a manner that is acceptable to Him.

> . . . Be not dismayed in your mind because my flesh has suffered a little while; for now the good heavenly Father has tried my faith, as gold in the fire, whether I would also trust and fear and love Him in the severest conflict. And now that He has found me faithful, from one tribulation to the other, so that through the grace of God I have overcome the rulers of this world (wherein I have greatly rejoiced from the heart) . . . henceforth there is laid up for me the crown of eternal life.   Jan Wouterss
> Tortured & Burned Alive by Catholic decree, A.D. 1572[1]

There are no short cuts here. The Lord simply will not rest till our bedrock confidence in Him (with or without additional props) is both sure and secure.

> O My child, thou has thought in thine heart that thou wouldst run from Me. But lo, I am everywhere before thee, and thou has only run into My arms. For I care for thee . . . and I seek to do [a complete work].[2]

In numberless ways God will bring us back to the same
point over and over again. He never tires of bringing us
to the one point [of our departure from Him] until we
learn the lesson, because He is producing the finished
product. . . . Again and again, with the most persistent
patience, God . . . [will bring] us back to . . . . the one
thing that is not entirely right. . . . Watch the slipshod
bits — "Oh, that will have to do for now." Whatever it is,
God will point it out with persistence until we are
entirely His.[3]

God's Paternal Love

Believers with whom God is dealing that attempt to dodge
the full outworking of this wondrous Way of the Cross amidst
their adversities by turning to the world for a seemingly "less
costly" and "more expeditious" path to relief are sure to be
confounded.

". . . In vain shalt thou use many medicines; for thou shalt not
be cured."   Jeremiah 46:11b

And even if one were to find a moment's reprieve by opting
out of the fires of testing prematurely, it would be at the
expense of intimacy with Jesus, a blessing too precious to
relinquish for *any* cause.

"And He gave them their request; but sent leanness into their
soul."   Psalms 106:15

The nature of God's paternal love is such that He won't let
up on us till every possible means has been exhausted in an
effort to put us in a position to address our weaknesses; and if
we have strayed, to draw us back to the bosom of His Love
(Lev. 26:21, 23-24, 40-42a, etc.).

"How shall I give thee up, Ephraim? how shall I deliver thee,
Israel? how shall I make thee as Admah? how shall I set thee as

Zeboim? mine heart is turned within me, my repentings are
kindled together."   Hosea 11:8

"For I will be unto Ephraim as a lion, and as a young lion to the
house of Judah: I, even I, will tear and go away; I will take
away, and none shall rescue him. I will go and return to my
place, till they acknowledge their offence, and seek my face: in
their affliction they will seek me early. Come, and let us return
unto the LORD: for he hath torn, and he will heal us; he hath
smitten, and he will bind us up."   Hosea 5:14-6:1

Hidden Evidence

Shortly after tucking away the shoes, I was out on a walk,
praying in my heavenly language, worshipping the Lord in
song and reflecting on God's promises. All of a sudden, the
Holy Spirit brought to mind my unbelief and the loathsome
fruit of hypocrisy it begets. Immediately, I bolted back to our
camper — shocked and shamed.

Love... You'll never believe what I did!

Then, with wide open eyes that said: *"Could it really be THAT
bad?"* Edwin gave me his full attention.

*...When you weren't looking I hid the receipt for the new shoes
you bought me, fearing that my feet are never going to recover
and we could take them back and get a refund.*

"What?!!" he replied in horror. *"Go get it – 'pronto,'* meaning
ASAP. *"Let's take it outside and burn it – NOW!"*

Absolutely! Let's destroy it!

And so we did! ...All from a posture of repentance, in the
Mighty Name of Jesus. By coming together in that manner we
were standing in agreement against the unbelief still resident in
my life *(Mt. 18:19)*, just as Jesus stood against it when He put

out the scorners before giving a twelve year old damsel in the sleep of death the command to "*arise.*"

"And he cometh to the house of the ruler of the synagogue, and seeth the tumult, and them that wept and wailed greatly. And when he was come in, he saith unto them, Why make ye this ado, and weep? the damsel is not dead, but sleepeth. And they laughed him to scorn. But when he had put them all out, he taketh the father and the mother of the damsel, and them that were with him, and entereth in where the damsel was lying. And he took the damsel by the hand, and said unto her, Talitha cumi; which is, being interpreted, Damsel, I say unto thee, arise. And straightway the damsel arose, and walked; for she was of the age of twelve years. And they were astonished with a great astonishment." Mark 5:38-42

Thank the Lord for trying my faith and for giving me another chance, as He is this day, to "*tread without stumbling*" on the "Highway of Holiness and Health."

It will happen then that from time to time we stumble and for a moment fall. We shall slip from the highway down the steep slope, and become bruised on the sharp stones. Old fears and old failures may return which we thought to have left behind. We shall learn in such moments, instantly to return and to seek the help of our Guide. We shall find that He is strong at once to rescue. Step by step He will show us how to climb, that we may reach once more the ridge. He will show us where and why we fell, that another time we may tread without stumbling by the same place. Thus we shall walk, unafraid despite the heights, rejoicing in the heights, under divine orders along the highway of God.[4]

CHAPTER NINETEEN

Unbelief: The Traitor's Gate

If you haven't already guessed, the trial was still in progress and Apostle Edwin was primed to keep the ball moving forward on the court. "Town Day" was coming up and it was time to pull the shoes out of hiding, put them on and head towards Jesus on the water. Burning the receipt was a step in the right direction, but it was time to advance by faith on the battlefield, though outward indicators were minimal.

". . . Hope that is seen is not hope: for what a man seeth, why doth he yet hope for?"   Romans 8:24b

The rhythm of my heartbeats picked up and thoughts began racing. Unbelief from within and satanic suggestions from without were closing in on me.

The pain will be too much. This is premature. It's reckless. Puss is going to spurt out of your toenails. Edwin is being insensitive. He has no idea what you're going through. If the tables were turned and it was him and not you that was suffering, he wouldn't be initiating such a move.

Oh, what grievous contention unbelief can create!

Dear Lord, "Purge me with hyssop, and I shall be clean: wash me, and I shall be whiter than snow" (Ps. 51:7).

Mutiny in My Soul

The war that broke out in my soul was indescribable. The rancor of it all shot through my being like poison. All the old enemies of faith were in a rage: fear, resentment, evil surmisings, self-pity, pride. And "prince" over them all was the

"I know better than you" attitude. The whole clan was barking calumnies. I even sensed myself reaching out in the spirit for "common sense" reasonings and sympathies from the unbelieving world to buttress my inward inclination to shrink back and lay down my Cross. From the background of the clamor, I could hear the voices of people who had abandoned the Cross in their own crises beckoning me to "throw in the towel," too, in hopes that my faint-heartedness would somehow justify their own weakness and failure.

My Heavenly Father knew it all before I ever saw the horror of all this inward potential for betrayal for myself.

"Thou knowest my downsitting and mine uprising, thou understandest my thought afar off."   Psalms 139:2

He was still profoundly at work humbling my proud heart, testing the veracity of my surrender, taming my spirit and *"[reduc]ing"*[1] me, as Gurnall so aptly put it, to the *"obedience of faith"* (Rom. 16:26). *"Bind me to the altar,"* I cried, in like manner as Little Miss "Much-Afraid," when she was tried.[2]

How often have I "turned traitor" under fire when the going gets tough ...my will gets crossed ...faith actions and natural reason collide ...or, I am not in agreement with particular decisions made by those that God sets in authority over my life; namely, my beloved husband?! It is a terribly wicked and dangerous streak in my character—a reflex reaction common to unregenerated souls. ...Something I have battled for years to overcome. In times of great reproach, it has even caused me to cave into castigation and fall in league with the enemy. If love and faith (fear's conquerors) were yet my fundamental "stock," such evil surmisings towards my brethren (or my God!!), would never find *any* credibility whatsoever in my thoughts.

. . . One property of love [is] 'to think no evil,' 1 Cor. xiii. 5; that is, a man will neither plot any evil against him whom he loves, nor easily suspect any evil to be plotted by him against himself. Love . . . interprets all he doth with so much sweetness and simplicity, that those passages in his behaviour towards her, which to another would seem . . . suspicious, are plain and pleasing to her, because she ever puts the most favourable sense upon all he doeth. . . . . And as love will not suffer him to turn traitor against a good God [or fellow believers], so neither will it suffer him to harbour any . . . [evil] thoughts of God's heart towards him; as if he who was the first lover, and taught the soul to love him . . . could, after all this, frame any plot of real unkindness against it. No; this thought, though Satan may force it in a manner upon the Christian, and violently press for its entertainment under the advantage of some frowning providence . . . can never find welcome so far as to be credited in the soul where love to God hath anything to do.[3]

Thank the Lord for bringing this blemish to the surface once again. Unwillingness to step out in faith on any issue is, in effect, rebellion. As such, it is a major impasse to healing (actually to salvation itself) and will most certainly keep believers turning circles in the wilderness, rather than crossing over the Jordan into the Promised Land.

Despising Dominion — Jude 1:8

"Charity [love] thinketh no evil" (1 Cor. 13:5). Yet, there I was, entertaining Satan while he put the worst spin imaginable upon my husband's character, motivations and ability under the guidance of the Holy Spirit to lead us into victory.

"Wherefore the people did chide with Moses, and said, Give us water that we may drink. And Moses said unto them, Why chide ye with me? Wherefore do ye tempt the LORD? And the people thirsted there for water; and the people murmured against Moses, and said, Wherefore is this that thou hast brought us up out of Egypt, to kill us and our children and our cattle with thirst? And Moses cried unto the LORD, saying, What shall I do unto this people? They be almost ready to stone me."
Exodus 17:2-4

In reality, this wasn't a personal struggle between Edwin and I at all. My actual controversy was with the Lord. He wanted me crossing the Jordan and becoming a conqueror; yet unbelief and the fear it begets had me tied to the banks of the river in my "civvies."

"He therefore that despiseth, despiseth not man, but God, who hath also given unto us his holy Spirit."   1 Thessalonians 4:8

"Why doth thine heart carry thee away? And what do thy eyes wink at, that thou turnest thy spirit against God, and lettest such words go out of thy mouth?"   Job 15:12-13

I don't believe that I went so far as to let *such words go out of [my] mouth.*" But only by the grace of God! Shamefully, prior to that particular incident of chastisement, I had been guilty of that, too. Either way: both deed and heart are of great concern to our Lord *(Mt. 5:27-28; Acts 8:19-23).*

The Spirit of Antichrist

Plain and simple: I was looking for ways (albeit unknowingly) to use my husband's *"earthen"* frame (i.e. his humanity) as an alibi to reject the counsel of Almighty God *(2 Cor. 4:7).* My precious Lord Jesus was reaching out to me in love with human hands and I was denying that His Spirit was the Source of their animation.

"Hereby know ye the Spirit of God: Every spirit that confesseth that Jesus Christ is come in the flesh is of God: and every spirit that confesseth not that Jesus Christ is come in the flesh is not of God: and this is that spirit of antichrist, whereof ye have heard that it should come; and even now already is it in the world."   1 John 4:2-3

No doubt about it. The Lord was using this extended trial to reveal another evil impeding my healing: the spirit of antichrist. I have since renounced it (in Jesus' Mighty name), and with a vengeance!

In a nutshell, I was judging my husband *"as if [he] walked according to the flesh,"* yet he was actually warring in the spirit *(2 Cor. 10:1-6)*. He was leading us out onto the battlefield against a demonic stronghold of unbelief that had kept me hostage to fear and self-preservation as long as I can remember *(Heb. 2:15)*.

The Ringleader of Sins

As soon as the finger of God reached down and touched that sore spot still resident in my life, my outlook on Apostle Edwin dramatically changed hue. Gone were the days when I was as eager as the household of Cornelius awaiting the arrival of Peter to hear from my husband's mouth *"all things that are commanded . . . of God" (Acts 10:33)*. Suddenly, the Word of Truth (which he has delivered with such passion, particularity and authority since the first day I heard him till now) was called (in measure) into question. ...NOT because of any error in disposition or doctrine on his part; God knows!! But rather, because the counsel He had received from the Holy Spirit stood in opposition to the evils still working in my own heart. Impenitence caused me to strip my husband of his apostolic mantle and censure his guidance, as though the step of faith he laid out emanated from the mere whim of a carnally oriented man. I was as fickle as the Jews when Christ walked the earth. One day they were shouting: *"Hosanna in the Highest"* and on another they were crying: *"Away with this man, and release unto us Barabbas" (Mt. 21:9; Lk. 23:18)*. God forgive me this wrong!

"For this cause also thank we God without ceasing, because, when ye received the word of God which ye heard of us, ye received it not as the word of men, but as it is in truth, the word of God, which effectually worketh also in you that believe."
                                                    1 Thessalonians 2:13

Gurnall was "spot on" when he tagged unbelief as *"the traitor's gate, at which all other sins"* enter.[4]

The strength of the whole body of sin lies in this lock of unbelief. There is no mastering of a [soul] while unbelief is in power....It is a ring-leading sin, a sin-making sin. . . . It is a sin that doth keep the field — one of the last of all others; that which the sinner is last convinced of and the saint ordinarily last conqueror of. It is one of the chief strengths and fastnesses unto which the devil retreats when other sins are routed."[5]

Can you imagine!?! As soon as "the rubber met the road" and my confession of repentance was brought to the touchstone, it was proven to be only surface level. Roll back a little further and you can see all the *"dead men's bones"* that unbelief fosters and the fiery darts from hell that it entertains *(Mt. 23:27; Eph. 6:16; Jam. 3:14-15)*. Those evils were actually stirring within me when I reached out with a phony smile and accepted the shoes from my husband's hands.

"The words of his mouth were smoother than butter, but war was in his heart: his words were softer than oil, yet were they drawn swords."   Psalms 55:21

There I was, almost four decades into a glorious Christian marriage (and only a day out from my acknowledgement of the unbelief that had driven me to hide the receipt) tricked to turn against the most endeared and respected person in my life.

"Ye know how through infirmity of the flesh I preached the gospel unto you at the first. And my temptation which was in my flesh ye despised not, nor rejected; but received me as an angel of God, even as Christ Jesus. Where is then the blessedness ye spake of? for I bear you record, that, if it had been possible, ye would have plucked out your own eyes, and have given them to me. Am I therefore become your enemy, because I tell you the truth?"   Galatians 4:13-16

Still worse, I had departed from my Lord and my God.

"Take heed, brethren, lest there be in any of you an evil heart of unbelief, in departing from the living God."   Hebrews 3:12

CHAPTER TWENTY

Restoring Honor

When speaking of the *"unfruitful works of darkness"* wrought in *"secret"* (even the secret chambers of our hearts), the Apostle Paul said: It is a *"shame even to speak"* of them *(Eph. 5:12)*. Amen! I am ashamed ...ashamed ...ashamed. ...A thousand times over, ashamed!

One of the greatest desires of my heart has been to take part in restoring Christ's End-Time Remnant Church to its original New Testament glory; and to recover (not attack and undermine) respect for the divinely appointed authority built into its structure.

"After this I will return, and will build again the tabernacle of David, which is fallen down; and I will build again the ruins thereof, and I will set it up."   Acts 15:16

Sadly, for the most part, such leaders have been rejected by our modern church culture in favor of hireling shepherds that cater to lusts and preach a domesticated *"jesus"* that has little (if any) controversy with sin, lawlessness, or false doctrine *(2 Cor. 11:4)*. That inner working of rebellion, in its secular outworking, is on display in our streets. Nowadays, for example, headlines feature police in leftist strongholds of the USA being faced down with impunity and threatened with death by teenage criminals, while local magistrates do nothing; or still worse, support the anarchists.

So much reverence has been lost (not only for our leaders) but above all else—for God. You can't have one without the other.

". . . And all the people greatly feared the LORD *and* Samuel."
                                                    1 Samuel 12:18b

Scripture says that when young men saw Job they *"hid themselves: and the aged arose, and stood up. . . . Nobles held their peace. . . . Men gave ear . . . . [And] after [his] words they spake not again"* *(Job 29:8, 10, 21, 22)*. But now???

Long years of indoctrination in "pick your own gospels" have created a lawless and pampered people, quick to receive, defend and even fawn over false prophets, but slow to recognize and honor God's own *(2 Cor. 11:4b, 19-20)*.

"My tabernacle is spoiled, and all my cords are broken: my children are gone forth of me, and they are not: there is none to stretch forth my tent any more, and to set up my curtains. For the pastors are become brutish, and have not sought the LORD: therefore they shall not prosper, and all their flocks shall be scattered."   Jeremiah 10:20- 21

Yet, time and again, snared by my weakness, I have been guilty of falling into their number by pulling down the pillars of the very House that I long to build up.

"Every wise woman buildeth her house: but the foolish plucketh it down with her hands."   Proverbs 14:1

No more! May that pattern cease forever, in Jesus' name, amen. We need to be *praying* for our leaders, our elders, and our husbands—not rebelling against their guidance; and then tearing them down by virtue of harbored misgivings and alliances made with evil spirits that supernaturally empower the imposition of self-will.

"And Samuel said, Hath the LORD as great delight in burnt offerings and sacrifices, as in obeying the voice of the LORD? Behold, to obey is better than sacrifice, and to hearken than the fat of rams. For rebellion is as the sin of witchcraft, and stubbornness is as iniquity and idolatry. Because thou hast rejected the word of the LORD, He hath also rejected thee from being king."   1 Samuel 15:22-23

The Five Fold Ministry Offices

There is "*no price too high*" that can be put on the shepherds that God anoints to lead His people in triumph *(Jer. 3:15).*

They are "gifts" that were given to us when Christ ascended up "on High," so as to reveal the magnificence of His own Person by means of our sanctification under their discipling (Psa. 68:18; Eph. 4:8-10).[1]

"And he gave some, apostles; and some, prophets; and some, evangelists; and some, pastors and teachers; for the perfecting of the saints, for the work of the ministry, for the edifying of the body of Christ: till we all come in the unity of the faith, and of the knowledge of the Son of God, unto a perfect man, unto the measure of the stature of the fulness of Christ."

Ephesians 4:11-13

This is what our trials are all about; rounding off our rough edges so we can be perfectly fitted together as "*lively stones*" into a "*spiritual house,*" giving corporate witness to Christ amidst a "*perverse and crooked*" generation unto whom we have been called to "*shine as lights*" *(Phil. 2:15; Eph. 5:25-27; 1 Pe. 2:5).*

"Unto him be glory in the church by Christ Jesus throughout all ages, world without end. Amen." Ephesians 3:21

All five of the previously listed ministry offices are of great value — especially in those pivotal seasons of chastisement when the Sword of the Lord comes down like the rod of Moses upon the rock *(Num. 20:11)*; smiting our consciences; cleaving the boulders of our hard hearts; dividing the "*waves*" of our lusts; and bringing us "*out from under the power of sin and Satan.*"[2] This is the time that the soil of our hearts is most fertile for spiritual growth and our thought processes most supple for renewal and transformation *(Rom. 12:2; Eph. 4:23; Col. 3:10)*. But it is also a time that we are exceptionally vulnerable to deception and in greatest need of the strong hand they have to offer so as to keep us on track, and warn us of the danger of returning to the fleshpots of Egypt when the going gets tough.

> When Israel left Egypt, they rejoiced greatly, that they were delivered from bondage; but when they came into the wilderness, where it did not please the flesh, they were very discontented and murmured, so that they wanted to return . . . Willem Droogsheerder,
> Tortured & Slain for the Testimony of Jesus, A.D. 1557[3]

"They on the rock are they, which, when they hear, receive the word with joy; and these have no root, which for a while believe, and in time of temptation fall away." Luke 8:13

What a gift! What a calling! What an accountability such men carry *(Heb. 13:17)*!

"But rise, and stand upon thy feet: for I have appeared unto thee for this purpose, to make thee a minister and a witness both of these things which thou hast seen, and of those things in the which I will appear unto thee; delivering thee from the people, and from the Gentiles, unto whom now I send thee, to open their eyes, and to turn them from darkness to light, and from the power of Satan unto God, that they may receive forgiveness of sins, and inheritance among them which are sanctified by faith that is in me." Acts 26:16-18

Confrontation of the Cross

David Wilkerson called our confrontation with the Cross a "*crisis.*"[4] Indeed, it is! So much so that we need to give ourselves every possible advantage for remaining glued to it; not the least of which is intimate association with a Cross-bearing body of believers (if we know of one); and submission to the oversight of renewed and trustworthy leaders that cannot be bullied to lighten up on sin *(2 Tim.4:2-3)*.

". . . This is a rebellious people . . . . which say to the seers, See not; and to the prophets, Prophesy not unto us right things, speak unto us smooth things, prophesy deceits." Isaiah 30:9a, 10

...Or still worse, be pressured to ignore it altogether.

"I have not sent these prophets, yet they ran: I have not spoken to them, yet they prophesied. But if they had stood in my counsel, and had caused my people to hear my words, then they should have turned them from their evil way, and from the evil of their doings."   Jeremiah 23:21-22

"Preach the word; be instant in season, out of season; reprove, rebuke, exhort with all longsuffering and doctrine. For the time will come when they will not endure sound doctrine; but after their own lusts shall they heap to themselves teachers, having itching ears; and they shall turn away their ears from the truth, and shall be turned unto fables."   2 Timothy 4:2-4

These men are *"faithful"* stewards like the early apostles — wholly submitted to the Lord amidst a crucible of divine dealings uniquely tailored to their own personal need for ongoing refinement *(1 Cor. 4:2; Phil. 3:12-14; 2 Cor. 6:3-10)*.
Scripture says:

". . . Know them which labour among you, and are over you in the Lord, and admonish you; and to esteem them very highly in love for their work's sake. And be at peace among yourselves."
1 Thessalonians 5:12b-13

That's a command we don't need to shy away from, even though we rarely see God-fearing men that are worthy of our trust. We are taught to "try" them by the Word and then look for its outworking in their lives, households and church oversight *(1 Tim. 3:1-13; Mt. 7:15-20)*. If they be found faithful, we can then be assured that our souls are safe under their care.

"But thou hast fully known my doctrine, manner of life, purpose, faith, longsuffering, charity, patience." 2 Timothy 3:10

If not, we are to avoid them like the plague *(1 Tim. 6:3-5)*.

"Now I beseech you, brethren, mark them which cause divisions and offences contrary to the doctrine which ye have learned; and avoid them. For they that are such serve not our

Lord Jesus Christ, but their own belly; and by good words and fair speeches deceive the hearts of the simple." Romans 16:17-18

"I know thy works, and thy labour, and thy patience, and how thou canst not bear them which are evil: and thou hast tried them which say they are apostles, and are not, and hast found them liars." Revelation 2:2

Vain glory is one thing and bona fide godly esteem working in tandem with reverence for the Lord is quite another. Never are our leaders to teach others "*to think of men above that which is written*" *(1 Cor. 4:6; 2 Cor. 12:6)*; but always they are to uphold the honor of God by commanding respect for His Presence and the operation of His Spirit when He ministers through them.

"These things speak, and exhort, and rebuke with all authority. Let no man despise thee." Titus 2:15

...And not through their lives only, but also through fellow believers, of whatever stature or level of maturity they may be.

"How is it then, brethren? When ye come together, every one of you hath a psalm, hath a doctrine, hath a tongue, hath a revelation, hath an interpretation. Let all things be done unto edifying." 1 Corinthians 14:26

Rescued

Broken at the Cross, my rebellion was changed into surrender. The evil thoughts towards my husband were replaced by meditations of appreciation for his shepherding and remorse over my stumbling. There we were again, with our love intact, yet more firmly bonded than ever by the blood of the Lamb and the outworking of His Cross. Once repentance was restored, I no longer opposed my own greater good and Edwin's guidance turned from heartache to sheer delight.

"Obey them that have the rule over you, and submit yourselves: for they watch for your souls, as they that must give account, that they may do it with joy, and not with grief: for that is unprofitable for you."   Hebrews 13:17

Oh, brethren, God is good!

"And the servant of the Lord must not strive; but be gentle unto all men, apt to teach, patient, in meekness instructing those that oppose themselves; if God peradventure will give them repentance to the acknowledging of the truth; and that they may recover themselves out of the snare of the devil, who are taken captive by him at his will."   2 Timothy 2:24-26

Back in the Saddle

The next day resolve was in full swing. A divided heart when it comes to difficult steps of obedience only serves to prolong chastisement and amplify pain. After prayer, we were ready to proceed with Faith-step One: Squeeze into the new shoes. Step Two: Shout a big *"thank you"* unto the Lord for His wonderful care and provision, refusing the temptation to murmur or act like a martyr.

"I will bless the LORD at all times: His praise shall continually be in my mouth."   Psalms 34:1

I did a little tap dance in demonstration of my acceptance of the Lord's promise of succoring and good health. ...Did my feet hurt? Yes, *"mucho"*! Did it matter? *"No!"* I was suffering the tough side of our gracious (but greatly to be feared) Heavenly Father's normally tender hands. Dare I complain?

"Wherefore doth a living man complain, a man for the punishment of his sins? Let us search and try our ways, and turn again to the LORD."   Lamentations 3:39-40

"Behold therefore the goodness and severity of God: on them which fell, severity; but toward thee, goodness, if thou continue in his goodness: otherwise thou also shalt be cut off."
                    Romans 11:22

Consider what others have suffered (and still suffer) in their race for the crown (not as a reaping of sin, as was I) but honorably, for Christ's name sake and the glory of God.

"For this is thankworthy, if a man for conscience toward God endure grief, suffering wrongfully. For what glory is it, if, when ye be buffeted for your faults, ye shall take it patiently? but if, when ye do well, and suffer for it, ye take it patiently, this is acceptable with God. For even hereunto were ye called: because Christ also suffered for us, leaving us an example, that ye should follow his steps."   1 Peter 2:19-21

Suffering is a necessary and beautiful part of change.

"Before I was afflicted I went astray: but now have I kept thy word."   Psalms 119:67

". . . We glory in tribulations also: knowing that tribulation worketh patience; and patience, experience; and experience, hope: and hope maketh not ashamed . . ."   Romans 5:3-5a

It is God's chosen means for crucifying our sins; and at its end, if we hold our faith *(Heb. 3:6, 14)*, lies greater intimacy with Jesus and the *"salvation of our souls" (1 Pe. 1:9)*.

"That I may know him, and the power of his resurrection, and the fellowship of his sufferings . . ."   Philippians 3:10a

"Forasmuch then as Christ hath suffered for us in the flesh, arm yourselves likewise with the same mind: for he that hath suffered in the flesh hath ceased from sin; that he no longer should live the rest of his time in the flesh to the lusts of men, but to the will of God."   1 Peter 4:1-2

Healed from the Inside, Out

Nothing mattered at that time other than the reality that Apostle Edwin and I were side-by-side moving in faith; ready for the water to turn to wine; our empty nets to burst; our twelve baskets of leftover bread *(Jn. 2:6-11; Lk. 5:4-9; Mt. 14:13-21)*. The "*King of Glory*" was with us and we were with Him *(Ps. 24:7-10)*. The sun and the moon were standing still *(Jos. 10:12-14)*. We were like Peter after Christ's resurrection when he and a handful of others caught a multitude of fishes at the word of a mystery man on the shoreline. Once he realized it was Jesus, his miracle took a "back seat." Overcome with joy, he "*cast himself into the sea*" and made a "beeline" to his Saviour *(Jn. 21:7)*.

That night my toes oozed with puss. Was I in "*I told you so*" mode? "*No!*" The haughty crown of pride that used to adorn my persona was coming off and making way for the "*ornament of a meek and quiet spirit, which is in the sight of God of great price*" *(1 Pe. 3:4)*. Patience was having her "*perfect work*" *(Jam. 1:4)*. God was changing my heart. Faith was getting the upper hand. The "*power of the Lord was present to heal*" me, once again, from the inside, out *(Lk. 5:17)*!

My recovery from that ordeal was truly remarkable. Without any medication, the fungus stopped its climb from my toes to the top of my ankles and began dissipating instead, until it disappeared altogether. My left leg returned to normal. My toenails dried up, came off and grew brand new. But most importantly, I was becoming the woman of faith and surrender God created me to be. Thank you Jesus! By Your stripes, we are healed *(1 Pe. 2:24)*.

A passage from Job that the Holy Spirit plucked from the Bible and planted in my heart in the heat of the trial came to fruition. My skin cleared. My disposition changed ...And in no uncertain terms I was brought back "*from the pit.*"

"His flesh shall be fresher than a child's: he shall return to the days of his youth: he shall pray unto God, and He will be favourable unto him: and he shall see his face with joy: for he will render unto man his righteousness. He looketh upon men, and if any say, I have sinned, and perverted that which was right, and it profited me not; he will deliver his soul from going into the pit, and his life shall see the light. Lo, all these things worketh God oftentimes with man, to bring back his soul from the pit, to be enlightened with the light of the living."

Job 33:25-30

CHAPTER TWENTY-ONE

He Teacheth My Hands
to War & My Fingers to Fight

Fast forward. Back to the present storyline — the *"Strange Outbreak"* that launched this book. ...Onward we marched in our epistle to the saints in Zimbabwe. We were like the Jews in the aftermath of their Babylonian captivity when rebuilding the walls of Jerusalem: one hand *"wrought in the work"* and the other *"held a weapon" (Neh. 4:17)*. It was war on the foreign field helping our brethren to walk out their trial; and war on the home front in our personal lives. Decked in full military regalia, Satan and the armies of hell were vaunting themselves *(Eph. 6:10-12)*. They were like Sanballat and Tobiah, the Jews' enemies, working overtime to sabotage our efforts to restore the broken link uniting faith with repentance *(Neh. 4:1-8)*; the divine connection that binds God's promises to their Covenant conditions.

Fearful thoughts kept ambushing me, even after I had initiated a no compromise initiative against them. I had all those years of victory behind me. ...One miraculous healing after another. Yet there I was back on the battlefield challenged, again. ...And when any of the darts found their way into a crack in my armor I got stung with dreadful feelings of despair and abandonment.

It was at that time that the Holy Spirit tossed me a lifeline. It dropped from heaven in the form of two great big question marks.

Number One:

How much of this is springing out of my own imagination?

"For from within, out of the heart of men, proceed evil thoughts."   Mark 7:21a

...And, Number Two:

How much of it is nothing but sheer flack from the devil, harassing me and blaspheming God?

"And he opened his mouth in blasphemy against God, to blaspheme his name, and his tabernacle, and them that dwell in heaven. And it was given unto him to make war with the saints . . ." Revelation 13:6-7a

Next, I was reminded of an autobiography that I read when Apostle Edwin and I were trying to help a sister break free from opiate addiction. The author, having been a prescription drug addict herself, shared about the dark thoughts of suicide she suffered when taking her so called "*medications*." They also popped up during the season of withdrawals she underwent once she made the choice to seek freedom from their tyrannical grip. All kinds of bizarre hallucinations and impulses inclining her heart to suicide surfaced. Finally she "put two and two together" realizing that something outside of herself was activating the barrage.

I in no wise wanted to divorce myself from responsibility by taking a "*the devil made me do it*" type posture. That kind of defense doesn't hold up before the Judgment Seat of Christ. Plus, self-deception is not the route to liberty. It only belabors our struggles and sets us up for more severe dealings. Yet conversely, I didn't want to be a fool in the devil's hand (2 Cor. 2:11; 11:3; Eph. 6:12).

Distinguishing Between Self & Satan

The Lord answered my cry in an especially precious way. I hadn't even "formally" addressed my enquiry to Him. Yet there He was with my answer in black and white. Glorious!

"And it shall come to pass, that before they call, I will answer; and while they are yet speaking, I will hear." Isaiah 65:24

Tokens like that are an indescribable encouragement! The same great Great God (so high and lifted up!), and so "near-and-dear" to the faithful amongst my forefathers, actually bowed the heavens (so to speak) so as to put that line of questioning in my heart. Thank you Jesus!

"Blessed be the LORD God of our fathers, which hath put such a thing as this in the king's heart . . ."   Ezra 7:27a

Detectives for Christ

I picked up *The Christian in Complete Armour* and the page opened to a list of three interrogations for deciphering between self and Satan. The issue Gurnall calls to judgment is whether or not we have a *"sincere"* or *"hypocritical"* and divided heart.

Test One: What is our *"comportment and behavior"* when the arrows fly?

What friendly welcome have such thoughts . . .?[1]

Good question.

Are these the guests thou hast welcomed and trimmed thy room for? Didst thou go to duty to meet those friends, or do they unmannerly break in upon thee, and forcibly carry thee—as Christ foretold of Peter in another case—whither thou wouldest not? If so, why shouldst thou bring they sincerity into dispute?. . . Suppose . . . as you are kneeling down to prayer, a company of roisters [revelers] should stand under your window, and all the while you are praying, they should be roaring and hallooing . . . ? Would you from the disturbance they make . . . question your sincerity in . . . duty?[2]

Test Two: How do we respond once they barge in?

Dost thou sit contented with this company, or use all the means thou canst to get rid of them, as soon as may be?

Sincerity cannot sit still to see such doings in the soul; but, as a faithful servant when thieves break into his master's house, though [so] overpowered with their strength and multitude, that he cannot with his own hands thrust them out of doors, yet he will send out secretly for help, and raise the town upon them. Prayer is the sincere soul's messenger. It posts to heaven with full speed . . . counting itself to be no other than in the belly of hell with Jonah, while it is yoked to such thoughts, and as glad when aid comes to rescue him out of their hands, as Lot was when Abraham recovered him from the kings that had carried him away prisoner.[3]

After examining my thoughts in light of those two tests, the clouds of condemnation began rolling back. The thoughts hounding me were not welcome in the least. I had no affinity or affection for them; and when they paraded across my mind, I wasn't docile, but fought back. Admittedly, however, I suffered the temptation to entertain them and waned in my resistance, at times. But overall, I longed for freedom.

Magnificent Purposes

...*Still*, however, I was bothered by concerns about my own culpability.

Lord, is there a doorway of sin not yet disclosed to me through which the enemy is entering? If, indeed, my heart is right with You, and You have received my plea for deliverance, why are the sores still present on my ear and neck? And, why are the missiles of fear still bombarding me with such intensity?

Impatience was getting the upper hand and opening my ear to the "*doubtful disputations*" of Bildad, one of Job's chief accusers.

"If thou wert pure and upright; surely *now* he would awake for thee, and make the habitation of thy righteousness prosperous."

Job 8:6

The devil's cunning insertion of the word "*now*" into this wise man's otherwise skillful rehearsal of God's Law of Righteous Judgment had my conscience all tangled up. Who can expect good from God, if his heart is not upright in His sight?

> Holy Job proves that he is not a hypocrite, as his friends uncharitably charged him, by this confidence he had on God in the depth of all his afflictions. Job xiii. 15, 16 [Job 13:15, 16]. 'Though he slay me, yet will I trust in him. I will maintain my ways before him. He also shall be my salvation: for a hypocrite shall not come before him.' As if he had said. If I were not sincere, I durst not appeal thus to God, and comfortably believe . . . he would yet save me: 'for a hypocrite shall not come before Him;' that is . . . he would never come in his sight. His conscience tells him, God knows him too well to intend him any good.[4]

"For if our heart condemn us, God is greater than our heart, and knoweth all things."   1 John 3:20

But once again, the Lord rescued me from falling prey to the devil's exploitation of the troubling of my conscience; this time by virtue of Gurnall's third interrogatory.

Test Three: Could there be multiple purposes for this trial?

In it he addressed our Heavenly Father's wonderful purposes (from time to time) for allowing our trials to wax on. Edwin has preached End-Time refinement and faith-building ever since I've known him, and we've walked in it together. Yet, it was so refreshing for us to have the very same message plainly confirmed to us through the pen of another. No doubt about it: William Gurnall was a friend of the Cross.

> He [the Lord] doth not by . . . [the long continuance of the trial] show thee to be a hypocrite, but gives thee a fair advantage of proving thyself sincere — not much unlike

his dealing with the Israelites, before whom he did not, as they expected, hastily drive out the nations, but left them as thorns in their sides. And why? Hear the reason from God's own mouth, 'That through them I may prove Israel, whether they will keep the way of the Lord to walk therein, as their fathers did keep it, or not,' Ju. ii:22 [Ju. 2:22]. Thus God leaves these corruptions in thee, to prove whether thou wilt fall in and be friends with them, or maintain the conflict with them, and continue praying against them; by which perseverance thou wilt prove thyself to be indeed upright. A false heart will never do this. . . . Observe therefore the behaviour of thy heart in prayer, and judge thyself sincere, or not sincere, by that, not by the present success it hath.[5]

Something "clicked." Another piece of the puzzle fell into place. I was being proven again (as we shall be till the end), like all of God's people, from the foundations of the world.

"For Thou, O God, hast proved us: thou hast tried us, as silver is tried."   Psalms 66:10

"Yea, the whole volume of holy Scriptures seems to be nothing else," but testimonials of the *"conflicts and triumphs"* of the Lord's overcomers: believers whose hearts were made pure (and whose faith was made sure) in the fiery furnace of affliction. [6]

. . . If God send thee to the sea and promise to go with thee and to bring thee safe to land, he will raise up a tempest against thee, to prove whether thou wilt abide by his word, and that thou mayest feel thy faith [personally experience its outworking] and perceive his goodness, for if it were always fair weather and thou never brought into such jeopardy whence His mercy only delivered thee, thy faith should be but a presumption . . .[7]

Plus, in a deeper way, I was being taught on the battlefield how to distinguish between Holy Spirit conviction and the castigations and accusations of the devil—an indispensible lesson that no Christian conqueror can do without.

> If the devil wants to reach that sense of sin which lies upon our conscience, so does the Holy Spirit. But how differently He works! . . . While Satan accuses only to bring despair, bondage and striving, the Holy Spirit convicts . . . to bring comfort, freedom and rest. . . . He takes . . . [our] sin, and us with it, to Calvary, to Jesus our door. There He shows us that that sin, and much else, was anticipated and settled by the Lord Jesus in His death upon the cross. . . . The worst that the devil can ever say about us is not comparable to the dark depths of sin that swept over Jesus on the cross. There the most self-condemned one [that is genuinely penitent] finds nothing but forgiveness, cleansing and comfort [unless such an one has gone so far as to blaspheme the Holy Ghost—Mt. 12:31-32]. The fact, then, that we are the sinners we are—of which the devil loves to accuse us—is only a half-truth. The other half of the truth is that Jesus died for us and did a complete work for us [that we could be set free, if we repent, amend our ways and follow His path to liberty]. That is something the devil never tells us. Only the gentle Holy Spirit tells us that![8]

The Breastplate of Righteousness

This was a priceless blessing. I was learning anew the secret to the endurance of Job; a penitent man approved of God as *"perfect"* and *"upright,"* though assailed by the devil and engulfed by manifold afflictions that stood in contradiction to that imprimatur.

"And the LORD said unto Satan, Hast thou considered My servant Job, that there is none like him in the earth, a perfect and an upright man, one that feareth God, and escheweth evil?"

Job 1:8

God used this giant of our faith to show us what it looks like under trial to walk in a spirit of repentance, while at the same time fending off unwarranted condemnation. ...So zealous for righteousness was he, that even amidst the most excruciating losses and vetting imaginable, he still had the courage and confidence to cry out:

".. . Let come on me what will." Job 13:13

I shudder! And Job is not the only one that chose that degree of threshing. So did King David, another one of our Lord's most valiant overcomers: truly *"a man after . . . [God's] own heart"* *(Acts 13:22).*

"O LORD my God, If I have done this; if there be iniquity in my hands; if I have rewarded evil unto him that was at peace with me; (yea, I have delivered him that without cause is mine enemy:) let the enemy persecute my soul, and take it; yea, let him tread down my life upon the earth, and lay mine honour in the dust. Selah."   Psalm 7:3-5

...And so did Paul.

"But in all things approving ourselves as the ministers of God, in much patience, in afflictions, in necessities, in distresses, in stripes, in imprisonments, in tumults, in labours, in watchings, in fastings; by pureness, by knowledge, by longsuffering, by kindness, by the Holy Ghost, by love unfeigned, by the word of truth, by the power of God, by the armour of righteousness on the right hand and on the left, by honour and dishonour, by evil report and good report: as deceivers, and yet true; as unknown, and yet well known; as dying, and, behold, we live; as chastened, and not killed; as sorrowful, yet alway rejoicing; as poor, yet making many rich; as having nothing, and yet possessing all things."   2 Corinthians 6:4-10

These God-fearing men would rather have their sins show up in the "here and now" so they could repent and amend while there was yet time, than to suffer the eternal consequence of exposure at the day of the Lord's judgment when nothing more can be done.

> For whatever remains unjudged now will come up before Him in that day.[9]

"And as it is appointed unto men once to die, but after this the judgment." Hebrews 9:27

Here is Job acknowledging his corruption and seeking holiness at the altar:

"Behold, I am vile. . . . Wherefore I abhor myself, and repent in dust and ashes." Job 40:4a; 42:6

"How many are mine iniquities and sins? make me to know my transgression and my sin." Job 13:23

And here he is, defending his uprightness in God's sight; letting "*no man,*" no, not spouse nor friend, (not even the devil himself!), steal his "*crown*" *(Rev. 3:11; Job 2:3b).*

"God forbid that I should justify you: till I die I will not remove mine integrity from me. My righteousness I hold fast, and will not let it go: my heart shall not reproach me so long as I live." Job 27:5-6

Emboldened by a clear conscience "*sprinkled*" in blood *(Heb. 10:22),* and determined (come what may!) to do his utmost to maintain a righteous life in the eyes of his Creator *(Job 1:5; 23:11-12),* this "*just*" man patiently and penitently endured the proving process until the day of his vindication was come and his faith in God was proven true *(Job 42:7-17; Heb. 12:22-24).*

"Behold now, I have ordered my cause; I know that I shall be justified." Job 13:18

"And the LORD turned the captivity of Job, when he prayed for his friends: also the LORD gave Job twice as much as he had before. Then came there unto him all his brethren, and all his sisters, and all they that had been of his acquaintance before, and did eat bread with him in his house: and they bemoaned him, and comforted him over all the evil that the LORD had brought upon him: every man also gave him a piece of money, and every one an earring of gold. So the LORD blessed the latter end of Job more than his beginning . . ."   Job 42:10-12a

...And by God's grace, he did it with a hopeful eye towards personal sanctification; and both ears tuned to the Last Trump, when "*the dead shall be raised incorruptible, and we shall be changed*" *(1 Cor. 15:52b).*

"But he knoweth the way that I take: when He hath tried me, I shall come forth as gold."   Job 23:10

"For I know that my redeemer liveth, and that He shall stand at the latter day upon the earth: and though after my skin worms destroy this body, yet in my flesh shall I see God: whom I shall see for myself, and mine eyes shall behold, and not another; though my reins be consumed within me."   Job 19:25-26

"Proving" My Armour—1 Samuel 17:39

This was advanced "field training" in the purpose and proper usage of the "*breastplate of righteousness*"; the primary piece of armour given to us, as Christian soldiers, for the preservation and defense of our spiritual "*vitals*"; namely, the heart and conscience *(Eph. 6:10-18).*

"Stand therefore, having your loins girt about with truth, and having on the breastplate of righteousness."   Ephesians 6:14

The breastplate preserves the most principal part of the body, and that is the breast, where the very vitals of man are closely couched together, and where a shot and stab is more deadly than in other parts that are remote from the fountain of life. A man may outlive many wounds received in the arms or legs, but a stab in the heart or other vital parts is the certain messenger of death approaching. Thus righteousness and holiness preserve the principal part of a Christian, his soul and conscience; we live or die spiritually, yea, eternally, as we look to our souls and consciences.[10]

"Consider mine enemies; for they are many; and they hate me with cruel hatred. O keep my soul, and deliver me: let me not be ashamed; for I put my trust in thee. Let integrity and uprightness preserve me; for I wait on thee."   Psalm 25:19-21

In a very precious way, the Lord of Hosts was "schooling" me in the finer points of spiritual warfare, so that I (in turn) could minister more effectively with my husband by drawing from the wells of our own personal combat.

God hath a design in [allowing] . . . Satan to trounce some of his saints by temptation, to train them up into a fitness to succour their fellow-brethren in the like condition: he sends them hither to school, (where they are under Satan's . . . lash,) that his cruel hand over them may make them study the word and their own hearts, by which they get experience of Satan's policies [devices], till at last they commence masters in this art of comforting tempted souls.[11]

"Blessed be the LORD my strength which teacheth my hands to war, and my fingers to fight."   Psalms 144:1

If this fundamental piece of armour be compromised by our own breach of Covenant and failure to respond in thorough repentance; or, by the blindness of our hearts to the operation of sin at work in our lives; or, by our unwitting acceptance of the enemy's castigations and relentless efforts to convince us that his wicked thoughts are our own (and that the charges he brings against us are valid); then we are robbed of our confidence with God, and subject to "fits" of faint-heartedness and defeat on the battlefield (Ps. 40:12; Lam. 5:16-17).

. . . A naked breast exposeth the unarmed soldier to a trembling heart, whereas one, otherwise cowardly, having his breast defended with a plate of proof, will more boldly venture upon the pikes. Thus righteousness, by defending the conscience, fills the creature with courage in the face of death and danger; whereas guilt, which is the nakedness of the soul, puts the stoutest sinner into a shaking fit of fear.[12]

"The wicked flee when no man pursueth: but the righteous are bold as a lion."   Proverbs 28:1

If our conscience be *"void of offence toward God, and toward men"* by virtue of ongoing soul searching and repentance *(Acts 24:16)*; and thereby cleansed and covered by the blood of Jesus; THEN our confidence in God is sure and our faith soars.

"And hereby we know that we are of the Truth, and shall assure our hearts before him. . . . Beloved, if our heart condemn us not, then have we confidence toward God. And whatsoever we ask, we receive of him, because we keep his commandments, and do those things that are pleasing in His sight."   1 John 3:19, 21-22

We are "suited up," not in a coat of arms crafted by man's device, but in the *"armour of light"* which puts us beyond the devil's shot *(Rom. 13:12)*. ...Not that our bodies are promised to be spared amidst persecution; but rather, that our spirits and souls are in the Lord's safe keeping *(Mt. 10:28-31)*.

. . . If the heart is cleansed by the love of Jesus Christ, and if the heart loves Him, one can resist all tortures.[13]

"The night is far spent, the day is at hand: let us therefore cast off the works of darkness, and let us put on the armour of light. Let us walk honestly . . ."   Romans 13:12-13a

"O GOD the Lord, the strength of my salvation, thou hast covered my head in the day of battle."   Psalms 140:7

In this posture of right standing we "know that we know" that God is on our side, no matter how severe the testing.

"When I cry unto thee, then shall mine enemies turn back: this I know; for God is for me."   Psalms 56:9

"For the Lord GOD will help me; therefore shall I not be confounded: therefore have I set my face like a flint, and I know that I shall not be ashamed. He is near that justifieth me; who will contend with me? let us stand together: who is mine adversary? let him come near to me. Behold, the Lord GOD will help me; who is he that shall condemn me?"   Isaiah 50:7-9a

It is this coveted assurance that we all need in order to be overcomers in these Last Days (and always). It turns ordinary soldiers into conquerors when in the throes of affliction, enabling them to "*run*" with David through whatever "*troop*" of accusations the devil sends, and come out safely with Job on the other side of the gauntlet "wearing" the reproach with dignity *(2 Sam. 22:30)*.

"Oh that one would hear me! . . . and that mine adversary had written a book. Surely I would take it upon my shoulder, and bind it as a crown to me."   Job 31:35- 36

...Yea, with honor, like Jesus when He was crowned in thorns *(Mt. 27:28-31)*.

"If ye be reproached for the name of Christ, happy are ye; for the spirit of glory and of God resteth upon you: on their part he is evil spoken of, but on your part he is glorified. But let none of you suffer as a murderer, or as a thief, or as an evildoer, or as a busybody in other men's matters. Yet if any man suffer as a Christian, let him not be ashamed; but let him glorify God on this behalf."   1 Peter 4:14-16

...Oh to be counted (along with the martyrs and others) in that blood washed army of penitents *(Rev. 7:13-17; 12:11)*!

I care not what my haters say, so free my conscience is.[14]

"And I heard a loud voice saying in heaven, Now is come salvation, and strength, and the kingdom of our God, and the power of his Christ: for the accuser of our brethren is cast down, which accused them before our God day and night."

Revelation 12:10

...Men and women of faith, abiding in the atonement and ready to defend their "ground" in Christ with the tenacity of David's "mighties" when challenged by the devil. ...Soldiers of the Cross so zealous for victory that they can "go it alone" (if need be) and *"fight the good fight of faith"* till the very "swords" that they hold (metaphorically speaking) *"cleave"* to the palms of their hands.

"And after him was Eleazar the son of Dodo the Ahohite, one of the three mighty men with David, when they defied the Philistines that were there gathered together to battle, and the men of Israel were gone away: he arose, and smote the Philistines until his hand was weary, and his hand clave unto the sword: and the LORD wrought a great victory that day; and the people returned after him only to spoil. And after him was Shammah the son of Agee the Hararite. And the Philistines were gathered together into a troop, where was a piece of ground full of lentiles: and the people fled from the Philistines. But he stood in the midst of the ground, and defended it, and slew the Philistines: and the LORD wrought a great victory."

2 Samuel 23:9-12

...So free and clear in conscience that we, with Paul (if it be God's engineering), can take our case with all boldness to the highest court in the land.

"Then said Paul, I stand at Caesar's judgment seat, where I ought to be judged: to the Jews have I done no wrong, as thou very well knowest. For if I be an offender, or have committed any thing worthy of death, I refuse not to die: but if there be none of these things whereof these accuse me, no man may deliver me unto them. I appeal unto Caesar." Acts 25:10-11

Yea, higher still: To the Judgment Seat of Christ. Not because we are defending the "*old man*" who must at all costs be acknowledged as corrupt and reckoned "*dead*" *(Eph. 4:22; Rom. 6:11)*. Nor, because we are depending on our own righteousness to deliver us *(Tit. 3:5)*. God forbid! But rather, because our faith is rightly placed in the righteousness of the One under whose blood we (by virtue of ongoing repentance and amendment) have chosen to stand *(Rom. 14:4)*.

"Who shall lay any thing to the charge of God's elect? It is God that justifieth. Who is he that condemneth? It is Christ that died, yea rather, that is risen again, who is even at the right hand of God, who also maketh intercession for us."

Romans 8:33-34

A Chink in My Breastplate

Inspired by what I read, I reached out to Edwin and acknowledged my urgent need to be covered by this "*armour of righteousness,*" free from personal bias and/or blindness in regards to my actual soul state *(2 Cor. 6:7; Rom. 13:12)*.

"He that trusteth in his own heart is a fool: but whoso walketh wisely, he shall be delivered." Proverbs 28:26

Sin has a power that blinds us to its nature and workings; this is what makes sin so deceptive. This answers why we so easily overlook our own sin and call it something else by giving it a more respectable label. . . . If it were not for the crucified Christ, the assessment of our own morality and sin would always be favorable. In other words, we will always pronounce a sentence lighter than what is deserved. We will always justify ourselves when we are our own judges. We will make our own assessments of our condition. We will rationalize and dismiss the case against ourselves. We will always give a self-flattering subjective evaluation."[15]

I was desperately hungering for righteousness; for authentic peace with God; not a projection of my own imagination which amounted to little more than relief from conflict and deliverance from suffering; but rather, the real thing; an uncondemned conscience and 100% confidence and steadfast belief in the reconciliation wrought through my Saviour's redeeming blood *(Eph. 1:6-7)*. I also yearned for my place amidst His God-fearing Remnant of penitents under the shadow of His healing wings.

"For, behold, the day cometh, that shall burn as an oven; and all the proud, yea, and all that do wickedly, shall be stubble: and the day that cometh shall burn them up, saith the LORD of hosts, that it shall leave them neither root nor branch. But unto you that fear my name shall the Sun of righteousness arise with healing in his wings; and ye shall go forth, and grow up as calves of the stall."   Malachi 4:1-2

With my husband's help, I then submitted my life afresh to the Holy Spirit for examination and as we did an old wound came into view. Hallelujah! The lights came on! It was the chink in my protective gear through which the enemy, time and again, has accessed my life, eroding my faith, and causing such havoc in my soul. Praise God! Jesus Christ is the Light of the world!

"For thou wilt light my candle: the LORD my God will enlighten my darkness."   Psalms 18:28

CHAPTER TWENTY-TWO

Flashback

A t the age of eleven I lost my mother to cancer. It was one of the most traumatic experiences of my youth, second only to the divorce of my parents when I was three. I still get a pang of remorse when I am reminded of the day my dad came home and I jumped into his arms, saying: *"Guess what, I'm getting a new daddy!"* I had no idea I was plunging a knife into his heart. Apparently my mother thought it would buffer the impact of the news if she presented the rending of their marriage as a "good thing." I wish I could take back those words.

Anyhow, hard as I tried, I could not figure out how my parents could so deeply care for my brother and I and yet no longer love one another? Everlasting faithfulness is the very essence of God, yet the two people on the planet that I most revered bore witness by their lives to a complete repudiation of that reality. My brother and I learned to get along. Couldn't they? Not sure, but I think the seeds of rebellion and unbelief that took hold in my life may be tied directly to that root. I just couldn't accept divorce. There was something wrong in the universe that needed fixing. We were a family! It just couldn't be true that love stops being love ...packs up ...and goes away.

Grandpa, tell me 'bout the good old days . . .
Did families really bow their heads and pray
Did daddies really never go away?[1]

When I got older my brother and I would spend weekends with my dad and his new wife in their home. It had one of those sunken living rooms, but it hadn't yet been fully furnished, so the only thing in it was a wooden stereo console with really big speakers. I'd go in there, plop down on the carpet, pull out our Glen Campbell 33 record album, turn up the volume and listen to him wailing lyrics about a father breaking the news to his kids about divorce while I cried. Can't recollect the whole song, but I do remember, somewhat, lines like: *"Sometimes things happen that we just can't foresee"* and: *"Your mama is stayin', but I'm goin' away."* [2]

Thank God for using my own marriage to show me a *"more excellent way" (1 Cor. 12:31)*. It can be summed up in three words snugged up side-by-side: *"Charity never faileth" (1 Cor. 13:8)*. The love of God is eternal. Here's another more up-to-date lyric that really captures what I'm trying to express. It has always resonated with Apostle Edwin and I.

So what's the glory in living?
Doesn't anybody ever stay together anymore?
And if love never lasts forever
Tell me, what's forever for? [3]

All of our controversies with one another start with a breakdown in our relationship with the Lord. If two believers get it right with Him (and keep it right through daily repentance), then breaches as wide as the deep blue sea can be healed forever. God's love conquers all Divorce was never His plan. It was only an "afterthought" for coping with the fallen nature of man.

"And the Pharisees came to him, and asked him, Is it lawful for a man to put away his wife? tempting him. And he answered and said unto them, What did Moses command you? And they said, Moses suffered to write a bill of divorcement, and to put her away. And Jesus answered and said unto them, For the hardness of your heart he wrote you this precept. But from the beginning of the creation God made them male and female. For this cause shall a man leave his father and mother, and cleave to his wife; and they twain shall be one flesh: so then they are no more twain, but one flesh. What therefore God hath joined together, let not man put asunder."   Mark 10:2-9

Unbelief: Stamped On My Soul

My mother was the "wind beneath my wings," so to speak, and very involved in just about every aspect of my life. I'll never forget the last time I saw her alive wearing a pink silky house vest overlaid with lace. I was eleven years old. She was propped up in a hospital bed trying to look well by putting on her best smile; all the while crying through the helpless look in her eyes. Bewildered and broken, the next time I saw her was at a viewing in our home where she lay in repose in an open casket while family and friends passed by paying their final respects. I couldn't seem to register what was going on. Her body was there but her loving spirit was gone. Inside her casket I placed a piece of pottery that I had made for her at school and a note that read: *"Everybody Loves You, Especially Me."*

Oh how I regretted the times that I struck out at her when I didn't get my way. Now there was no chance of letting her know how much I loved her; that I missed her terribly; and that I didn't really mean any of the hateful things I said to her over the years. I whispered it in her ear, but could she hear? *"Please, please, don't close the casket and lock her inside all alone."*

The imprint such a loss stamped on my soul was one of 100% UNBELIEF. It was one of utter helplessness in the face of an overwhelming evil from which there was no hope of escape. It was abrupt separation from someone I deeply loved and relied upon for counsel and confidence. I do not recall any prayers being lifted in her behalf by family members, or in a temple setting, throughout the term of her illness. Perhaps they were and I just don't remember? If so, they left no impression whatsoever. What I do remember is this: the look in my step-father's normally stoic steel grey eyes. They were swimming in two puddles of tears and looked as vacant ...as quizzical ...and as despondent as mine.

Where was God? ...If there was a God? Or, did I even think of God? No one pointed me to the Lord Jesus or spoke plainly to me from the entire volume of Old Testament Scripture on the issues of eternity. Why? Because we, as a people, couldn't see the treasure concealed in its pages: Yeshua Ha'Mashiach; God's unspeakable Gift of Eternal Life to our people *"first"* and then to the world at large.

"Ye are the children of the prophets, and of the covenant which God made with our fathers, saying unto Abraham, And in thy seed shall all the kindreds of the earth be blessed. Unto you first God, having raised up his Son Jesus, sent him to bless you, in turning away every one of you from his iniquities."

Acts 3:25-26

We did not understand the reasons for the curses that were following us, either; namely our lack of conformity to the entire writ of Mosaic Law; and our corporate rejection of our Messiah.

"Cursed be he that confirmeth not all the words of this law to do them. And all the people shall say, Amen."

Deuteronomy 27:26

"Pilate saith unto them, What shall I do then with Jesus which is called Christ? They all say unto him, Let him be crucified. And the governor said, Why, what evil hath he done? But they cried out the more, saying, Let him be crucified. When Pilate saw that he could prevail nothing, but that rather a tumult was made, he took water, and washed his hands before the multitude, saying, I am innocent of the blood of this just person: see ye to it. Then answered all the people, and said, *his blood be on us, and on our children.*" Matthew 27:22-25

The Chosen People

Throughout the years of my rearing I often heard that we were *"God's chosen people."* But the big question was: *"chosen"* for what???

"For thou art an holy people unto the LORD thy God: the LORD thy God hath chosen thee to be a special people unto himself, above all people that are upon the face of the earth."

Deuteronomy 7:6

Yes, we were given the Holy Land, the Law and the promises *(Rom. 3:1-2)*; and it was through our lineage that Messiah was prophesied to come *(Rom. 9:4-5)*. But why all the sickness; the antisemitism; and above all else, the Holocaust?

Plain and simple: We had lost our Biblical lodestar and had settled in our quest for excellence for a worldly alternative; putting our priority on secular education, the arts, entertainment, science, sports, wealth and a thousand other pursuits, rather than maintaining our original God-given calling to be a *"Light to the Gentiles,"* that they too, might learn to *"set their hope in God" (Isa. 49:6; Acts 13:47; Ps. 78:7)*. Sadly, much of today's church has fallen from a similar perch.

> . . . As soon as a little breathing time set in, they again began to lean towards the world; the parents became rich, the children luxurious and wanton; the world caressed them, and in course of time they became respected and lifted up; the reproach of the cross was relinquished, and the honor of this world stepped into its place.[4]

Plus, we failed to connect the dots — not realizing that being a *"chosen"* people also meant being an "accountable" people; for divine love is not sealed unto salvation, unless it is both received and reciprocated by obedience to the One who first loved us *(1 Jn. 4:10)*.

". . . For unto whomsoever much is given, of him shall be much required . . ."   Luke 12:48

"He that hath my commandments, and keepeth them, he it is that loveth me . . . . He that loveth me not keepeth not my sayings . . ."   John 14:21a, 24a

In other words, the favor we had been given was not a "freebie." Receipt of it was conditioned upon our conformity to the terms of a Covenant so sacred that it was given by the *"disposition of angels"* and sealed in blood *(Acts 7:53)*.

"For when Moses had spoken every precept to all the people according to the law, he took the blood of calves and of goats, with water, and scarlet wool, and hyssop, and sprinkled both the book, and all the people, saying, This is the blood of the testament which God hath enjoined unto you."

Hebrews 9:19-20

Blessings and Curses

As soon as our forefathers agreed to the Covenant, they entered into a blessing if they kept it and a curse if they did not; implicating not only themselves, but also us, as their posterity.

"And Moses took half of the blood, and put it in basons; and half of the blood he sprinkled on the altar. And he took the book of the covenant, and read in the audience of the people: and they said, All that the LORD hath said will we do, and be obedient. And Moses took the blood, and sprinkled it on the people, and said, Behold the blood of the covenant, which the LORD hath made with you concerning all these words."

Exodus 24:6-8

"Neither with you only do I make this covenant and this oath; but with him that standeth here with us this day before the LORD our God, and also with him that is not here with us this day."   Deuteronomy 29:14-15

The word "favor" does not even come close to describing the surpassing goodness the God of our fathers had in store for us. If we kept the Covenant made at Sinai and confirmed again at Moab, we would be the most blessed people in the world — invincible among the nations and completely disease free.

"No weapon that is formed against thee shall prosper; and every tongue that shall rise against thee in judgment thou shalt condemn . . ."   Isaiah 54:17a; See also Deuteronomy 11:25

"Wherefore it shall come to pass, if ye hearken to these judgments, and keep, and do them, that the LORD thy God shall keep unto thee the covenant and the mercy which he sware unto thy fathers: and he will love thee . . . . Thou shalt be blessed above all people . . . . and the LORD will take away from thee all sickness, and will put none of the evil diseases of Egypt, which thou knowest, upon thee; but will lay them upon all them that hate thee."   Deuteronomy 7:12-13a, 14a, 15

But if we broke it, we'd be open to an equivalent curse — unless (and that's a big "*unless*") we repented and responded to our transgression by means of the prescribed sacrifice outlined in the Law.

"Behold, I set before you this day a blessing and a curse; a blessing, if ye obey the commandments of the LORD your God, which I command you this day: and a curse, if ye will not obey the commandments of the LORD your God, but turn aside out of the way which I command you this day, to go after other gods, which ye have not known."   Deuteronomy 11:26-28

The Law, however, with its meticulous directives for sacrifice was never intended to go on into perpetuity. Rather, it was to serve as a standard bearer and a provisionary means by which we could receive atonement when we fell short of that measure, *until* Messiah came and took away our sins by the sacrifice of Himself forever *(Heb. 9:10)*.

"Wherefore then serveth the law? It was added because of transgressions, till the seed should come to whom the promise was made . . ."   Galatians 3:19a

"But before faith came, we were kept under the law, shut up unto the faith which should afterwards be revealed. Wherefore the law was our schoolmaster to bring us unto Christ, that we might be justified by faith. But after that faith is come, we are no longer under a schoolmaster."   Galatians 3:23-25

"And not only so, but we also joy in God through our Lord Jesus Christ, by whom we have now received the atonement."
                    Romans 5:11

One of the many curses brought down upon us by our forefathers when they as a people rejected our Messiah was a life riddled with fear—the very thing that our Lord Jesus, by His "amazing grace," is still (layer by layer) removing from my life, along with the spiritual blindness that goes with it. King David, being a prophet, forewarned us of its crippling effects in one of his Messianic psalms.

"They gave me also gall for my meat; and in my thirst they gave me vinegar to drink. Let their table become a snare before them: and that which should have been for their welfare, let it become a trap. Let their eyes be darkened, that they see not; and make their loins continually to shake."   Psalm 69:21-23

Unspeakable Loss

Every year my family opened the door and put out a chair and glass of wine for Elijah at our annual Passover Celebration. It was our statement of faith in his anticipated announcement of the pending arrival of our promised Messiah.

"Behold, I will send you Elijah the prophet before the coming of the great and dreadful day of the LORD: and he shall turn the heart of the fathers to the children, and the heart of the children to their fathers, lest I come and smite the earth with a curse."
Malachi 4:5-6

Though dutiful with our Seders,[a] however, we were not well versed in the hundreds of other Messianic prophecies that had already identified John the Baptist as Malachi's "Elijah" and Jesus of Nazareth as our anticipated Passover Lamb *(Acts 2:22-36; 1 Cor. 5:7)*.

---

[a] Seder: a Jewish home or community service including a ceremonial dinner held on the first or first and second evenings of the Passover in commemoration of their epic Exodus from Egypt.

". . . John seeth Jesus coming unto him, and saith, Behold the Lamb of God, which taketh away the sin of the world."

John 1:29

The Scriptures matched perfectly all the way down to the last "*jot*" and "*tittle*" *(Mt. 5:18).*

"And he [John the Baptist] shall go before him [Jesus] in the spirit and power of Elias [Elijah], to turn the hearts of the fathers to the children, and the disobedient to the wisdom of the just; to make ready a people prepared for the Lord."

Luke 1:17

"For all the prophets and the law prophesied until John. And if ye will receive it, this is Elias, which was for to come."

Matthew 11:13-14; See also Matthew 17:10-13

Yet we failed to recognize both our "Elijah" and our Messiah Himself.

"This is the stone which was set at nought of you builders, which is become the head of the corner."   Acts 4:11; Ps. 118:22

In our naiveté, for example, we thought that the whole account of Christ's miraculous birth in Bethlehem was a "Gentile thing." I had no idea that it was the fulfillment of a series of prophecies passed down to our people by our own prophets, and then from us to the rest of the world *(Acts 13:46-47; Rom. 9:4-5).*

"Therefore the Lord himself shall give you a sign; Behold, a virgin shall conceive, and bear a son, and shall call his name Immanuel."   Isaiah 7:14

"Behold, a virgin shall be with child, and shall bring forth a son, and they shall call his name Emmanuel, which being interpreted is, God with us."   Matthew 1:23

"But thou, Bethlehem Ephratah, though thou be little among the thousands of Judah, yet out of thee shall he come forth unto me that is to be ruler in Israel; whose goings forth have been from of old, from everlasting." Micah 5:2

Unbelief and an uncanny blindness foretold in Old Testament Scripture as a punishment for our persistent waywardness had shut us out *(Ps. 69:21-28; Rom. 11:8-10)*.

"But their minds were blinded: for until this day remaineth the same vail untaken away in the reading of the old testament; which vail is done away in Christ. But even unto this day, when Moses is read, the vail is upon their heart." 2 Corinthians 3:14-15

"And in them is fulfilled the prophecy of Esaias, which saith, By hearing ye shall hear, and shall not understand; and seeing ye shall see, and shall not perceive: for this people's heart is waxed gross, and their ears are dull of hearing, and their eyes they have closed; lest at any time they should see with their eyes and hear with their ears, and should understand with their heart, and should be converted, and I should heal them." Matthew 13:14-15; Isaiah 6:9-10

We did not know, nor believe, the voices of our prophets.

"Then he [Jesus] said unto them, O fools, and slow of heart to believe all that the prophets have spoken." Luke 24:25

The New Testament

Throughout the pages of our Scriptures our prophets heralded a New Covenant, sealed in our Messiah's blood, that (if kept) would open us up to receive what the *"blood of bulls and of goats"* never could *(Heb. 9:12-14; Heb. 10:4)*: a brand new heart, engraved with His Law; and a brand new spirit inclining us to obey our beloved Lord, always. Miracle of miracles! In the Latter Days, the ten commandments originally etched by the *"finger of God"* into *"tables of stone" (Deu. 9:10)*, were (by that same finger) going to be written into *"fleshly tables of the heart"* *(2 Cor. 3:3).*

"Behold, the days come, saith the LORD, that I will make a new covenant with the house of Israel, and with the house of Judah: not according to the covenant that I made with their fathers in the day that I took them by the hand to bring them out of the land of Egypt; which my covenant they brake, although I was an husband unto them, saith the LORD: but this shall be the covenant that I will make with the house of Israel; After those days, saith the LORD, I will put my law in their inward parts, and write it in their hearts; and will be their God, and they shall be my people. And they shall teach no more every man his neighbour, and every man his brother, saying, Know the LORD: for they shall all know me, from the least of them unto the greatest of them, saith the LORD: for I will forgive their iniquity, and I will remember their sin no more."

Jeremiah 31:31-34

"A new heart also will I give you, and a new spirit will I put within you: and I will take away the stony heart out of your flesh, and I will give you an heart of flesh. And I will put my spirit within you, and cause you to walk in my statutes, and ye shall keep my judgments, and do them."   Ezekiel 36:26-27

Ponder the blessedness that we missed! *"A new and living way"* into the very Presence of God had been opened to us through the blood of Jesus, but we couldn't see it *(Heb. 10:20).* Jesus fulfilled the Old Testament foreshadow. No longer was a high priest of the Aaronic priesthood going to go behind the veil into the *"holiest of all"* in the Temple when it still stood in Jerusalem once per year with the blood of animals to atone for his own sins and the sins of the people *(Heb. 9:8);* but Jesus (as our High Priest) went into the actual Presence of God by means of the sacrifice of Himself so as to redeem whosoever would repent and believe on Him (Jew or Gentile) to the Father of Lights forever.

"But Christ being come an high priest of good things to come, by a greater and more perfect tabernacle, not made with hands, that is to say, not of this building; neither by the blood of goats and calves, but by his own blood he entered in once into the holy place, having obtained eternal redemption for us."

Hebrews 9:11-12

The picture of future glory that the Apostle John recorded in Revelation Chapter 21 is but a detailed portrait of a sketch that had been made known to our people generations earlier in the book of Isaiah. Who can fathom the bliss to come?! ...No more suffering. No more tears. No more death.

"He will swallow up death in victory; and the Lord GOD will wipe away tears from off all faces; and the rebuke of his people shall he take away from off all the earth: for the LORD hath spoken it. And it shall be said in that day, Lo, this is our God; we have waited for him, and he will save us: this is the LORD; we have waited for him, we will be glad and rejoice in his salvation. For in this mountain shall the hand of the LORD rest."   Isaiah 25:8-10a

"And I saw a new heaven and a new earth: for the first heaven and the first earth were passed away; and there was no more sea. And I John saw the holy city, new Jerusalem, coming down from God out of heaven, prepared as a bride adorned for her husband. And I heard a great voice out of heaven saying, Behold, the tabernacle of God is with men, and he will dwell with them, and they shall be his people, and God himself shall be with them, and be their God. And God shall wipe away all tears from their eyes; and there shall be no more death, neither sorrow, nor crying, neither shall there be any more pain: for the former things are passed away. And he that sat upon the throne said, Behold, I make all things new . . ."   Revelation 21:1-5a

In a word, "*there shall be no more curse*" (*Rev. 22:3a*). Just think: Revelation 22 is only a tiny glimpse into the future that awaits us in our promised Shangri-La.

"But as it is written, Eye hath not seen, nor ear heard, neither have entered into the heart of man, the things which God hath prepared for them that love him."   1 Corinthians 2:9; Isaiah 64:4

Without a Sacrifice

A supernatural phenomenon occurred when Jesus "*yielded up the ghost*" at His crucifixion. The veil of the Temple was "*rent in twain from the top to the bottom,*" thus confirming the fulfillment of the Old Covenant established by Moses and the initiation of the New *(Mt. 27:50-54; Mk. 15:37-38)*. Shortly thereafter, by a series of providences, the Temple in Jerusalem was destroyed, making it impossible for our people to perpetuate in any wise a biblically validated atonement *(Deu. 12; Lev. 16)*. The Lord Jesus Christ, by His unspeakable death and resurrection, had brought it to a close.

"For Christ is the end of the law for righteousness to every one that believeth."   Romans 10:4

Yet, in our ignorance (and perhaps even rebellion), we were still relying on the innovation of Jewish Tradition ...living our "best life" ...our affiliation with the local synagogue ...and participation in a modified version of Yom Kippur (the Day of Atonement), even though it was utterly void of its central feature: animal sacrifice as mandated in the Mosaic Law for our righteousness and atonement.

"For the life of the flesh is in the blood: and I have given it to you upon the altar to make an atonement for your souls: for it is the blood that maketh an atonement for the soul."
Leviticus 17:11

We were sitting under the condemnation of cumulative sin that had never been covered or forgiven and reaping the consequence of our separation from God in our ailing bodies and in our ruptured family relationships.

"If thou wilt not observe to do all the words of this law that are written in this book, that thou mayest fear this glorious and fearful name, THE LORD THY GOD; then the LORD will make thy plagues wonderful, and the plagues of thy seed, even great plagues, and of long continuance, and sore sicknesses, and of long continuance. Moreover he will bring upon thee all the diseases of Egypt, which thou wast afraid of; and they shall cleave unto thee. Also every sickness, and every plague, which is not written in the book of this law, them will the LORD bring upon thee, until thou be destroyed."   Deuteronomy 28:58-61

"Thou shalt betroth a wife, and another man shall lie with her."
Deuteronomy 28:30a

Without a Covering

Year after year we brought to remembrance the first Passover and the Exodus of our people from Egyptian captivity, yet the Destroyer was no longer "passing over" us as he did then and we weren't asking why *(Heb. 11:28)*.

"Then Moses called for all the elders of Israel, and said unto them, Draw out and take you a lamb according to your families, and kill the passover. And ye shall take a bunch of hyssop, and dip it in the blood that is in the bason, and strike the lintel and the two side posts with the blood that is in the bason; and none of you shall go out at the door of his house until the morning. For the LORD will pass through to smite the Egyptians; and when he seeth the blood upon the lintel, and on the two side posts, the LORD will pass over the door, and will not suffer the destroyer to come in unto your houses to smite you."   Exodus 12:21-23

Just like our wayward forefathers when Christ walked the earth, we failed to recognize the *"time of [our] visitation"* and did not turn to our Messiah in repentance *(Lk. 19:44)*, beseeching Him on the veracity of His promises to undertake.

"Behold, I will bring it health and cure, and I will cure them, and will reveal unto them the abundance of peace and truth."

Jeremiah 33:6

He told us point blank:

". . . I am the LORD that healeth thee." Exodus 15:26b

Yet, we went to court to solve our issues and to doctors for our remedy, only to suffer the sad disappointment of hope misplaced.

"When Ephraim saw his sickness, and Judah saw his wound, then went Ephraim to the Assyrian, and sent to king Jareb: yet could he not heal you, nor cure you of your wound."

Hosea 5:13

Repentance & Redemption

The only thing that could have saved us from that fate was (and still is) genuine repentance on par with what was witnessed at Pentecost in the aftermath of Peter's preaching when *"about three thousand souls"* gave their lives to Christ *(Acts 2:41)*; a repentance centered around our corporate *"acknowledgement of that sin which is the summation of all our sins — [namely] the crucifixion of [our] Messiah."*[5]

"Therefore let all the house of Israel know assuredly, that God hath made the same Jesus, whom ye have crucified, both Lord and Christ. Now when they heard this, they were pricked in their heart, and said unto Peter and to the rest of the apostles, Men and brethren, what shall we do? Then Peter said unto them, Repent, and be baptized every one of you in the name of Jesus Christ for the remission of sins, and ye shall receive the gift of the Holy Ghost. For the promise is unto you, and to your children, and to all that are afar off, even as many as the Lord our God shall call."   Acts 2:36-39

CHAPTER TWENTY-THREE

Betrothed to Christ

When I came into womanhood, I didn't get involved in any serious relationships with men. It was my way of "protecting" myself from the possibility of suffering a "love lost," thus awakening the wounds incurred during my childhood years. During the first year at a university several hundred miles from home, however, I was swept off my feet by a very aggressive suitor. Taken up by romance, I swung wide open the doors of a heart rusted shut only to have it shattered into pieces once again; this time, by the infidelity of my projected "prince charming." I was *"lookin' for love in all the wrong places,"*[1] not knowing that the insatiable drive for love that God has built into our frame is there for the express purpose of bringing us to His Son.

> This instinct for love, so firmly implanted in the human heart, is the supreme way by which we learn to desire and love God Himself above all else.[2]

> There is only one Being Who can satisfy the last aching abyss of the human heart, and that is the Lord Jesus Christ.[3]

My father had discouraged me from engaging in the relationship, but rebel that I was, I chose not to honor my father *(Exo. 20:12)*. I had no ears for his counsel and lived to see his warning played out:

Sweetheart... I just don't want to see you get hurt.

Again, I faced the agony of rejection and feelings of despair and helplessness in the face of circumstances out of my control.

I was like a Mexican piñata with a big dent from my former wounding, but now split wide open with all of my remaining innards spread out on the ground. We can't "make" others love us, nor can we bind them to us throughout eternity. The whole world knows that. That's why the old Beetle song "Money Can't Buy Me Love" was such a smash. Sacred blessedness of that kind is a gift of God and entirely dependent upon His grace. He puts it in the heart. And if it's going to last forever, then it's got to be founded in our common bond, as faithful believers, with Jesus as our *"first"* and *"exceeding"* great love *(Rev. 2:4; Gen. 15:1).*

There is a pagan rhyme that perfectly describes my condition at that pivotal time in my life. It's about a storybook character in children's literature who at one time was a popular name in American households. It goes like this:

Humpty Dumpty sat on a wall,
Humpty Dumpty had a great fall,
All the kings horses and all the kings men,
Couldn't put Humpty together again.[4]

Conversion

Little did I know that my Heavenly Father was at work amidst such a devastating providence, using it to good, by stripping away my atheistic and Judaic biases and opening my being for the reception of His Son *(Rom. 8:28).* I was in the Hawaiian Islands at the time yearning to start a new life, taking in the spectacular beauty and experiencing great stirrings in my heart "God-ward." In those days, hitchhiking and bicycling with a backpack and sleeping bag were the "in" thing to do.

Out of seemingly nowhere, a Jewish Christian by the name of Gil came into view wearing red shorts, carrying a black Bible, and walking the shoreline preaching the Kingdom of God. He had been a guru in upstate New York before his conversion to our Messiah and was bold as a lion, with no concern as to how he appeared in the eyes of others.

Just my speed. I was very closed minded to "Christianity" (whatever my concept of that was???), though open to eastern mysticism and all kinds of other spiritual paths. I needed someone to speak into my life that hadn't been cut from the institutional cloth because I held it in such disdain. Unfortunately, like so many other Jews (not all, of course), I had classed just about everyone that professed a "*jesus*" *(2 Cor. 11:3-4; 1 Cor. 8:4-5)*, of whatever denomination or drift, and regardless of the integrity of his character (or lack thereof), into one reprehensible category reserved for losers, hypocrites, greedy-graspers and potential participants in a future Holocaust.

With this Christian brother's encouragement, I knelt in the sand, gathered up all the "mustard seed faith" I had, and reached up to receive Yeshua Ha'Mashiach (Jesus the Anointed One) as my Messiah.

My prayer was nothing fancy. ...Just a few floundering words. Actually, the whole scenario was so foreign to me that I needed a believer on knee level to guide me. His eagerness to help reminds me of a cherished quote from Andrew Murray's outstanding book on prayer:

> No one can teach like Jesus. A pupil needs a teacher who knows his work, who has the gift of teaching, who in patience and love will descend to the pupil's needs. Blessed be God! Jesus is all this and much more.[5]

Through the love of this stranger, Jesus was knocking, and by the stirring of a supernatural Presence that seemed to be completely outside of myself, I was ready to open the door.

I repent and welcome You into my heart. Jesus, please be my Lord.

"Behold, I stand at the door, and knock: if any man hear my voice, and open the door, I will come in to him, and will sup with him, and he with me." Revelation 3:20

I was ripe for conversion. I was in an unfamiliar place. I had no career ambitions; no intimate relationships to speak of; very little interaction with my family; no particular place in the world I wanted to go; and above all else, I was broken. Plus, I had a consuming desire to start my life anew; so much so, that I was even juggling ideas about changing my name. The Lord saw it all (both my yearning and my confusion) and used the occasion to capture me with His love.

"Now when I passed by thee, and looked upon thee, behold, thy time was the time of love; and I spread my skirt over thee, and covered thy nakedness: yea, I sware unto thee, and entered into a covenant with thee, saith the Lord GOD, and thou becamest mine."   Ezekiel 16:8

Not only did I become His, but He became mine.

"I am my beloved's, and my beloved is mine . . ."
Song of Solomon 6:3a

"Whom have I in heaven but thee? And there is none upon earth that I desire beside thee. My flesh and my heart faileth: but God is the strength of my heart, and my portion for ever."
Psalm 73:25-26

The new life I was seeking had begun.

"Therefore if any man be in Christ, he is a new creature: old things are passed away; behold, all things are become new."
2 Corinthians 5:17

Golden Nuggets

Gil gave me two landmark gems of guidance that day. Number One: *"Get yourself a Bible and start reading."* Number Two: *"Seek out baptism by immersion in water."* I followed up on step one right away. The lady at the bookstore gave me the strangest look when I asked her if she had anything containing the words of Christ. I didn't realize that the Old and New Testaments had been bound together into one perfectly meshed book.

"So foolish was I, and ignorant . . ." Psalms 73:22a

Baptism, however, was still pending. Being Jewish and very naive, I did not know how to go about it, nor did I understand its significance. The one thing I did know was that I wanted to make a public declaration of my faith, with heaven and earth as witnesses of my love for Jesus and my willingness (as far as I understood it) to surrender my will to His with the same passion as a bride would her groom.

It was only later, as I matured in the Lord, that I came to appreciate the significance of obedience to that New Testament command — one that is so important that the Son of God, though He is without sin, surrendered to it as an example for us and went so far as to tie it directly to salvation.

"Then cometh Jesus from Galilee to Jordan unto John, to be baptized of him. But John forbad him, saying, I have need to be baptized of thee and comest thou to me? And Jesus answering said unto him, Suffer it to be so now: for thus it becometh us to fulfil all righteousness. Then he suffered him." Matthew 3:13-15

"He that believeth and is baptized shall be saved; but he that believeth not shall be damned."   Mark 16:16

The Baptism of Repentance

How glorious to have that understanding now! Water baptism is first and foremost a *"baptism of repentance"* (Lk. 3:3). It is an external visible sign representative of a wondrous work of transformation that the power of God begins to effect within us by the *"washing of regeneration, and renewing of the Holy Ghost"* (Tit. 3:5). This takes place when we repent of our waywardness and reckon *"dead"* everything in our lives that is contrary to God, choosing instead to walk in *"newness of life"* reflective of the *"divine nature"* (Rom. 6:3, 4, 11; 2 Pe. 1:4). This all takes place through a windfall of fiery trials like the ones going on in the lives of true believers worldwide. These providences work like a winnowing fan sifting through the chambers of our lives and separating the wheat from the chaff.

"I [John the Baptist] indeed baptize you with water unto repentance: but he [Christ] that cometh after me is mightier than I, whose shoes I am not worthy to bear: He shall baptize you with the Holy Ghost, and with fire: Whose fan is in his hand, and he will throughly purge his floor, and gather his wheat into the garner; but he will burn up the chaff with unquenchable fire."   Matthew 3:11-12

I love the way the Apostle Paul, being an Israelite, put his teaching on baptism in pictures that fellow Jews like myself could readily grasp. In his sketch, he placed the New Testament ordinance of baptism right on top of the Old Testament foreshadow in circumcision. In so doing, he brought our Father's highest purposes into view *(Deu. 10:16; Jer. 4:4);* namely, that every trace of self-centeredness corrupting our lives would be cut off like the foreskin of a man's private parts. Then, we would be free and unencumbered by the flesh to love and worship Him in the *"beauty of holiness"* with the abandon and reverence He is due *(Ps. 29:2).*

"In whom also ye are circumcised with the circumcision made without hands, in putting off the body of the sins of the flesh by the circumcision of Christ: buried with him in baptism, wherein also ye are risen with him through the faith of the operation of God, who hath raised him from the dead."   Colossians 2:11-12

"And the LORD thy God will circumcise thine heart, and the heart of thy seed, to love the LORD thy God with all thine heart, and with all thy soul, that thou mayest live."
                                                    Deuteronomy 30:6

Hallelujah! Twenty years into my life and I finally discovered what being Jewish is all about.

"For he is not a Jew, which is one outwardly; neither is that circumcision, which is outward in the flesh: but he is a Jew, which is one inwardly; and circumcision is that of the heart, in the spirit, and not in the letter; whose praise is not of men, but of God."   Romans 2:28-29

My Baptism

I maintained the discipline of study, but the Bible read more like a textbook than like the living Word that Gil described. It was only after my baptism in water and subsequent baptism in the Holy Ghost that the *"vail"* lifted and the Bible came alive *(2 Cor. 3:14-16)*. Then, every word of God breathed and seemed to speak directly to my need.

Within a short time I bumped into Gil on another beach and expressed my zeal for baptism. Immediately, he took me out into the crashing waves of the Pacific Ocean and baptized me from head to toe in the name of the Father, His Son Jesus Christ and the Holy Spirit *(Mt. 28:19)*. When I came up out of the water and made it back to the shoreline, I was greeted by the reproach of my peers.

Who are you to be telling us that Jesus is the "only" way? How do you know?

In other words: Who selected you out of our number and set you up as the big spiritual muckety-muck? ...My answer was simple and straightforward: *"I just know."*

"The Spirit itself beareth witness with our spirit, that we are the children of God."   Romans 8:16

Had I been further along in my walk I could have used the testimony of Messiah Himself to validate my claim.

"Jesus saith unto him, I am the way, the truth, and the life: no man cometh unto the Father, but by me."   John 14:6

Born Again!

It was a transformational day. Speaking to a Jewish leader, Jesus said:

". . . Verily, verily, I say unto thee, Except a man be born of water and of the Spirit, he cannot enter into the kingdom of

God. That which is born of the flesh is flesh; and that which is born of the Spirit is spirit." John 3:5-6

I had become what some people call a "completed Jew," meaning that in addition to being a Jew by bloodline, I am a Jew (and a Christian!!!) by *"adoption"* too, because the Spirit of Christ lives in my life *(Gal. 4:4-6).*

"But when the fulness of the time was come, God sent forth his Son, made of a woman, made under the law, to redeem them that were under the law, that we might receive the adoption of sons. And because ye are sons, God hath sent forth the Spirit of his Son into your hearts, crying, Abba, Father." Galatians 4:4-6

Hallelujah! Graffed into Christ, I had become part of a beautiful and diverse body of believers—my God given spiritual family.

"And they [the Jewish people] also, if they abide not still in unbelief, shall be graffed in: for God is able to graff them in again." Romans 11:23

"For we are members of his body, of his flesh, and of his bones." Ephesians 5:30

"For by one Spirit are we all baptized into one body, whether we be Jews or Gentiles, whether we be bond or free; and have been all made to drink into one Spirit." 1 Corinthians 12:13

Immediately, fruit appeared on the vine. For the first time in my life I was not moved by the approval (or disapproval) of either friends or family. The Spirit of Christ had made its home where rejection once ruled and the love of Jesus was profusely *"shed abroad"* in my broken heart now on the mend *(Rom. 5:5).* Just like Ezekiel prophesied, God put a *"new spirit"* within me *(Eze. 36:26).* Praise His name forever! I was now hearing a new voice (or, better said, I was receiving impressions from a Presence within) teaching me how to order my steps. In very practical ways this inner *"unction"* was telling me just what my Heavenly Father would have me to do *(1 Jn. 2:20).*

"And thine ears shall hear a word behind thee, saying, This is the way, walk ye in it, when ye turn to the right hand, and when ye turn to the left." Isaiah 30:21

When He wanted me to go right and I chose left, a dark cloud of oppression would overshadow me. Contrariwise, when He impressed it upon my heart to go right and I yielded right (even if it was not my preferred path and required the relinquishment of certain pleasures and treasures) I experienced *"joy unspeakable and full of glory"* *(1 Pe. 1:8).* That beautiful verse which says: *"He will teach us of his ways, and we will walk in his paths"* was no longer a mere sentence on a page. It was becoming reality in my life *(Isa. 2:3; Mic. 4:2).*

Without me realizing what was going on, the Lord Jesus was teaching me about the *"two contrary natures"* within described by William Gurnall in Chapter Eight; one from earth, *"earthy"*; and the other from heaven, *"heavenly"* *(1 Cor. 15:47-49).* When I yielded, even in thought only, to the tug pulling on my old earthy nature, I went out from God's Presence back under the dominion of Satan, sensing again my separation from the Father and the loneliness it begets. And when I put that tug off and chose instead to yield to the inclination of the new woman, born of the Spirit of Christ, the sweet peace of Jesus enveloped me. How true is the saying: *"He is altogether lovely"* *(Son. 5:16)!* No doubt about it: I still had (and have) a long way to go before apprehending *"that for which also I am apprehended of Christ Jesus"* *(Phil. 3:12);* but it was a beginning.

The Baptism of the Holy Spirit

Shortly after my baptism in water, God (in His great love), led me to a Christian ministry that had a farm on the Kona Coast. There I received the baptism of the Holy Spirit; a spiritual baptism, distinct from my initial external baptism by immersion in water *(Acts 1:8).*

"Now when the apostles which were at Jerusalem heard that Samaria had received the word of God, they sent unto them Peter and John: who, when they were come down, prayed for them, that they might receive the Holy Ghost: (For as yet He was fallen upon none of them: only they were baptized in the name of the Lord Jesus.) Then laid they their hands on them, and they received the Holy Ghost."   Acts 8:14-17

I didn't initially speak with tongues as an evidence of that experience, yet my cup ran over with praises that *"magnified God."* He *"put a new song in my mouth, even praise unto our God" (Ps. 40:3a)*.

"While Peter yet spake these words, the Holy Ghost fell on all them which heard the word. And they of the circumcision which believed were astonished, as many as came with Peter, because that on the Gentiles also was poured out the gift of the Holy Ghost. For they heard them speak with tongues, and magnify God. Then answered Peter, Can any man forbid water, that these should not be baptized, which have received the Holy Ghost as well as we?"   Acts 10:44-47

Later, those praises became sprinkled with *"new tongues"* and continued to well up like rivers of *"living water"* in my inmost being *(Jn. 4:10)*. *"Hungry and thirsty"* I devoured the Word *(Ps. 107:5)*. All the lights seemed to come on! Night after night I was up following the trail of references in my King James Thompson Chain Bible. Hours on end I sang, poured out my heart to Jesus and bathed in the Scriptures. As I did, God's Spirit swept through me in waves, breaking the shackles of sin and Satan, and leading me onward on the Road to Glory.

"What is it then? I will pray with the spirit, and I will pray with the understanding also: I will sing with the spirit, and I will sing with the understanding also."   1 Corinthians 14:15

I can't begin to express how exciting all this was for me, as a Jew. The words of our prophets (long hidden from my view) were becoming reality in my life.

"And in that day shall the deaf hear the words of the book, and the eyes of the blind shall see out of obscurity, and out of darkness. The meek also shall increase their joy in the LORD, and the poor among men shall rejoice in the Holy One of Israel."   Isaiah 29:18-19

The Bruised & Broken Hearted

Divorce, death and infidelity can leave debilitating wounds invisible to the natural eye. Those three blows bruised my soul and kept me in a perpetual cycle of rejection. Afraid to suffer the loss of love and afraid to be at the mercy of disease, I've been "*subject to bondage*" my whole life long.

There has also been another fear working in my heart. ...A fear greater than any other, and yet common to us all, though I was out of contact with it: an inherent fear of God. ...The fear of having to answer to my Judge for secret sins not yet atoned.

> This makes . . . [us] afraid of every disease that comes to town, pox or plague, lest it should arrest . . . [us], and bring . . . [us] by death to judgment.[6]

"Forasmuch then as the children are partakers of flesh and blood, he also himself likewise took part of the same; that through death he might destroy him that had the power of death, that is, the devil; and deliver them who through fear of death were all their lifetime subject to bondage."

Hebrews 2:14-15

Things began to change, however, when our Precious Jesus came into my life and began to set me free through a series of trials like the ones described in this book. Through one divinely orchestrated providence after another, the deeply embedded seeds of rebellion and unbelief at the base of my fears have been uncovered, acknowledged in repentance, and overcome through the wonderworking power of my Saviour's atoning blood. It's the Way of the Cross. Praise God! I cannot frame words to thank Him enough!

Sing, oh, sing of my Redeemer,
With His blood He purchased me,
On the cross He sealed my pardon,
Paid the debt, and made me free.[7]

From this day forward, it is my determined purpose to cling to the Cross so as to keep this gateway sin of unbelief that has undermined my faith my entire Christian walk securely shut.

He Healeth the Brokenhearted

The betrayal I suffered was the coup de grâce that brought me to the feet of Jesus. I was bleeding inside from a sorrowful spirit and void of the ability to lift myself up. Even those closest to me couldn't provide adequate solace to suture the wound.

"The heart knoweth his own bitterness; and a stranger doth not intermeddle with his joy."   Proverbs 14:10

None but God Almighty could have *ever* come close to putting the pieces of my broken heart back together. None! Truly, Jesus is the Messiah that our Old Testament prophets assured us would come.

"And he [Jesus] came to Nazareth, where he had been brought up: and, as his custom was, he went into the synagogue on the sabbath day, and stood up for to read. And there was delivered unto him the book of the prophet Esaias. And when he had opened the book, he found the place where it was written [of Him], The Spirit of the Lord is upon me, because he hath anointed me to preach the gospel to the poor; he hath sent me to heal the brokenhearted, to preach deliverance to the captives, and recovering of sight to the blind, to set at liberty them that are bruised, To preach the acceptable year of the Lord."
                                                    Luke 4:16-19

"The LORD doth build up Jerusalem: he gathereth together the outcasts of Israel. He healeth the broken in heart, and bindeth up their wounds."   Psalm 147:2-3

This greatly loved song became a favorite:

Something beautiful, something good
All my confusion He understood
All I had to offer Him was brokenness and strife
But he made something beautiful of my life.[8]

Forgiveness and Freedom

It was about nine years after my mother's death that I came to understand what I never had in my youth: That Jesus, as the sacrificial lamb depicted in Isaiah Chapter 53 and foreshadowed in the Passover Feast, came to bring us into the bond of a New Covenant signed in His blood.

". . . For even Christ our passover is sacrificed for us."
1 Corinthians 5:7b

...That by the sacrifice of Himself, He paid the full price to set us free from every curse that has ever followed us.

"Christ hath redeemed us from the curse of the law, being made a curse for us: for it is written, Cursed is every one that hangeth on a tree: that the blessing of Abraham might come on the Gentiles through Jesus Christ; that we might receive the promise of the Spirit through faith."   Galatians 3:13-14

...And that now, whosoever (Jew or Gentile) that will come into the bond of the New Covenant with Christ, being born again of His Spirit; and aligning his/her life with the terms upon which He in His Gospel offers to save us from our sins; beginning with faith and repentance; can (as an heir of the promises given to Abraham) *"call God into the field for his help"* and experience victory in every area of his life.[9]

"Now to Abraham and his seed were the promises made. He saith not, And to seeds, as of many; but as of one, And to thy seed, which is Christ."   Galatians 3:16

What an awesome, awesome Truth! Had we known of it when my mother fell ill, there is a possibility we would have never seen her in such a state; nor felt so utterly impotent and helpless as her care givers. Instead, we could have repented of our sins and the sins of our fathers; received Jesus as our Atonement; and acknowledged Him in fullness as everything Scripture declares Him to be. ...Not only as a great teacher (though He is — *Isa. 2:3*); and not only as a prophet (though He's that, too — *Jn. 6:14*); but even more importantly, as THE *"Prophet"* that Moses promised would come; the Son of the Almighty God of Abraham, Isaac and Jacob; the Saviour of the world *(Acts 3:22-23)*.

"I will raise them up a Prophet from among their brethren, like unto thee, and will put my words in his mouth; and he shall speak unto them all that I shall command him. And it shall come to pass, that whosoever will not hearken unto my words which he shall speak in my name, I will require it of him."

Deuteronomy 18:18-19

Set free from the continuum of sin that followed us, and reconciled to the Father through the blood of Jesus, our family could then have circled my mother's bedside in fervent prayer, calling on the same Yeshua Ha'Mashiach that revealed Himself to Joshua as the *"Captain of the host"* and the *"whole militia of heaven"* would have engaged with us in the fight for her life *(Jos. 5:13-15).*[10]

What a foundation of faith that would have laid for my future! That's the kind of substance that David Wilkerson was nurtured up in from his youth. Can you imagine?! ...A twelve year old boy with a faith so lively that he outflanked the elders of his church when begging God from a coal bin in the basement for the life of his father!? He cried with such desperation and passion that it echoed through the pipes of his house and landed him shoulder-to-shoulder with his believing mother at his father's bedside where they witnessed a miracle.

...Mom read the Word of promise:

"And all things, whatsoever ye shall ask in prayer, believing, ye shall receive."   Matthew 21:22

...And David laid hands on his father's forehead.

Jesus, I believe what You said, Make Daddy well![11]

Here's David Wilkerson telling what happened next:

There was one more step. I walked to the door and opened it and said, loud and clear: "Please come, Dr. Brown. I have . . ." (it was hard) "I have prayed believing that daddy will get better." Dr. Brown looked down at my twelve-year-old earnestness and smiled a warm and compassionate and totally unbelieving smile. But that smile turned first to puzzlement and then to astonishment as he bent to examine my father. "Something has happened," he said. His voice was so low I could hardly hear. Dr. Brown picked up his instruments with fingers that trembled, and tested Dad's blood pressure. "Kenneth," he said, raising Dad's eyelids and then feeling his abdomen and then reading his blood pressure again. "Kenneth, how do you feel?" "Like strength is flowing into me." "Kenneth," said the doctor, "I have just witnessed a miracle."[12]

Praise be unto God! There is not a single account in the entire New Testament of a penitent soul with mustard seed faith (and especially a "*daughter of Abraham*") ever being turned away from Jesus in his/her quest for healing (*Lk. 13:11-17; Mt. 15:21-28*). Not one!

"When the even was come, they brought unto him many that were possessed with devils: and he cast out the spirits with his word, and healed ALL that were sick: that it might be fulfilled which was spoken by Esaias the prophet, saying, himself took our infirmities, and bare our sicknesses."   Matthew 8:16-17

CHAPTER TWENTY-FOUR

The Prayer of Faith

On September 16, 2018 Apostle Edwin and I finished "Faith our Alarm System," the ten page letter to our Zimbabwean brethren. Hallelujah! We bowed our heads in prayer, asked for God's blessing and sent it off via email. Two days later we broke camp and left the area. Time to move on.

On the day of departure, the affliction I was suffering showed no signs of recovery. But by God's grace, and with the support of my believing husband, I was resolved to keep my eyes on Jesus and *"hold fast"* to the *"faith"* we had outlined in our epistle *(Rom. 4:12)*.

"Let us hold fast the profession of our faith without wavering; (for he is faithful that promised)."   Hebrews 10:23

"Trust ye in the LORD for ever: for in the LORD JEHOVAH is everlasting strength."   Isaiah 26:4

Anything short of that mark, after sending off the letter, would have shown me up as a hypocrite.

"Thou therefore which teachest another, teachest thou not thyself?"   Romans 2:21a

Off we went to do chores before hitting the highway, one of which was laundry. Once we got things going, Edwin stepped out to work on our vehicle and was approached by a man asking for money for food. Not knowing whether or not he would use the money to get some nourishment, Edwin decided to drop what he was doing and take him to a restaurant where he bought him lunch and shared Christ *(Mt. 25:31-46)*.

While they were gone, the enemy magnified his assaults against me, pounding away at the bruising incurred in my youth. So much so, I became excessively distressed.

Dear Lord Jesus, My Great Physician, please forgive my weakness and cleanse me thoroughly from this persistent unbelief. Heal me, O Lord, body and soul.

First chance I got when Edwin returned I confessed my struggles and asked if he would anoint me with oil in the name of the Lord in conformity to the instructions left to the Church by the Apostle James *(Jam. 5:14-16)*. A look of astonishment came over his face. It was so out-of-character for him not to have initiated that course of action without any encouragement whatsoever at the outset of this trial. Perplexed and grieved by his inadvertent omission, he queried the Lord with persistence:

Why, oh why, Dear Lord, did I miss this important step?

We don't have all the answers. We do know, however, that it wasn't until several days into the trial that the root of unbelief at the base of my fears, going all the way back into my Jewish heritage, was laid bare and I was ready to own up with genuine remorse, repent and pursue the path of confession written into the Biblical prescription for prayers related to healing. Even though I was still looking through a *"glass darkly"* *(1 Cor. 13:12)*, I could see more clearly than ever the crippling effects of this blemish and the power it had to throw me down from the heights of my spiritual walk with the mere suggestion of disease. I also saw the leavening effects; how it wrought in me all manner of fears, disputations and doubts; turning me into a hypocrite; opening me up to lies (even about my own husband!?!); causing me to rebel against authority; and pressing upon me the great temptation to turn to the world, rather than to Christ and His Cross, for remedy. Once that revelation came to the fore (complete with its disclosure of unbelief as *"the traitor's gate"*), it then *"came into"* our hearts to take the vial of oil expressly set apart for times like this off the shelf and pray *"the prayer of faith"* *(Jam. 5:15)*.

"Is any sick among you? Let him call for the elders of the church; and let them pray over him, anointing him with oil in the name of the Lord: and the prayer of faith shall save the sick, and the Lord shall raise him up; and if he have committed sins, they shall be forgiven him. Confess your faults one to another, and pray one for another, that ye may be healed. The effectual fervent prayer of a righteous man availeth much." James 5:14-16

Wonderful lessons were learned in this trial. The *"prayer of faith,"* in combination with the *"steps of that faith,"* and thorough wholehearted repentance founded in absolute surrender to Christ opens us up to receive the fullness of Christ's promised redemption — spirit, soul and body.

I felt the warm oil wash over my forehead and then the weight of my husband's hands upon my head. We both renewed our repentance and then he voiced a short prayer for the restoration of my soul and the healing of my body, in the great Name of Jesus. ...Nothing elaborate. Just real. And most importantly, scriptural. I'm supremely grateful for Edwin's patience, love, stability, faith and example. He has long suffered right along with me through innumerable valleys and victories as God has purified and refined my faith (and his too) in all kinds of different ways. Four simple words spoken by the Lord Himself and echoed through my husband's lips in our times of greatest need have changed my outlook forever: *"Have faith in God"* (Mk. 11:22).

Back to work we went in preparation for the trip. My skin did not immediately clear, nor did the *"good fight of faith"* cease *(1 Tim. 6:12).* But something had changed.

. . . In some miraculous and mysterious way I had been lifted into a completely new mental and spiritual environment, out of the borderland of outer darkness, into the light and glory of heaven.[1]

I had *"touched"* Jesus; not the hem of His garment only; but the Lord Himself *(Mt. 9:20; 14:36).* And just like the woman with the issue of blood *(Mk. 5:29),* from that turning point onward, the plague affixed to my body was stanched and remission began until at last every lesion was gone.

> The disease was designed to bring us to complete severance from what God disapproves of in our life. When the Lord attains this purpose, He may remove the disease.[2]

Best of all, I sensed an inward change. A new surge of belief had entered my core—renewing my spiritual strength and inspiring me to tell the whole wide world what Jesus can do for the soul!

"I believed, therefore have I spoken . . ." Psalm 116:10a

I had been like Jonah in the belly of a huge fish and while there I was turned into a true believer. Once cast out onto dry ground I was ready to head back into *"Nineveh"* and speak with conviction, hoping that my testimony would serve as a catalyst to ignite belief and inspire the same wonderful *"works meet for repentance"* in the lives of others as did his *(Acts 26:20)*.

"And Jonah began to enter into the city a day's journey, and he cried, and said, Yet forty days, and Nineveh shall be overthrown. So the people of Nineveh believed God, and proclaimed a fast, and put on sackcloth, from the greatest of them even to the least of them. . . . And God saw their works, that they turned from their evil way; and God repented of the evil, that he had said that he would do unto them; and he did it not. . . . "   Jonah 3:4-5, 10

A string of scars remained along the backside of my chin for a couple of months in the aftermath of my healing. Each time I ran my hand over the calloused tissue to see whether or not they had disappeared, I was reminded of the shrinking of the sinew in Jacob's thigh at the Jabbok-river crossing and the limp that it caused in his gait from that time forward. It still serves to this very day as a testament in Jewish culture to this patriarch's night of wrestling until he prevailed with God and received His blessing. Perhaps this line-up of scars was my shrunken thigh?

The mere thought of the association of the two lifted my spirit sky high.

"And Jacob was left alone; and there wrestled a man with him until the breaking of the day. And when he saw that he prevailed not against him, he touched the hollow of his thigh; and the hollow of Jacob's thigh was out of joint, as he wrestled with him. And he said, Let me go, for the day breaketh. And he said, I will not let thee go, except thou bless me. And he said unto him, What is thy name? And he said, Jacob. And he said, Thy name shall be called no more Jacob, but Israel: for as a prince hast thou power with God and with men, and hast prevailed. And Jacob asked him, and said, Tell me, I pray thee, thy name. And he said, Wherefore is it that thou dost ask after my name? And he blessed him there. And Jacob called the name of the place Peniel: for I have seen God face to face, and my life is preserved. And as he passed over Penuel the sun rose upon him, and he halted upon his thigh. Therefore the children of Israel eat not of the sinew which shrank, which is upon the hollow of the thigh, unto this day: because he touched the hollow of Jacob's thigh in the sinew that shrank."

Genesis 32:24-32

Well... The scars are long gone, but the testimony lives on:

"Jesus Christ the same yesterday, and to day, and for ever."
Hebrews 13:8

He is still standing beside Jabbok's banks ready to meet anyone willing to wrestle with the two arms of faith and repentance till the "*break of day*" so as to receive their blessing.

The words of encouragement Betsie ten Boom whispered from a stretcher at Ravensbrück to her sister Corrie shortly before passing from time into eternity come to mind:

. . . Must tell people what we have learned here. We must tell them that there is no pit so deep that He is not deeper still. They will listen to us, Corrie, because we have been here.[3]

CHAPTER TWENTY-FIVE

Lo, I Am With You Alway

If we could only wrap our arms around the sacrificial love and forgiveness that pumps through the heart of both the Father and Son *(Eph. 3:14-19)*. We forsook God and went our own way, yet because Jesus bore that iniquity for us at Calvary, the Father promises never to forsake us—provided we do not forsake Him *(2 Pe. 2:15)*.

". . . The LORD is with you, while ye be with him; and if ye seek him, he will be found of you; but if ye forsake him, he will forsake you."   2 Chronicles 15:2b

Our blessed Saviour has gone before us and shown us the Way. Love Him. Adore Him. Fear Him. Believe in Him. Worship Him with all that is within us, holding nothing back. In our weakness, do the things that please Him and He will be with us always, even as the Father is with Him.

". . . He that sent me is with me: the Father hath not left Me alone; for I do always those things that please him."   John 8:29

"Teaching them to observe all things whatsoever I have commanded you: and, lo, I am with you alway, even unto the end of the world. Amen."   Matthew 28:20

And when we fall short, confess it out speedily and repent, with full confidence that *"a broken and a contrite heart . . . [He] wilt not despise"* *(Ps. 51:17)*.

If we put our whole hearts into loving the Lord ...doing God's Will ...and keeping His Word, He will be with us forever. "F O R E V E R"—as in now and throughout all eternity!

". . . He hath said, I will NEVER leave thee, nor forsake thee. So that we may boldly say, The Lord is my helper, and I will not fear . . ."   Hebrews 13:5b-6a

"Jesus answered and said unto him, If a man love me, he will keep my words: and my Father will love him, and we will come unto him, and make our abode with him."   John 14:23

WOW! What magnificent promises and beautiful conditions! *"God with us"* in the Person of Christ, if we would but love Him and keep His commandments *(Mt. 1:23)*.

"For this God is our God for ever and ever: he will be our guide even unto death."   Psalms 48:14

"Whither shall I go from thy spirit? or whither shall I flee from thy presence? If I ascend up into heaven, thou art there: if I make my bed in hell, behold, thou art there. If I take the wings of the morning, and dwell in the uttermost parts of the sea; even there shall thy hand lead me, and thy right hand shall hold me."   Psalm 139:7-10

Hear it from the lips of our Lord Himself:

"I will not leave you comfortless: I will come to you." John 14:18

...When Jacob fled the wrath of Esau, God promised to be with him.

". . . Behold, I am with thee, and will keep thee in all places whither thou goest, and will bring thee again into this land; for I will not leave thee, until I have done that which I have spoken to thee of."   Genesis 28:15

When Moses cried out in much trembling regarding the commission entrusted to his charge, our gracious Father responded with the same assurance.

"And Moses said unto God, Who am I, that I should go unto Pharaoh, and that I should bring forth the children of Israel out of Egypt? And he said, Certainly I will be with thee . . ."

Exodus 3:11-12a

...And when David passed from peril to peril he trod upon fear like "*ashes*" under the soles his feet, and all for the same reason *(Mal. 4:3)*.

"Yea, though I walk through the valley of the shadow of death, I will fear no evil: for thou art with me; thy rod and thy staff they comfort me."   Psalm 23:4

"What shall we then say to these things? If God be for us [and with us], who can be against us?"   Romans 8:31

Victory in Jesus

You see this same theme in the testimonies of faith-filled overcomers of all generations: Christ with us (and in us) is our sure hope of victory *(Col. 1:27)*.

"Then," said the Shepherd, speaking very gently again, "I am going to lead you through danger and tribulation, Much-Afraid, but you need not be the least bit afraid, for I shall be with you. Even if I lead you through the Valley of the Shadow itself you need not fear, for my rod and my staff will comfort you." Then He added, "Thou shalt not be afraid of terror by night; nor for the arrow that flieth by day; nor for the pestilence that walketh in darkness; nor for the destruction that wasteth at noon day. Though a thousand fall at thy side, and ten thousand at thy right hand, it shall not come nigh thee ... For I will cover thee with My feathers, and under My wings shalt Thou trust" (Psa. 91:4-7).[1]

Hallelujah! Jesus is our glory and Crown. Of ourselves we can expect nothing but weakness. But through Christ, "*we shall do valiantly: for he it is that shall tread down our enemies*" (Ps.

60:12). Even the *"gates of hell"* shall not prevail against us *(Mt. 16:18).*

> . . . Caleb and Joshua trusted in God, and said: "God is with us; their defense is taken from them; we shall devour them like bread." Num. 14:9. And by their faith they overcame everything, and entered into the promised land. Jos. 3:17. Thus . . . also our enemies are great, strong and numerous; but if we have a faith like Caleb and Joshua, so that we do not see our own strength, but go out from ourselves, and rely upon Him with the whole heart, then we shall come off conquerors; for David says: "Commit thy way unto the Lord; trust also in Him; and He shall bring it to pass." Ps. 37:5.
>
> Jelis Strings, Beheaded by Catholic decree, A.D. 1562[2]

"Not that we are sufficient of ourselves to think any thing as of ourselves; but our sufficiency is of God."   2 Corinthians 3:5

"And he said unto me, my grace is sufficient for thee: for my strength is made perfect in weakness. Most gladly therefore will I rather glory in my infirmities, that the power of Christ may rest upon me. Therefore I take pleasure in infirmities, in reproaches, in necessities, in persecutions, in distresses for Christ's sake: for when I am weak, then am I strong."

2 Corinthians 12:9-10

To this, the whole body of witnesses agree.

> . . . It is not great men who change the world, but weak men in the hands of a great God.[3]

"But we have this treasure in earthen vessels, that the excellency of the power may be of God, and not of us."

2 Corinthians 4:7

As long as we are firmly joined to the love of Jesus at the Cross of Repentance—with no sin dividing us asunder from Him—and are willing to engage in the *"good fight of faith,"* we can remain stable and faithful (come what may) till the very End *(1 Tim. 6:12).*

> Through this love they overcame all things, and performed glorious deeds beyond the power of man. . . . Knowing their own weakness, they experienced the strength of God in the cross, so that they could take upon themselves with a composed yea, with a joyful mind, that from which human nature beyond measure seemed to recoil and flee. Yea, they were filled with such an exuberant and great joy, begotten in them through the unhindered contemplation of the heavenly glory in faith and hope, that they would have preferred no royal banquet to this parting feast. They were endowed with such strength that even cruel and inhuman torture could not extort from them the names of their fellow brethren, so that, filled with divine and brotherly love, they sacrificed their bodies for their fellow believers.[4]

Plus, we can be used of God (as were they) to awaken souls to their need for Jesus and with His blessing even bring some of our greatest opponents, *"to reflection, and thus to investigation, and ultimately to conversion."*[5] *"Let it be, dear Lord, let it be."*

"And they that be wise shall shine as the brightness of the firmament; and they that turn many to righteousness as the stars for ever and ever." Daniel 12:3

Absolute Surrender to Christ

Martin Luther King Jr., the now deceased figurehead of the Civil Rights Movement here in America, gave some stirring speeches before his assassination. In his last, he spoke of having been to the *"mountaintop,"* and after catching a glimpse in the Spirit of the *"Promised Land,"* was stripped of every ambition other than an all consuming passion to *"do God's Will."*

> . . . Longevity has its place. But I'm not concerned about that now. I just want to do God's will. And He's allowed

me to go up to the mountain. And I've looked over. . . . So . . . I'm not worried about anything. I'm not fearing any man. Mine eyes have seen the glory of the coming of the Lord.[6]

That kind of abandon lends itself to super-human acts of faith and power; in his case, martyrdom. It also gives place to great patience in times when hope fulfilled seems a great way off. No price is too costly for those who walk with a clear conscience in the sight of God and have resolved to surrender all at Christ's Cross. ...No road is too narrow. No mountain too high to climb for men and women (even youth) that have been captured by the love of Jesus and have (as a result) given themselves to Him with that kind of unfettered faith and resolve. This is where all of our present trials — including our health issues — are intended to lead us. When we finally get there, then, with the Apostle Paul, we shall be ready to exchange the "*old rugged Cross*" for our promised "*crown.*"[7]

"I have fought a good fight, I have finished my course, I have kept the faith. Henceforth there is laid up for me a crown of righteousness, which the Lord, the righteous judge, shall give me at that day: and not to me only, but unto all them also that love His appearing."   2 Timothy 4:7-8

Embracing the Cross

That common ambition to please God and do His Will at whatever cost was at the ground floor of the faith of the martyrs *(2 Cor. 5:9)*; though most likely, if they were here with us, they would tell us not to speak too highly of their devotion; being that none of us have yet been tested to our uttermost extremity; and only God knows the thresholds of self-preservation that still lurk within.

"Wherefore let him that thinketh he standeth take heed lest he fall."   1 Corinthians 10:12

This is one reason why we all so desperately need each others' prayers.

> . . . Help us pray to God, that we may gain the victory of a good fight, that God will now teach my fingers to war and my arm to bend the bow of steel, so that by faith I may break through a troop, and leap by my God over a wall (Ps. 18:34, 29); so that we may say with Paul: The fight is fought, the course is finished, the crown of life is laid up for us. II Tim. 4:8.   Hendrick Verstralen,
> Slain by Catholic decree, A.D. 1571[8]

It's also why our apprehensions about trials, testings and chastisements need to be overcome by acceptance of (and thanksgiving for) all the circumstances that our Father allows NOW so as to free us from worldly entanglements; purge us from sin; and fortify our faith. Those that have gone before us understood this well. Over and over you see it in their prayers.

> May the Lord, according to His great mercy, give us what will tend to our salvation.   Conrad Koch,
> Secretly Beheaded by Catholic decree, A.D. 1565[9]

When Jesus put forth His parable on perseverance, saying *"men ought always to pray, and not to faint" (Lk. 18:1-8)*, He asked an eternally consequential question of us all:

> ". . . When the Son of man cometh, shall he find faith on the earth?"   Luke 18:8b

Dear Lord, let our answer, one-and-all, be a resounding: "YES!"

God *"knoweth our frame; He remembereth that we are dust"* and promises never to allow any difficulty to come to us, without providing a way to *"bear"* it *(Ps. 103:14)*. That's where choices come into play. Will we recognize and take His way of escape?

"There hath no temptation taken you but such as is common to man: but God is faithful, who will not suffer you to be tempted

above that ye are able; but will with the temptation also make a
way to escape, that ye may be able to bear it."   1 Cor. 10:13

Trials can be an indescribable blessing if valued and
embraced in faith.

The Mark of the Beast is coming and it is going to be a
beautiful time [of growth and sanctification] for those
who remain faithful. Persecution and suffering are going
to bring God's family together into true unity and at the
same time separate the insincere. For the early
Anabaptists the main issues were water baptism and the
Lord's Supper [versus infant baptism and the Mass]. For
this last generation, the bottom line will be receiving the
Mark of the Beast or refusing it. I've known it for a long
time. The Tribulation has got to come.[10]

"Faith-challenges" of every kind are marvelous "*training*" for
the "*perilous times*" that lie just ahead *(1 Tim. 3:1)*.

I have been in countries where the saints are already
suffering terrible persecution. In China the Christians
were told, 'Don't worry, before the Tribulation comes,
you will be translated--raptured.' Then came a terrible
persecution. Millions of Christians were tortured to
death. Later I heard from a bishop from China say, sadly,
'We have failed. We should have made the people strong
for persecution rather than telling them Jesus would
come first.' Turning to me he said, 'You still have time.
Tell the people how to be strong in times of persecution,
how to stand when the Tribulation comes--to stand and
not faint.' I feel I have a divine mandate to go and tell the
people of this world that it is possible to be strong in the
Lord Jesus Christ. We are in training for the Tribulation.

Corrie ten Boom

Can't help but reflect on some of the statements made by
David Wilkerson when he delivered his 1973 Vision describing
the cataclysmic events he saw on the horizon and zeroing in on

the persecution madness to come. Standing before a sea of faces; some stunned; and many frightened; some new in the Lord; and others in their midnight years; he thundered:

> It better dawn on you soon. The ends of the world are upon us. This is the hour we have all preached about. . . . I look at some of you grey haired folks and some of you preachers here, white hair, you've been preaching this for years. . . . . I think this is the most exciting time in the world to watch the last generation unfold. . . . All the things we've seen and read about over the centuries [are] coming to pass right before our eyes and some of you are sitting there and still not knowing what's happening.[11]

Then, after pausing, in a matter-of-fact (but joyous) sort of a way, he answered the perplexed and troubled look in the eyes of his audience with a single statement. "*Friends,*" he said:

> . . . Jesus is coming and He's getting His house in order![12]

Amen and amen! He's getting us ready, to go out and meet Him when He breaks through the clouds.

"For the Lord himself shall descend from heaven with a shout, with the voice of the archangel, and with the trump of God: and the dead in Christ shall rise first: Then we which are alive and remain shall be caught up together with them in the clouds, to meet the Lord in the air: and so shall we ever be with the Lord."   1 Thessalonians 4:16-17

"That he might present it to himself a glorious church, not having spot, or wrinkle, or any such thing; but that it should be holy and without blemish."   Ephesians 5:26-27

Hallelujah! We have nothing to fear as we head into the refining fires, as long as we remain in submission to God and don't take our eyes off Jesus.

"I have set the LORD always before me: because he is at my right hand, I shall not be moved."   Psalms 16:8

CHAPTER TWENTY-SIX

Door of Hope

Beloved Readers... We have now come full circle. The prophet's dream has come true. Jody's secret desire has been fulfilled, too. ...God gave us a platform to testify of His healing grace in a book. Plus, my conviction that such a book would need a particular depth to it if it were to have any power has likewise had its outworking. Of necessity, it had to tie healing directly into the *"Way of Truth"* (i.e. the Way of the Cross) spoken of by the Apostle Peter *(2 Pe. 2:20).* That special *"Way"* links faith together with daily repentance, thus addressing our most urgent need: the healing of the whole man; spirit, soul and body; *"to the end"* that our hearts be established *"unblameable in holiness before God, even our Father, at the coming of our Lord Jesus Christ with all his saints"* *(1 Th. 3:13).* Absolutely nothing is more important than that! ...Getting ready for the First Resurrection and Eternal Life with the Father and the Son should be the number one priority of us all *(Mt. 25:10-12; Rev. 21 & 22).*

Many of you that are coming to these pages are broken and needy. You're in the Valley of Achor, sinking in the mire of unconfessed sin and are longing to lay hold of soul prosperity; the golden key hanging from the prophet's chain so as to open a Door of Hope.

Some do not know Jesus and many of those who do, don't know Him in intimacy and power; nor in transparency and Truth. ...Only as a historic figure. ...A distant Saviour preached at church. ...A lifeless picture on a wall. We encourage you (no time wasted!) to kneel down where you are, [a] repent, open your

---

[a] See Chapter 23: "Betrothed to Christ."

heart in all simplicity to the Spirit of Christ, and yield unto Him the reigns of your life.

Others here with us are in desperate need of deliverance and healing. You're like the impotent man by the pool of Siloam that's been waiting seemingly forever for the stirring of the water, hoping to be the first to step in, but suffering the grave disappointment of *"hope deferred"* *(Pro. 13:12)*.

Still others are like the woman with the issue of blood that exhausted all her living on physicians, only to grow worse, and for that reason have lost hope altogether. Or, perhaps your concerns lie with the welfare of a colleague, a neighbor, or a brother? You're like the Syrophenician mother begging for the deliverance of her daughter; or, like the four friends of the paralytic who stopped at nothing (even breaking through the roof of a house!) so as to get their ailing friend into the Presence of Jesus.

Whatever the case or cause, like Betsie ten Boom whispered from her stretcher: *"There is no pit so deep that He's not deeper still."* ...Not "terminal" cancer. Not depression or demon possession. Not addiction. Not COVID 19. Jesus heals *"all manner of sickness and all manner of disease"* *(Mt. 10:1)*.

"God is no respecter of persons" *(Acts 10:34)*. The healing that Jesus purchased with His own blood is available to YOU, just like it's been for us and countless others throughout history. All accounts tell the same story: *"As many as touched Him,"* — even only *"the hem of His garment"* — *"were made perfectly whole"* *(Mk. 6:56; Mt. 14:36)*.

Oh, Dear Reader, we beseech you, *"in Christ's stead"* *(2 Cor. 5:20)*: Go out to meet Jesus at the Jabbok crossing. Reach up with the two arms of faith and repentance and don't let go till the break of day when you receive your blessing.

Follow Naaman the Syrian leper to the banks of the Jordan River and dip seven times in the waters of repentance — continuing onward in that way of life, even after your miraculous cleansing. Stretch forth your withered hand, though all the world, including doubting Thomases of the Christian profession, hold you in derision and the hordes of hell parade across your mind thundering doubt and calling you a fool.

Do you remember the passage that dropped into Jody's heart when she was crying out for the *"faith of Jesus"* so she could minister with me in power?

"And as ye go, preach, saying, The kingdom of heaven is at hand. Heal the sick, cleanse the lepers, raise the dead, cast out devils: freely ye have received, freely give."   Matthew 10:7-8

Well, here we are, side-by-side, with a cloud of witnesses surrounding us, ready to pray with YOU:

Heavenly Father... We come in obedience to your Word, laying hands in the Spirit on all sincere penitents coming to you with a "true heart" confessing their sins, and ready not only to pray the "prayer of faith," but also, to walk in the "steps" of that "faith" from this present Hour till their final breath. Unto these that "fear" Your name, may the Son of Righteousness arise "with healing in His wings" (Mal. 4:2). Empower these cherished ones, O Lord, to stay close to You and each other through all the trials, tribulation and temptations ahead, until at last, we see You "coming in the clouds of heaven with power and great glory" to take us home (Mt. 24:30).
...In Jesus' name, we pray, amen.

"And these signs shall follow them that believe; In my name shall they cast out devils; they shall speak with new tongues. They shall take up serpents; and if they drink any deadly thing, it shall not hurt them; they shall lay hands on the sick, and they shall recover."   Mark 16:17-18

Healing and deliverance are promises. And like our friend Velma tells anyone who will listen:

God *always* keeps His promises.

". . . Be not afraid, only BELIEVE." Mark 5:36b

END NOTES

Chapter 1: A Dream Come True

1. Leona Choy, *Andrew Murray The Authorized Biography*, (Fort Washington, PA, USA: CLC Publications, 2000). Andrew Murray lost his voice for two years until at last he was *"healed by the Lord so completely that never again was he troubled by any weakness of throat or voice,"* p. 149.
2. Ibid., p. 164.
3. Thieleman J. van Braght, *The Bloody Theater or Martyrs Mirror of the Defenseless Christians*, (Scottdale, PA, USA: Herald Press, 1749), p. 1031.
4. David Wilkerson, "They Have Done Away with the Cross," *Times Square Church Pulpit Series*, (Lindale, TX, USA: World Challenge), Dec. 23, 1986.
5. Art Katz, *The Anatomy of Deception*, (Bemidji, MN, USA: Burning Bush Press, 2008), p. 54.
6. Thieleman J. van Braght, *Martyrs Mirror*, p. 865.
7. Ibid., p. 676.
8. Alexander Maclaren, *Maclaren's Expositions of Holy Scripture*, "Hosea 2:15," https://biblehub.com/commentaries/hosea/2-15.htm.
9. Leona Choy, *Andrew Murray The Authorized Biography*, p. 162.
10. Edwin & Jody Mitchell, *The Two Headed Dragon of Africa*, (Santa Fe, NM, USA, 1991).
11. "Matthew Henry Commentary on 2 Chronicles 16," https://www.blueletterbible.org/Comm/mhc/2Ch/2Ch_016.cfm.

Chapter 2: And Then the World Changed

1. "Black Lives Matter: Understanding Its Origins, History and Agendas July 12, 2016, *Right Side News*, July 12, 2016, https://rightsidenews.com/life-and-science/culture-wars/black-lives-matter-understanding-origins-history-agendas/.
2. "Spiritual Disobedience in China," *Voice of the Martyrs Magazine*, (Bartlesville, OK, USA: The Voice of the Martyrs), March 2020.
3. "Bill Gates And Intellectual Ventures Funds Microneedle Vaccine Technology That Injects Luciferase Ink, Marking Vaccinated People," *Humans are Free*, May 20, 2020, https://humansarefree.com/2020/05/bill-gates-and-intellectual-ventures-funds-microchip-implant-vaccine-technology.html.
4. Editor Gary Kah, "A Number for Everyone," *Hope for the World Update*, (Noblesville, IN, USA), garykah.org, Fall Issue 2021, p. 6.
5. Ibid., "Practical Advice," p. 9. See also Emerald Robinson, "What is Luciferase: How a firefly enzyme that glows might herald the end of the world," *Emerald Robinson's the Right Way*, November. 4, 2021,

https://emeralddb3.substack.com/p/what-is-luciferase.

6   Ibid., "The COVID Agenda & Mark of the Beast Technology," pp. 2-3.

7   "Starbucks Is Dropping Cash to Protect Customers and Staff: Why we can expect more contactless experiences soon," *Inc.com*, May 7, 2020. https://www.inc.com/don-reisinger/starbucks-is-dropping-cash-to-protect-customers-staff.html.

8   Pastor Glenn A. Guest, *Steps Towards the Mark of the Beast*, (Belleville, Ontario, Canada: Essence Publishing, 2007), p. 69.

9   Thieleman J. van Braght, *The Bloody Theater or Martyrs Mirror of the Defenseless Christians*, (Scottdale, PA, USA: Herald Press, 1749), p. 700.

10   David Wilkerson, *The Vision*, (New York, NY, USA: A Jove Book, Berkeley Publishing Group, 1977), p. 60.

11   Ibid., p. 60.

12   Ibid., p. 75.

13   Ibid., p. 60.

14   Thieleman J. van Braght, *Martyrs Mirror*, p. 730. From *The Proof of Faith*, one of two books written by Valerius during his long imprisonment.

15   Ibid., p. 691, 694.

16   Charles John Ellicott, *Ellicott's Commentary for English Readers*, "2 Chronicles 32:21," https://biblehub.com/commentaries/2_chronicles/32-31.htm.

17   Thieleman J. van Braght, *Martyrs Mirror*, p. 910.

18   Ibid., p. 856.

19   Ibid, p. 504. Quoted is Jerome Segers, a devout martyr tortured and burned at the stake by Catholic decree in A.D. 1551.

Chapter 3: O Magnify the Lord with Me

1   C. Irving Benson, *The Eight Points of the Oxford Groups*, (Melbourne, London, Edinburgh, Toronto, Bombay and Madras: Humphrey Milford, Oxford University Press, 1938), p. 58.

2   Leona Choy, *Andrew Murray The Authorized Biography*, (Fort Washington, PA, USA: CLC Publications, 2000), pp. 143, 145.

3   Ibid., pp. 208-209.

4   Robert Stearns, *No, We Can't Radical Islam, Militant Secularism and the Myth of Coexistence*, (Bloomington, MN, USA: Chosen Books, 2011), p. 81.

5   David Wilkerson, *The Cross and the Switchblade*, (Old Tappan, NJ, USA: Spire Books, 1963), p. 42.

6   Ibid., p. 36.

7   William Gurnall, *The Christian in Complete Armour*, (Peabody, MA, USA: Hendrickson Publishers, 2016), Vol. 2, p. 435.

8   Steve Gallagher, *At the Altar of Sexual Idolatry*, (Dry Ridge, KY, USA: Pure Life Ministries, 1986), p. 50-51.

Chapter 4: The Old Time Gospel

1   Edwin & Jody Mitchell, "Faith Our Alarm System," 26 Sept. 2018, p. 6.

2 Smith Wigglesworth, *Ever Increasing Faith*, (Springfield, MO, USA: Gospel Publishing House, Original Copyright 1924, Revised Edition 1971), p. 46.
3 C. Irving Benson, *The Eight Points of the Oxford Groups*, (Melbourne, London, Edinburgh, Toronto, Bombay and Madras: Humphrey Milford, Oxford University Press, 1938), p. viii.
4 Ibid., pp. x, ix.
5 Edited by Elizabeth Jay, *The Journal of John Wesley, A Selection*, (Oxford, NY, USA: Oxford University Press, 1987), p. 131.
6 Andrew Murray, *Divine Healing*, (Fort Washington, PA, USA: CLC Publications, 1971), pp. 12-13.
7 Ibid., 9.
8 Geoffrey Allen, *He That Cometh*, (New York, USA: MacMillan Company, 1933), p. 143.
9 Art Katz, *The Anatomy of Deception*, (Bemidji, MN, USA: Burning Bush Press, 2008), pp. 25-26.
10 Art Katz, *True Fellowship: Church as Community*, (Bemidji, MN, USA: Burning Bush Press, 2009), p. 32.
11 Art Katz, *The Anatomy of Deception*, p. 26.
12 Hannah Hurnard, *Hearing Heart*, (Wheaten, IL, USA: Tyndale House Publishers, 1978) p. 50.
13 Roy Hession, *We Would See Jesus*, (Fort Washington, PA, USA: CLC Publications, 1958), p. 22.
14 Ibid., p.23.
15 Ibid.
16 Art Katz, *The Anatomy of Deception*, pp. 54-55.
17 Roy & Revel Hession, *We Would See Jesus*, p. 22-23.
18 Art Katz, *And They Crucified Him*, (Bemidji, MN, USA: Burning Bush Press, 2011), p. 25.
19 William Gurnall, Revised and corrected by John Campbell, *The Christian in Complete Armour*, (London, England: R. Griffin & Company, 1745), p. 299.
20 Simeon Shofar, Jan. 27, 1997.
21 Ibid.
22 Ibid.
23 Ibid.
24 Ibid.
25 Art Katz, *The Anatomy of Deception*, p. 25.
26 Art Katz, *And They Crucified Him*, p. 20.
27 Editor David Daniell, *William Tyndale The Obedience of a Christian Man*, (London, England: Penguin Books, 2000), p. 7.

Chapter 5: The Just Shall Live by Faith

1 William Gurnall, Revised and corrected by John Campbell, *The Christian in Complete Armour*, (London, England: R. Griffin & Company, 1745), p. 619.
2 Thieleman J. van Braght, *Martyrs Mirror*, p. 826.
3 Rabbi Hillel.
4 Geoffrey Allen, *He That Cometh*, (New York, USA: The Macmillan

Company, 1933), p. 85.

5   Editor David Daniell, *William Tyndale The Obedience of a Christian Man*, (London, England: Penguin Books, 2000), p. 10.

6   Ibid., p. 8.

7   Geoffrey Allen, *He That Cometh*, pp. 111-112.

8   John Bunyan, *Pilgrim's Progress*, (Grand Rapids, MI, USA: Spire Book, Fleming H. Revell, Part One originally published in 1678, Part Two in 1685), pp. 9, 14.

9   Ibid., pp. 14-15.

10   Editor David Daniell, *William Tyndale The Obedience of a Christian Man*, p. 23.

11   Ibid., p. 15.

12   Corrie ten Boom with John & Elizabeth Sherrill, *The Hiding Place*, (Old Tappan, NJ, USA: Spire Books, 1971), pp. 213-214.

13   Ibid., p. 215.

14   David McCasland, *Oswald Chambers: Abandoned to God*, (Grand Rapids, MI, USA: Discovery House Publishers, Distributed by Thomas Nelson Publishers, Nashville, TN, USA, 1993), pp. 63, 198.

15   Frances Chan, *Crazy Love: Overwhelmed by a Relentless God*, (Colorado Springs, CO, USA: David C Cook, 2013), pp. 112.

16   William Gurnall, Revised and corrected by John Campbell, *The Christian in Complete Armour*, p. 14.

17   Ibid.

18   Editor David Daniell, *William Tyndale The Obedience of a Christian Man*, pp. 6-7.

19   William Gurnall, *The Christian in Complete Armour*, (Peabody, MA, USA: Hendrickson Publishers, 2016), Vol. 2, pp. 281-282.

20   Thieleman J. van Braght, *Martyrs Mirror*, p. 44.

21   Edwin & Jody Mitchell, "Faith our Alarm System," Sept. 16, 2018, pp. 8-9.

22   Matthew Henry, *Matthew Henry's Concise Commentary*, "1 Kings 15:18," https://biblehub.com/commentaries/1_kings/15-18.htm.

Chapter 6: Covenant Conditions Attached

1   William Gurnall, *The Christian in Complete Armour*, (Peabody, MA, USA: Hendrickson Publishers, 2016), Vol. 2, p. 438.

2   Steve Gallagher, *At the Altar of Sexual Idolatry*, (Dry Ridge, KY, USA: Pure Life Ministries, 1986), p. 13. From foreword by Edwin Louis Cole.

3   Thieleman J. van Braght, *The Bloody Theater or Martyrs Mirror of the Defenseless Christians*, (Scottdale, PA, USA: Herald Press, 1749), p. 396.

4   Steve Gallagher, *At the Altar of Sexual Idolatry*, p. 132.

5   Ibid., p. 133.

6   Frances Roberts, *On the Highroad to Surrender*, (Ojai, CA, USA: King's Press, 1973), pp. 78-79. A prophetic word.

Chapter 7: The Spirit of Fear

1   Thieleman J. van Braght, *The Bloody Theater or Martyrs Mirror of the Defenseless Christians*, (Scottdale, PA, USA: Herald Press, 1749), p. 705.

2   Roy Hession, *The Calvary Road*, (Fort Washington, PA, USA: CLC Publications, original copyright 1950, new material added in 1990, this printing 2000), p. 36.

3   William Gurnall, *The Christian in Complete Armour*, (Peabody, MA, USA: Hendrickson Publishers, 2016), Vol. 1, p. 557.

4   Ibid.

5   Frances Chan, *Crazy Love: Overwhelmed by a Relentless God*, (Colorado Springs, CO, USA: David C Cook, 2013), p. 196.

6   Rich Higgins, "In Just Four Months," July 26, 2020. Higgins served in the Trump Administration as the NSC Director of Strategic Planning.

7   "It's Happening: France Vaccine Pass Required in Public Spaces from August 1st," *Investment Watch Blog*, July 13, 2021, https://www.investmentwatchblog.com/its-happening-france-vaccine-pass-required-in-public-spaces-from-august-1st/.

8   Scholl, Inge, *The White Rose: Munich 1942-43*, (Middletown, CT, USA: Wesleyan University Press, 1970, 1983), pp. 63-65. Originally published in German in 1952. Kurt Huber was put on trial with members of the White Rose resistance group, pronounced guilty of "high treason" and executed July 13, 1943. The quotation is from "The Final Statement of the Accused."

9   Gerhard Schoenberner, *The Yellow Star*, (New York, NY, USA: Bantam Book, Transworld Publishers, 1973), pp. 14, 15.

10   Editor Gary H. Kah, "The COVID Agenda & Mark of the Beast Technology," *Hope for the World Update*, (Noblesville, IN, USA), garykah.org, Fall 2021 Issue, p. 3. Quoted is Vatican insider Archbishop Carlo Maria Vigano in an open letter to President Trump, Oct. 10, 2020.

11   "Australian state to seize savings, homes, driver's licenses of people with unpaid COVID fines," *Natural News*, November 7, 2021, https://www.naturalnews.com/2021-11-07-australian-state-to-seize-savings-homes-covid-fines.html.

12   Editor Gary H. Kah, "Spiritual Prep," *Hope for the World Update*, Fall 2021 Issue, p. 10.

13   Ibid., "Creeping Authoritarianism," p. 9.

14   Ibid., "Spiritual Prep," p.10.

15   Bishop Raymore, Zimbabwe, March 2020.

16   Edwin & Jody Mitchell, *Purified, Made White and Tried*, (Whitefish, MT, USA: Josiah Publishing, 2007), p. 42.

17   William Gurnall, Revised and corrected by John Campbell, *The Christian in Complete Armour*, (London, England: R. Griffin & Company, 1745), p. 55.

18   Hannah Hurnard, *Hinds' Feet on High Places*, (Carol Stream, IL, USA: Living Books, Tyndale House, 1975), pp. 122-123.

Chapter 8: Spiritual Warfare

1   Thieleman J. van Braght, *The Bloody Theater or Martyrs Mirror of the Defenseless Christians*, (Scottdale, PA, USA: Herald Press, 1749), p. 907.
2   William Gurnall, Revised and corrected by John Campbell, *The Christian in Complete Armour*, (London, England: R. Griffin & Company, 1745), p. 83.
3   Frances Roberts, *Come Away My Beloved*, (Ojai, CA, USA: King's Farspan, Copyright Renewal 2001), p. 93. A prophetic word.
4   H.A. Walter, *Soul Surgery*, (stepstudy press, www.stepstudy.com), p. 112. Walter quotes Fosdick, *The Meaning of the Faith*, p. 253.
5   William Gurnall, Revised and corrected by John Campbell, *The Christian in Complete Armour*, p. 107.
6   William Gurnall, *The Christian in Complete Armour*, (Peabody, MA, USA: Hendrickson Publishers, 2016), Vol. 1, p. 124.
7   Jesse Penn-Lewis with Evan Roberts, *War on the Saints*, Unabridged, Ninth Edition, (New York, NY, USA: Thomas E. Lowe, 1973), pp. 190-191.
8   Steve Gallagher, *At the Altar of Sexual Idolatry*, (Dry Ridge, KY, USA: Pure Life Ministries, 1986), pp. 188-189.
9   Achilles is a character in Greek mythology said to be physically invulnerable in all points except his heel.
10 Thieleman J. van Braght, *Martyrs Mirror*, p. 623.

Chapter 9: Don't Be in Such a Hurry

1   Leona Choy, *Andrew Murray The Authorized Biography*, (Fort Washington, PA, USA: CLC Publications, 2000), p. 163.
2   William Gurnall, Revised and corrected by John Campbell, *The Christian in Complete Armour*, (London, England: R. Griffin & Company, 1745), p. 24.
3   Andrew Murray, *With Christ in the School of Prayer*, (Springdale, PA, USA: Whitaker House, 1981), pp. 122- 123.
4   Thieleman J. van Braght, *The Bloody Theater or Martyrs Mirror of the Defenseless Christians*, (Scottdale, PA, USA: Herald Press, 1749), p. 801.
5   Viktor E. Frankl, *Man's Search for Meaning*, (Boston, MA, USA: Beacon Press, 2006), p. ix.
6   William Gurnall, *The Christian in Complete Armour*, (Peabody, MA, USA: Hendrickson Publishers, 2016), Vol. 1, p. 567.
7   William Gurnall, Revised and corrected by John Campbell, *The Christian in Complete Armour*, p. 618.
8   Brother Yun & Paul Hattaway, *The Heavenly Man*, (Carlisle, United Kingdom: Piquant, Special Edition, Copyright 2012), p. 313.
9   Steve Gallagher, *At the Altar of Sexual Idolatry*, (Dry Ridge, KY, USA: Pure Life Ministries, 1986), pp. 119-120.
10 Brother Yun & Paul Hattaway, *The Heavenly Man*, p. 312.

Chapter 10: Enough is Enough

1   Steve Gallagher, *At the Altar of Sexual Idolatry*, (Dry Ridge, KY, USA: Pure Life Ministries, 1986), p. 12. From foreword by Edwin Louis Cole.
2   Ibid., p. 13.
3   William Gurnall, Revised and corrected by John Campbell, *The Christian in Complete Armour*, (London, England: R. Griffin & Company, 1745), p. 87.
4   Corrie ten Boom with John & Elizabeth Sherrill, *The Hiding Place*, (Old Tappan, NJ, USA: Spire Books, 1971), pp. 194-195.
5   Lyrics attributed to Richard of Chichester. See hymnary.org.
6   Frances Roberts, *Come Away My Beloved*, (Ojai, CA, USA: King's Farspan, Copyright Renewal 2001), pp. 126-127. A prophetic word.
7   Thieleman J. van Braght, *The Bloody Theater or Martyrs Mirror of the Defenseless Christians*, (Scottdale, PA, USA: Herald Press, 1749), p. 106. When asked why he continually spoke the Name of Jesus, Ignatius replied: *"My dear Jesus, my Saviour, is so deeply written in my heart, that I feel confident, that if my heart were to be cut open and chopped to pieces, the name of Jesus would be found written on every piece."* Hallelujah!
8   Written by Johnson Oatman, Jr., 1897.
9   William Gurnall, *The Christian in Complete Armour*, (Peabody, MA, USA: Hendrickson Publishers, 2016), Vol. 2, p. 450.
10 Jordan S. Rubin, *The Maker's Diet,* (Lake Mary, FL, USA: Siloam, 2004), pp. 162-163.
11 Frances Roberts, *Come Away My Beloved*, p. 27. A prophetic word.
12 Ibid., p. 118. A prophetic word.
13 William Gurnall, *The Christian in Complete Armour*, Vol. 2, p. 461.
14 Oswald Chambers, *My Utmost for His Highest*, (Ulrich, OH, USA: Barbour Publishing, 1935, Renewed 1963), August 12th entry.

Chapter 11: To the Cross I Flee

1   C. Irving Benson, *The Eight Points of the Oxford Group*, (Melbourne, London, Edinburgh, Toronto, Bombay and Madras: Humphrey Milford, Oxford University Press, 1938), p. 20.
2   Roy Hession, *The Calvary Road*, (Fort Washington, PA, USA: CLC Publications, original copyright 1950, new material added in 1990, this printing 2000), p. 42.
3   William Gurnall, *The Christian in Complete Armour*, (Peabody, MA, USA: Hendrickson Publishers, 2016), Vol. 1, p. 510.
4   Art Katz, *And They Crucified Him*, (Bemidji, MN, USA: Burning Bush Press, 2011), p. 17.
5   Roy & Revel Hession, *We Would See Jesus*, (Fort Washington, PA, USA: CLC Publications, 1958, this printing 2017), p. 61.
6   Art Katz, *And They Crucified Him*, p. 15.
7   Edwin & Jody Mitchell, *Becoming a True Christian*, (Whitefish, MT, USA: Josiah Publishing, Updated Edition April 2000), p. 5.
8   Roy & Revel Hession, *We Would See Jesus*, pp. 21-22.

9   Edwin & Jody Mitchell, *Becoming a True Christian*, pp. 5-6.
10 Roy & Revel Hession, *We Would See Jesus*, p. 66.
11 Edwin & Jody Mitchell, *Becoming a True Christian*, p. 8.
12 Ibid., p. 8.
13 Roy & Revel Hession, *We Would See Jesus*, p. 62.
14 C. Irving Benson, *The Eight Points of the Oxford Group*, p. 7.
15 Roy & Revel Hession, *We Would See Jesus*, p. 60.
16 Elizabeth Clephane, "Beneath the Cross of Jesus," hymn, 1868.
17 Charles Wesley, 1747. A hymn.
18 Thieleman J. van Braght, *The Bloody Theater or Martyrs Mirror of the Defenseless Christians*, (Scottdale, PA, USA: Herald Press, 1749), p. 727.

Chapter 12: Praying with Resignation

1   Thieleman J. van Braght, *The Bloody Theater or Martyrs Mirror of the Defenseless Christians*, (Scottdale, PA, USA: Herald Press, 1749), p. 924.
2   David McCasland, *Oswald Chambers: Abandoned to God*, (Grand Rapids, MI, USA: Discovery House Publishers, Distributed by Thomas Nelson Publishers, Nashville, TN, USA, 1993), p. 42.
3   Art Katz, *True Fellowship: Church as Community*, (Bemidji, MN, USA: Burning Bush Press, 2009), p. 36.
4   Frances Chan, *Crazy Love: Overwhelmed by a Relentless God*, (Colorado Springs, CO, USA: David C Cook, 2013), p. 170.
5   Hannah Hurnard, *Hinds' Feet on High Places*, (Carol Stream, IL, USA: Living Books, Tyndale House, 1975), p. 145.
6   Thieleman J. van Braght, *Martyrs Mirror*, p. 580.
7   David McCasland, *Oswald Chambers: Abandoned to God*, p. 86.
8   Thieleman J. van Braght, *Martyrs Mirror*, p. 746.
9   Andrew Murray, *Divine Healing*, (Fort Washington, PA, USA: CLC Publications, 1971), pp. 7, 9.
10 Ibid., p. 7.
11 William Gurnall, *The Christian in Complete Armour*, (Peabody, MA, USA: Hendrickson Publishers, 2016), Vol. 1, p. 522.

Chapter 13: The Awesome Power of Confession

1   C. Irving Benson, *The Eight Points of the Oxford Groups*, (Melbourne, London, Edinburgh, Toronto, Bombay and Madras: Humphrey Milford, Oxford University Press, 1938), p. 21.
2   Ibid.,p. 24.
3   Ibid., p. 24-25.
4   Thieleman J. van Braght, *The Bloody Theater or Martyrs Mirror of the Defenseless Christians*, (Scottdale, PA, USA: Herald Press, 1749), p. 696.
5   Dietrich Bonhoeffer, *Life Together*, (New York, NY, USA: HarperCollins Publisher, 1954), pp. 114, 113.
6   Art Katz, *True Fellowship: Church as Community*, (Bemidji, MN, USA: Burning Bush Press, 2009), p. 131.

7   Dietrich Bonhoeffer, *Life Together*, p. 114.

8   C. Irving Benson, *The Eight Points of the Oxford Group*, p. 26.

9   Steve Gallagher, *At the Altar of Sexual Idolatry*, (Dry Ridge, KY, USA: Pure Life Ministries, 1986), p. 70.

10 C. Irving Benson, *The Eight Points of the Oxford Group*, p. 23.

11 Ibid., p. 22.

12 Dietrich Bonhoeffer, *Life Together*, p. 116.

13 Steve Gallagher, *At the Altar of Sexual Idolatry*, p. 75.

14 Dietrich Bonhoeffer, *Life Together*, pp. 115-116.

15 Steve Gallagher, *At the Altar of Sexual Idolatry*, p. 71, 70.

16 Roy Hession, *The Calvary Road*, (Fort Washington, PA, USA: CLC Publications, original copyright 1950, new material added in 1990, this printing 2000), p. 41.

17 Roy & Revel Hession, *We Would See Jesus*, (Fort Washington, PA, USA: CLC Publications, 1958, this printing 2017), pp. 69-70.

18 Dietrich Bonhoeffer, *Life Together*, p. 114.

19 Art Katz, *True Fellowship: Church as Community*, p. 136.

20 Dietrich Bonhoeffer, *Life Together*, p. 118.

21 Art Katz, *True Fellowship: Church as Community*, p. 137.

22 William Gurnall, Revised and corrected by John Campbell, *The Christian in Complete Armour*, (London, England: R. Griffin & Company, 1745), p. 325.

23 Thieleman J. van Braght, *Martyrs Mirror*, p. 696.

24 Dietrich Bonhoeffer, *Life Together*, pp. 112-113.

25 Thieleman J. van Braght, *Martyrs Mirror*, p. 760.

26 Dietrich Bonhoeffer, *Life Together*, pp. 88-89.

27 Ibid., p. 89.

28 C. Irving Benson, *The Eight Points of the Oxford Group*, p. 128.

Chapter 14: Living in the Light of Christ

1   Geoffrey Allen, *He That Cometh*, (New York, USA: The Macmillan Company, 1933), p. 174.

2   William Gurnall, *The Christian in Complete Armour*, (Peabody, MA, USA: Hendrickson Publishers, 2016), Vol. 1, p. 475.

3   William Gurnall, *The Christian in Complete Armour*, Vol. 1, p. 510.

4   Ibid., Vol. 1, p. 522, 523, 524.

5   Martin Luther at the Imperial Diet of Worms, 1521.

6   Thieleman J. van Braght, *The Bloody Theater or Martyrs Mirror of the Defenseless Christians*, (Scottdale, PA, USA: Herald Press, 1749), p. 382. Article XI of the "Confession of Faith According to the Holy Word of God" maintained by the martyrs and set forth posthumously in about A.D. 1600.

7   William Gurnall, *The Christian in Complete Armour*, Vol. 1, p. 522.

8   H.A. Walter, *Soul Surgery*, (stepstudy press, www.stepstudy.com), p. 82.

9   Source unknown.

10 Roy & Revel Hession, *We Would See Jesus*, (Fort Washington, PA, USA: CLC Publications, 1958, this printing 2017), pp. 72-74.

11 Ibid., pp. 71-72.

Chapter 15: Abraham's Faith Steps

1   David McCasland, *Oswald Chambers: Abandoned to God*, (Grand Rapids, MI, USA: Discovery House Publishers, Distributed by Thomas Nelson Publishers, Nashville, TN, USA, 1993), p. 177.

2   Smith Wigglesworth, *Ever Increasing Faith*, (Springfield, MO, USA: Gospel Publishing House, Original Copyright 1924, Revised Edition 1971), p. 45.

3   William Gurnall, *The Christian in Complete Armour*, (Peabody, MA, USA: Hendrickson Publishers, 2016), Vol. 2, p. 282.

4   William Gurnall, Revised and corrected by John Campbell, *The Christian in Complete Armour*, (London, England: R. Griffin & Company, 1745), p. 440.

5   Thieleman J. van Braght, *The Bloody Theater or Martyrs Mirror of the Defenseless Christians*, (Scottdale, PA, USA: Herald Press, 1749), pp. 691, 694. Quoted is Matthias Servaes; a burning torch in a dark time; betrayed, tortured and beheaded by Catholic decree, A.D. 1565.

6   A phrase popularized by U.S. President Harry S. Truman referring to taking responsibility for one's actions.

7   Russell Kelso Carter, "Standing on the Promises," 1886. A hymn.

Chapter 16: Journey of Ever Increasing Faith

1   William Gurnall, *The Christian in Complete Armour*, (Peabody, MA, USA: Hendrickson Publishers, 2016), Vol. 1, p. 96.

2   Jordan Rubin, *Patient Heal Thyself*, (Shippensburg, PA USA: Destiny Images Publishers, 2016), Acknowledgement page.

3   Frances Roberts, *Come Away My Beloved*, (Ojai, CA, USA: King's Farspan, Copyright Renewal 2001), p. 93. A prophetic word.

4   Ibid., p. 93.

5   Ibid., pp. 93, 92.

6   Hannah Hurnard, *Hinds' Feet on High Places*, (Carol Stream, IL, USA: Living Books, Tyndale House, 1975), p. 11.

7   C. Irving Benson, *The Eight Points of the Oxford Groups*, (Melbourne, London, Edinburgh, Toronto, Bombay and Madras: Humphrey Milford, Oxford University Press, 1938), pp. 8, 9.

8   Lewis E. Jones, "Power in the Blood," 1899. A hymn.

9   Andrew Murray, *Divine Healing*, (Fort Washington, PA, USA: CLC Publications, 1971), p. 13.

10 Ibid., pp. 14-15.

11 Ibid., p. 15.

Chapter 17: He Turned Our Mourning into Dancing

1   Smith Wigglesworth, *Ever Increasing Faith*, (Springfield, MO, USA: Gospel Publishing House, Original Copyright 1924, Revised Edition 1971), p. 74.

2   William Gurnall, *The Christian in Complete Armour*, (Peabody, MA, USA: Hendrickson Publishers, 2016), Vol. 2, pp. 278-279.

3   Smith Wigglesworth, *Ever Increasing Faith*, pp. 40-41.
4   Thieleman J. van Braght, *The Bloody Theater or Martyrs Mirror of the Defenseless Christians*, (Scottdale, PA, USA: Herald Press, 1749), p. 453.
5   Mount Everest is located in Himalayas. It is the highest mountain above sea level on earth.
6   Frances Chan, *Crazy Love: Overwhelmed by a Relentless God*, (Colorado Springs, CO, USA: David C Cook, 2008), 200-201.

Chapter 18: Walking on Water with Jesus

1   Thieleman J. van Braght, *The Bloody Theater or Martyrs Mirror of the Defenseless Christians*, (Scottdale, PA, USA: Herald Press, 1749), p. 906.
2   Frances Roberts, *Come Away My Beloved*, (Ojai, CA, USA: King's Farspan, Copyright Renewal 2001), p. 109. A prophetic word.
3   Oswald Chambers, *My Utmost for His Highest*, (Ulrich, OH, USA: Barbour Publishing, 1935), July 31st entry.
4   Geoffrey Allen, *He That Cometh*, (New York, USA: The Macmillan Company, 1933), p. 114.

Chapter 19: Unbelief: The Traitor's Gate

1   William Gurnall, *The Christian in Complete Armour*, (Peabody, MA, USA: Hendrickson Publishers, 2016), Vol. 2, p. 29.
2   Hannah Hurnard, *Hinds' Feet on High Places*, (Carol Stream, IL, USA: Living Books, Tyndale House, 1975), p 212.
3   William Gurnall, Revised and corrected by John Campbell, *The Christian in Complete Armour*, (London, England: R. Griffin & Company, 1745), pp. 493-494.
4   Ibid., p. 439.
5   William Gurnall, *The Christian in Complete Armour*, (Peabody, MA, USA: Hendrickson Publishers, 2016), Vol. 2, pp. 23-24.

Chapter 20: Restoring Honor

1   Edwin & Jody Mitchell, *Welcome to the Church of the Two or More*, (josiahpub@hotmail.com), p. 11.
2   William Gurnall, *The Christian in Complete Armour*, (Peabody, MA, USA: Hendrickson Publishers, 2016), Vol. 2, p. 228.
3   Thieleman J. van Braght, *The Bloody Theater or Martyrs Mirror of the Defenseless Christians*, (Scottdale, PA, USA: Herald Press, 1749), p. 569.
4   David Wilkerson, "They Have Done Away with the Cross," *Times Square Church Pulpit Series*, (Lindale, TX, USA: World Challenge), Dec. 23, 1986.

Chapter 21: He Teacheth My Hands to War

1   William Gurnall, *The Christian in Complete Armour*, (Peabody, MA, USA: Hendrickson Publishers, 2016), Vol. 1, p. 352.

2   Ibid., Vol. 1, pp. 352-353.
3   Ibid., Vol. 1, p. 353.
4   William Gurnall, Revised and corrected by John Campbell, *The Christian in Complete Armour*, (London, England: R. Griffin & Company, 1745), p. 285.
5   William Gurnall, *The Christian in Complete Armour*, Vol. 1, p. 353.
6   Thieleman J. van Braght, *The Bloody Theater or Martyrs Mirror of the Defenseless Christians*, (Scottdale, PA, USA: Herald Press, 1749), p. 12.
7   Editor David Daniell, *William Tyndale The Obedience of a Christian Man*, (London, England: Penguin Books, 2000), p. 6.
8   Roy & Revel Hession, *We Would See Jesus*, (Fort Washington, PA, USA: CLC Publications, 1958, this printing 2017), pp. 104-105. 115.
9   Art Katz, *True Fellowship: Church as Community*, (Bemidji, MN, USA: Burning Bush Press, 2009), p. 134.
10   William Gurnall, Revised and corrected by John Campbell, *The Christian in Complete Armour*, pp. 293-294.
11   Ibid., p. 71.
12   Ibid., p. 294.
13   Richard Wurmbrand, *Tortured for Christ*, (Bartlesville, OK, USA: VOM Books, 1967, 1998, 2013), p. 41
14   Thieleman J. van Braght, *Martyrs Mirror*, p. 19.
15   Art Katz, *And They Crucified Him*, (Bemidji, MN, USA: Burning Bush Press, 2011), p. 16.

Chapter 22: Flashback

1   Holly Dunn, "Daddy's Hands," August 1986.
2   Sonny Bono, "You Better Sit Down Kids," 1971.
3   Rafe van Hoy, "What's Forever For," First Recording 1978.
4   Thieleman J. van Braght, *The Bloody Theater or Martyrs Mirror of the Defenseless Christians*, (Scottdale, PA, USA: Herald Press, 1749), p. 362.
5   Art Katz, *The Holocaust Where Was God?*, (Copyright 1998, 2008), artkatzministries.org, p. 88.

Chapter 23: Betrothed to Christ

1   Johnny Lee, "Lookin' for Love," 1980.
2   Hannah Hurnard, *Hinds' Feet on High Places*, (Carol Stream, IL, USA: Living Books, Tyndale House, 1975), p. 11.
3   Oswald Chambers, *My Utmost for His Highest*, (Ulrich, OH, USA: Barbour Publishing, 1935), July 30th entry.
4   The first recorded versions of this rhyme date back to late eighteenth century England. Its origins are obscure.
5   Andrew Murray, *With Christ in the School of Prayer*, (Springdale, PA, USA: Whitaker House, 1981), p. 13.
6   William Gurnall, *The Christian in Complete Armour*, (Peabody, MA, USA: Hendrickson Publishers, 2016), Vol. 2, p. 432.

7   P.P. Bliss, 1876. Bliss came to Christ at a Revival Meeting at age 12.
8   Gloria Gaither, 1971.
9   William Gurnall, *The Christian in Complete Armour*, Vol. 2, p. 438.
10   Ibid.
11   David Wilkerson, *The Cross and the Switchblade*, (Old Tappan, NJ, USA: Spire Books, 1963), p. 40.
12   Ibid., pp. 40-41.

Chapter 24: The Prayer of Faith

1   Hannah Hurnard, *Hinds' Feet on High Places*, (Carol Stream, IL, USA: Living Books, Tyndale House, 1975), p. 312.
2   Leona Choy, *Andrew Murray The Authorized Biography*, (Fort Washington, PA, USA: CLC Publications, 2000), p. 148.
3   Corrie ten Boom with John & Elizabeth Sherrill, *The Hiding Place*, (Old Tappan, NJ, USA: Spire Books, 1971), p. 217.

Chapter 25: Lo, I am With You Alway

1   Hannah Hurnard, *Hinds' Feet on High Places*, (Carol Stream, IL, USA: Living Books, Tyndale House, 1975), pp. 144-145.
2   Thieleman J. van Braght, *The Bloody Theater or Martyrs Mirror of the Defenseless Christians*, (Scottdale, PA, USA: Herald Press, 1749), p. 658.
3   Brother Yun & Paul Hattaway, *The Heavenly Man*, (Carlisle, United Kingdom: Piquant, Special Edition Copyright 2012), p. 13. Paul Hattaway is quoted.
4   Thieleman J. van Braght, *Martyrs Mirror*, p. 355. The author is quoting a fellow lover of the holy martyrs from former times.
5   Ibid., p. 356.
6   Martin Luther King Jr., "I've Been to the Mountaintop," speech delivered at Mason Temple Church of God in Christ Headquarters, April 3, 1968.
7   George Bennard, "The Old Rugged Cross," a classic hymn first introduced June 7, 1913 in Pokagon, MI, USA.
8   Thieleman J. van Braght, *Martyrs Mirror*, p. 877
9   Ibid., p. 688.
10   Testimonial given in Canada during the 1990's by a converted Hutterite.
11   David Wilkerson, "1973 Prophecy—The Vision," May 5, 2011, YouTube, https://youtu.be/l_R9I-qQEbs.
12   Ibid.

Made in the USA
Middletown, DE
29 December 2021